The diaries of
JAMES AGATE
newly edited by Tim Beaumont

None of the characters in this book is imaginary and whether any of them is real metaphysics has not yet determined.

James Agate

THE SELECTIVE
EGO

The diaries of
JAMES AGATE
newly edited by Tim Beaumont

HARRAP LONDON

FOR JILL

First Published in Great Britain 1976
by GEORGE G. HARRAP & CO. LTD
182–184 High Holborn, London WC1V 7AX

Copyright The Trustees of the Agate Estate
This selection © *Tim Beaumont* 1976

ISBN 0 245 52849 0

Composed in Monotype Times New Roman
and printed by Billing & Sons Ltd.
Guildford, Worcester and London
Made in Great Britain

PREFACE

"Time will show whether he will be remembered more for his diary than for his dramatic criticism." Thus *The Oxford Companion to the Theatre*.

The nine volumes of *Ego* have been out of print and unobtainable even through the most assiduous of second-hand booksellers for years. So have the three volumes of *A Shorter Ego* edited by Agate himself. More lately (1961) Herbert van Thal has edited *An Anthology* of Agate's work. I have edited this present condensation of the *Ego*s because I believe it to present Agate's work in the right form for this time. The *Anthology* is fascinating reading, particularly the introduction by Alan Dent, and we must all be grateful to Mr van Thal and Rupert Hart-Davis for keeping Agate's work alive in published form. But it merely whets the appetite for more, and in particular for more *Ego*.

I myself first came across the *Ego* volumes when my father, a right-wing Tory M.P. and a Master of Fox Hounds who, although a prolific reader, virtually never visited a serious theatre and never listened to serious music, read one and issued a general announcement to his family that, since the books were by then out of print, anyone finding one of them second-hand was at liberty to give it to him for Christmas. As a result *Ego* came back into my mind every time I entered a second-hand bookshop.

Eventually, going on a month's holiday, I decided that I must read them myself, and extracted the lot from the London Library. I read them all in a week, and saw immediately what made Agate at one time the favourite reading of so many different kinds of people. One of his volumes of dramatic criticism is called *Here's Richness*. How much more does that apply to his diaries.

PREFACE

To edit them has been a labour of love, and I owe a debt of gratitude to all those who have helped me.

That *Ego* itself will one day be reprinted in its entirety I have no doubt, and this is one of the reasons why I have not lumbered this volume with endless historical notes. All that will come when Agate is eventually recognized as one of the classic English Diarists. I have merely furnished brief notes at the end on some of the characters who appear most often.

Nor have I felt it necessary to indicate where I have cut. In reducing the material from nine volumes to one I have reluctantly not only had to cut diary entries wholesale but also within entries.

It could be argued that all that is needed is a reissue of *A Shorter Ego*, but even if Agate's selection was the best for his time it is not necessarily that which will most interest readers today.

I have tried in this selection to do two things. The first is to give as much space as is consonant with the balance of the book to Agate's writing about acting. He was not a great dramatic critic, if by a great dramatic critic one means someone who applies an original mind to plays, but he was arguably the best ever writer about *acting*.

And so in this book the reader will come back again and again, as Agate did, to Irving, Sarah Bernhardt and Rachel. But there is also much on the early Gielgud, Richardson and Olivier.

I have also tried to keep the feel of Agate the diarist and place the dramatic criticism in this context. I have had to sacrifice a great deal in the process, his patronage of talented young men who only too often were merely talented, his love of golf, his passion for hackney ponies, and his delight in the success of his great pony *Ego*.

But what is left, I believe, not only gives a portrait of the man but of the London in which he lived. It is interesting to compare the diaries with Harold Nicolson's. They cover much the same period, they are mainly set in the same city, their authors were both basically homosexual, both passionately interested in the arts. And yet they hardly overlap: Nicolson mentions Agate not at all, and Agate records meeting Nicolson once.

One world is the world of Bloomsbury, of Parliament, of the aristocracy; the other the world of the Savage, Fleet Street and the bourgeoisie. They are complementary.

As to the truth of the diaries, Alan Dent, as so often, has said the definitive word. "He was not exactly a liar. But in his writing he was inclined to soar into something which he defined and defended as 'the higher truth'. It consists in embroidery upon, or elaboration of, what actually happened or was said." And Dent quotes the accounts both of his own arrival (not in this volume since it occurs in the autobiography which forms the first part of *Ego* 1 and which precedes the diary) and of his departure (page 139) in evidence.

Agate was not necessarily an attractive man. Arnold Bennett describes him in his Journal as "rather coarse-looking and therefore rather coarse in some things. Fattish. Has reputation for sexual perversity." He was capable of meanness and malice. But as he rightly said of himself "His enemies will miss him". So did his friends. I hope this volume will create more.

Tim Beaumont
New Year's Day 1975

ACKNOWLEDGMENTS

My thanks are due to George Mathew and the late Stanley Rubinstein, James Agate's literary executors, for permission to undertake this work and to the above, to Alan Dent and to Peter Forster for information and assistance.

Extracts from entry in "The Oxford Companion to the Theatre"
edited by Phyllis Hartnoll [OUP Third Edition]:

AGATE, James Evershed (1877–1947), English dramatic critic. He began his journalistic career on the *Manchester Guardian* and from there moved to the *Saturday Review*. From 1923 until his death he was dramatic critic of the *Sunday Times*. His later publications include *Brief Chronicles* (1943), dealing with performances of Shakespearian and other Elizabethan plays which he had witnessed; *Red Letter Nights* (1944) dealing with the plays of later dramatists seen between 1921 and 1943; and *Immoment Toys* (1945), a survey of light entertainment on the London stage 1920–43. In *These were Actors* (also 1943) he edited a selection of contemporary criticism from a newspaper-cuttings book of 1811 to 1833. He also compiled *The English Dramatic Critics* (1932) an anthology of criticism written between 1660 and 1932.

In the numerous volumes of his *Ego* series Agate published the detailed diary of his life which he started in 1932. Time will show whether he will be remembered more for his diary than for his dramatic criticism. One thing is certain: he recorded the theatre of his time with more vigour and interest than any other critic, except Bernard Shaw, brought to any period.

CONTENTS

CONTENTS

EGO 1

June 1932–July 1934

June 2

To-day is the day on which my review of Arnold Bennett's *Journals* ought to have appeared in the *Express*. Kept out because of lists of winners in Irish Sweep for the Derby. Had considerable difficulty in getting consent to this review, on the theory that A. B. is no longer news. Am told that Beverley Baxter [then Managing Editor of the *Daily Express*] said to his staff four days after A. B.'s funeral: "Gentlemen, please understand that so far as the 'D.E.' is concerned Arnold Bennett is dead." The worst of it is that B. B. was right and in his place I should have had to do the same. But it hurts! It is A. B.'s diaries which have prompted this one, started by the writer in the fifty-fifth year of his age, which sounds like something on a tombstone! Am hoping this book will help to rid me of those *idées noires* with which I am too much obsessed.

But debt worries are legitimate hell. Have begun retrenching. Vacated the cottage at Beaconsfield and put up a "To Let" board; moved to smaller flat at £140 instead of £250 which was the rent at Palace Court; got rid of the chauffeur and now make Alfred Lester drive as well as valet. This is not his real name, but fits this six foot four of melancholy fine. His previous place was ducal, which accounts for him saying to me on his second day: "We have been looking through our suits, sir, and find we need two more." Upon my promising to consider the matter he said: "They are ordered, sir. I dress my gentlemen according to their age and shape! You will approve the patterns, sir, I feel sure."

June 3

Question. Why am I keeping this diary? Answer. Because it is part

1

of the insane desire to perpetuate oneself. Because there seem to be lots
of things I want to say that other writers put into novels and accepted
essayists into essays. Because it will be a relief to set down just what I
do actually think, and in the first words to hand, instead of pondering
what I *ought* to think and worrying about the words in which to express
the hammered-out thought. But I cannot and never could invent a
story, or be bothered to tell it, and have already published *five* books of
essays, not having to do with the theatre, that have been complete
and utter failures. So I am driven to this last ditch of expression.

June 4

I see that E. V. Lucas has been made a Companion of Honour. No
use to me! I want a knighthood, not because I should be the first
dramatic critic to have one, but to prove to the good folk of Manchester
that I am not a failure. Indeed, I promise His Majesty, if he will give
me one, not to use the title south of the Trent! Honours list, as usual,
wildly disappointing. But Monty Shearman [see Concise Biographies]
points out that not réclame nor money nor anything else except an
honour of sorts can come to one who has been Town Clerk of say
Middlesbrough for forty years. *A fortiori*, I suppose, magistrates in
Poona and sewage-inspectors in Kenya. But I still think it should be
Sir Ernest Newman and then Sir Desmond MacCarthy and then
Sir James Agate, if only for the fact that up to this date I have broadcast
oftener than anybody else except the announcers.

June 7

Went to Mills's circus last night and enjoyed every moment of it.
Alfred Lester had never seen a circus before, and laughed only when
somebody fell down. Didn't believe the zebras and thought they were
donkeys painted—"they're all the same pattern".

What a relief to be able to set down here *exactly* what I think,
and not to have to make an article out of it. How sick I am of being
whimsical *à la* Kenneth Grahame or erudite about Toulouse-Lautrec
or up-to-date with Dame Laura Knight—who sees pewter figures on
zinc horses—or still more up-to-date by knowing about Thérèse
Lessore whose circus pictures were praised by Frank Rutter last Sunday.

I kept seeing resemblances everywhere. One little dwarf—some
dwarfs are bigger than others—reminded me of Charles Laughton, one
of the clowns wearing a flaming aureole of silly yellow hair was very
like Gordon Craig, while one of the elephants was *exactly* like Eliza
Aria, and wore a mantilla just like hers, only it was the size of the
back of a kitchen chair. The other three elephants were all rather like
Y——, the pianist. Y—— dying a few weeks ago, but, I hear, is getting

better. He must weigh 24 stone, and at his worst was still eating whole chickens at a meal. One of the acrobats had a sore throat. Does Mills travel a hospital, and how do sick people who lead a rough life manage? Perhaps they aren't often ill?

There was one fellow in the show who did nothing except rope-spinning, but did it so well that we held our breaths. He was the ugliest handsome devil I have seen for years, with a squint or glide in one eye that went right round the back of his head. Watching him I wondered how we can have arrived at judging people by their morals, table manners, or other irrelevant standard.

The Wallendas gave their usual "sick-making" performance on the high wire. At Olympia last Christmas I sat next to Tom Webster who, when this was going on, dropped to his knees and hid his head in my lap. But what struck me most was the spick-and-spanness of this travelling show which was like a London first-night down to the ringmaster's gloves of new, white kid. One *expects* a circus at Olympia, but not in these fields. They were playing in York at 9.30 on Saturday night and the show was up and ready to open in this field in Harrogate at 4 o'clock on Sunday afternoon. The staff is 350 with 50 local labourers to pull down at one place and another 50 to set up in the next town. The whole thing beautifully stage-managed. I noticed that the Yorkshire audience did not acclaim a turn when it came on but waited till it had justified applause.

Mills has had a career anybody might envy. Carriage-builder. Then whip to Miss Ella Ross of Sale, Manchester. Used to drive her famous blacks in all the show-grounds of England—Grand Vulcan and that lot. Then the war, and Mills made a fortune. Then the circus. Was a bit cock-a-hoop at one time, to be expected in a man who has got on too well. Then came a dreadful illness—eczema from head to foot, literally from the soles of his feet to the crown of his head. Borne these two years with extraordinary courage and patience. That a career which began in funereal gloom should have reached these dazzling and Olympian heights recalls the story Coquelin used to tell of a rival of his young days who won the first prize for comedy at the Conservatoire and ultimately made a fortune in the *pompes funèbres*. Our Bertram has done it the other way round.

Somebody broke the window of the car in the car-park.

When we drove past the field on the way to town this morning there was our boss-eyed ruffian of the night before standing on a horse and spinning a rope in the sunlight. Now he looked exactly like a picture by Laura Knight, which makes me think that she paints her things in the day-time. This must be why they don't have the proper night effect.

June 8

Invited by two somebodies I don't know to attend a welcome

lunch to somebody I have never heard of returning from Australia, a country I am not interested in. Refused.

Invited by Violet, Duchess of Rutland, to an exhibition of her drawings. The invitation marked "Press", with a note on back of card: "I shall be all the afternoon in my own house in case you care to look in afterwards." Signed, "V. R." Am thinking of framing this after altering the address to Windsor Castle and ante-dating it.

Took Leo Pavia [see Concise Biographies] to lunch at Bertorelli's, having vowed last night to frequent Lyons in perpetuity. Minestrone, tournedos with mushroom sauce, excellent bottle of St Julien, cigar, 13s. 11d. Tip 1s., since I must economise somewhere. Leo is a pupil of Leschetizky and knew Brahms—i.e. he once opened the door to him. Likes to think he might have been the grandson of either Rossini or Meyerbeer, both of whom stayed at his grandparents' house in Regent Square in the 'fifties, but is afraid his grandmother was honest. Perpetually hard up, and a wit who spends his life pouring vinegar on troubled waters. Everybody's enemy except his own. At lunch today he said it was absurd for me to keep a diary and suggested a noctuary!

A paper for which I write under a pseudonym wanted me to notice the Camargo Ballet at the Savoy. Vaughan Williams's "Job", Walton's "Façade", some Scarlatti, and Ravel's "The Enchanted Grove". Beecham conducting. Would like to see this, but will not write about it if I can help it. Strongly object to ignoramuses writing about the drama, and realise that I know nothing about ballet. If people have mouths, why don't they speak through them instead of making signs? About as sensible, I suppose, as to ask why when we can get apples we want Cézanne to draw them. Don't defend my attitude, but stick to it.

The advantage of a male secretary is that you can go on working while you are dressing or undressing. Worked out an entire theory of ballet when I was in my pants, dressing for the play. Jock [Alan Dent. See Concise Biographies] says that in my pants I look exactly like those monstrosities which used to advertise Horne's, or somebody's, underwear on the coping of the building at the corner of Tottenham Court Road and New Oxford Street recently pulled down. The British public which will not have Epstein gazed on these for forty years with affection and appreciation!

Marie Tempest in *The Vinegar Tree* at the St James's Theatre. Brilliant and witty performance by this valiant and ageless lady. Celia Johnson in cast. Met her uncle on the first tee at a golf course recently. He said: "Is my niece as good as you say she is?" I said: "No!" drove off and walked away. I will *not* be talked to about the theatre when I am playing golf. Supper at Savoy with Shearman. Edith Shackleton and a friend came over for coffee. Edith is a tower of sympathy to people in trouble, and spends her quick and noble mind generously. M. S. had caviare and lager, plus a large port; I had cold tongue, a pint of Bollinger (N.V.) and a cigar. Monty offered to pay and I said No, regretfully. Bill £1 16s. 6d. Tip 3/6.

June 19

Champagne, good cold supper and bridge. During the game had one of those idiotic nerve-troubles that seize me sometimes. All my life I have been afraid I may have some sudden, uncontrollable impulse to do the thing I most want not to do. First noticed this at Southport when I was about eighteen and used to take May, who was three, for walks on the pier. I was terrified lest I should snatch her up and throw her into the sea! Was so worried about this that I consulted a doctor.

But that is a day-time worry; the sleep-walking fear is worse. I have never walked in my sleep in my life, but for fear I should do so I cannot sleep high up or with an open window unless there is a piece of furniture against it. I dislike houses with a staircase-well for the same reason. I cannot bear to have razors or matches in my bedroom, though I am not so nervous about poisons. At one time I forced myself to keep awake in railway carriages and would not travel in an empty one. Have several times consulted doctors and they all tell me that the people who actually do these things never have any previous fear that they may do them. The man who throws himself over Waterloo Bridge or in front of a train *for no reason* has never had any premonition of it. I suppose the whole thing comes from being over-strung. Have for years had "compulsional neuroses", like touching railings or lamp-posts, or not walking on the cracks in pavements. Have known myself turn out the gas four, eight, sixteen or thirty-two times, always in multiples of four. Have had to have sleeveless vests to avoid pulling at the sleeves, and lots of things like that, to get out of a habit. It started when I was about sixteen. I was changing for a lawn-tennis party, and went back to tidy the clothes I had left on the bed. I remember saying to myself: "If you do that, you will do it all your life!" I went back, and I have done it all my life. I sometimes take twenty minutes to leave a room through being obliged to do these things. It can't be drink or smoke or too much sex indulgence, because all this started when I had no experience of these. When I was a boy I had to read the last sentence in any chapter some dozen times "to make sure", and when I am below par I find myself doing this at the theatre, even if the following dialogue is a blank for five minutes. Impossible to describe the hell of all this, and to look at me nobody would believe it. My best cure is to repeat Macbeth's: "Then comes my fit again," and wait till the fit passes. Except for these attacks I also am "whole as the marble, founded as the rock".

June 23

Lunched at the Club with Ralph Richardson and Cedric Hardwicke, who had brought Boswell's *On the Profession of a Player* for me. A year or two ago Richardson had the habit of acting all his parts with his buttocks. I cured him of this, and his Henry V had no backside at all, though it reappeared, and rightly, in his next comic part.

August 19

The ordinary playgoer is semi-articulate. He will tell you that a play is "dreadful" and leave you to guess whether he means (*a*) that being socially below dinner-jacket level it does not interest him, and he is therefore not concerned with the accuracy or dramatic value of its observation, or (b) that the white-tie level being reached the piece would interest him if it were not that the plot is stupid and the character-isation feeble. This is like a traveller from a new country who should tell you that he found the climate "awful" without saying whether it was too hot or too cold, too wet or too dry.

August 20

One of the ways in which taste has changed most is in the attitude towards quotation. Montaigne has a passage about those authors "who, amidst their trivial compositions, intermingle and wrest in whole sentences taken from ancient authors, supposing by such filching-theft to purchase honour and reputation to themselves, doe cleane contrarie. For this infinite varietie and dissemblance of lustres make a face so wan, so ill-favored, and so uglie, in respect of theirs, that they lose much more than gaine thereby." Yet was there ever any other who quoted more than Montaigne? I suppose that his borrowings make up more than one-tenth of his total matter. Bacon in his *Essays* has 131 quotations from the Latin alone. Hazlitt . . . But then I could go on and cite any number of great quoters.

The modern attitude is, I suppose, something like this: "I want to know what James Agate thinks about this new play. Is it good or bad or just indifferent? Is it worth my while to see it? I do not want to know what Balzac thought about Talma, or whether he did or didn't see him. I don't want any second-hand opinions from Lessing or Lemaître or Lewes. I have these authors on my bookshelves and can take them down if I want. (This is a lie—they haven't and they can't.) I don't want to read what Agate thinks is fine writing any more than I want fine writing from a tipster who is going to tell me what will win the 3.30. I want Agate to tell me without embellishments whether last night's play did or did not win the 8.30!"

My answer is this: "You cannot dispose of a play by saying that it is either rotten or not rotten. A piece of writing by a playwright calls for a piece of writing by the critic. By this I do not mean fine writing, and the reason why all my life I have been so liberal in quotation has nothing to do with embellishment. The first object in writing is to impart information, and when I quote, it is because I desire to get into the reader's head something which is not there. The reader who remembers the lines:

> Against the blown rose may they stop their nose
> That kneel'd unto the buds

must lump the old thing being shoved down his throat again for the sake of the ninety-nine readers who do not know it, who haven't a Shakespeare handy, who wouldn't know where to look for the passage if they had, and who with the help of it will better grasp whatever point I am making.

There is a passage about *King Lear* which I have quoted *ad nauseam* and shall continue to quote though people nauseate me for it. In one scale is the informed reader's scorn at having the old thing trotted out again; in the other is the amazed delight of ninety-nine other readers making acquaintance with it for the first time. It is a passage from Karl von Holtei's *Reminiscences* and runs as follows:

> Devrient played with overwhelming, violent exaltation; it seemed to me that the emptiness of the house spurred him on to exert himself trebly in sheer defiance. After the second act there was a long wait. At last the stage-manager came before the curtain and informed the small audience that Herr Devrient had fallen down in a fit, and was quite unable to go on acting. The evening's performance must therefore unavoidably be considered at an end. The audience left quietly. I ran about in the street outside, driven by a deadly fear, keeping my eyes on the door by which the actors went out and in. . . . At last they brought him out, still dressed, in part, in the old king's costume. It was a strange scene. The disordered clothing, the pale face, the bright daylight. . . . It was as if they were carrying a dead man from the battle-field.

Jock says that this occurs in at least eleven of my twenty-two books, and I say that if I write twenty-two more it will re-occur in exactly half of them.

And then I am sick of those carpers who say: "Yes, James, it's all very well for Bacon and Montaigne. But they're different!" Now what do they mean by "different"? They mean, of course, that Bacon and Montaigne are better writers than I am, which should make them all the more annoyed at being fobbed off by quotations in these better writers. Why should they insist upon having the whole of, and nothing but, the infinitely poorer me?

I think the libraries have something to do with it. Having inherited a Montaigne or got it from The Times Book Club they don't mind if he quotes. But when they have paid with an actual twopence for the *Sunday Times*, they want their twopence-worth of original writing and feel themselves defrauded whenever they see a quotation. "We've paid money to have this fellow sweat his intellectual guts out, and sweat he shall!" I believe they calculate this to six places of decimals!

September 1

Letter from Leo with this passage:

> Which reminds me of my favourite story of you. Once I was in great trouble—something domestic, no doubt. Coming for sympathy and advice I found you in the throes of your weekly article for the *Saturday*, biting your pencil and saying, "I can't find the right adjective for this sentence. What I've got doesn't seem to fit. Can you think of something better?" I made a suggestion which was received with rapture and adopted. You then said, "Come on Leo, out with it!" I began, and your face assumed that benign smile which it wears when you are interested or amused. On I went, not noticing that your smile waned and was replaced by a look of worry. Finished, I said, "Well, Jimmie!" and waited. Presently, coming out of a dream, you said, "I *was* right. That first adjective will have to go back!"

October 13

'No plays worth seeing except *Children in Uniform*, about which I broadcast last night. All my colleagues try to explain Manuela on the grounds that she had no mother and was lonely. But how do they explain the young schoolmistress? Had she no mother either? And what may the Headmistress be supposed to mean by the categoric statement that Manuela is "just like a boy"? The truth is that Podsnap still rules this silly island.

October 14

Here's the stuff I broadcast about *Children in Uniform*:

> When a German is confronted with something outside normal experience he sits down to study it, whereas an Englishman in the same situation sends for a policeman. The German is perfectly willing to believe that something he has not previously encountered in the world may nevertheless be as old as the world itself, whereas your Englishman, meeting something for the first time, imagines that it must be the first time the thing has happened. This explains why the Germans are a race of philosophers and the English a collection of cricketers.
>
> The theme of *Children in Uniform* has been in existence ever since the world has had children, and you probably all know that it concerns what, in a schoolgirl, the English like to call *hero worship*

for her mistress. The theme is, we cheerfully admit, familiar enough in Germany, though we cannot imagine our own Becky Sharp viewing even the young Miss Pinkerton in this light.

Your Englishman, confronted by something abnormal will always pretend that it isn't there. If he can't pretend that, he will look through the object, or round it, or above it or below it, or in any direction except into it. If, however, you *force* him to look into it, he will at once pretend that he sees the object not for what it is but for something that he would like it to be. Show him an act of motor-banditry, and he will rejoice that the spirit of adventure still prevails with the young. Read to him out of the Sunday paper an account of some maniac who, for the fun of it, has put an old lady through her own mangle and then made off with the twopence-ha'penny yielded in the process, and he will not be horror-struck at the existence of people whose hobby is the outrage *qua* outrage, but deplore that to obtain twopence-ha'penny so much unnecessary violence was used.

Now translate the foregoing into terms of sex. The Englishman can get along with sex quite perfectly so long as he can pretend that it isn't sex but something else. Some little time ago I was asked to interest myself in a play about a young French girl who went into a nunnery at Étaples because of her spiritual and fragrant hero-worship of the Mother Superior. The Mother Superior being promoted to Paris, the young nun, who could not follow her, committed suicide.

To which I replied that I had written a play about a young man who had joined the London Midland and Scottish Railway as a porter because of his spiritual and fragrant hero-worship of the station-master at Rugby. The station-master being promoted to Euston, the porter put his head under the next train!

Now I cannot for the life of me see why a play about a nun should be awarded the Ballyhoo Prize for 1933, whereas the same play about a railway-porter would succeed in getting its author thrown out of every decent club in London. I do not see why if we are going to have plays showing Paul Dombey adoring Dr Blimber, David Copperfield gazing shyly at the flute-playing Mr Mell, and poor Smike cleaning the windows of Dotheboys Hall not for dear life but for dear Mr Squeers!

Mind you, I am not asking for, and I do not particularly want, queer plays. All I ask, apropos of *Maedchen in Uniform*, is for some uniformity in that old maid, Mrs Grundy. I think I am correct in saying that in its play form the film has been watered down. There is a scene in which a young girl trembles at first sight of the sympathetic mistress, and the explanation is offered that it is because she has lost her mother!

This brings me back to that policeman who is the British cure for everything. There is a story of an English peer who was waiting to take his ticket at a railway booking-office, when his valet, who was standing by with the usual bags, rugs, papers and so forth, ventured to call his master's attention to the fact that the man in front of his lordship had fallen down dead. "Rubbish!" said the nobleman. "Fetch a policeman!"

That, of course, is our attitude to any fact of sex, biology or even Nature herself. I have not the slightest doubt that the Englishman considers the amoeba's habit of splitting in two as highly improper, and would stop it if he could. He is firmly convinced that there ought to be a gentleman-amoeba and a lady-amoeba—and if there aren't such things, then the amoeba is not nice to know.

The Englishman, you see, divides the entire universe into things nice to know and things not nice to know—the only remaining category being things nice not to know.

It only remains to be said that *Children in Uniform* as presented at the Duchess Theatre, is an intensely moving little tragedy of sex and nothing whatever else, and that it is to be praised for handling a difficult subject with the greatest possible delicacy.

Now when an Englishman says a subject has been exquisitely handled he always means exquisitely avoided. This is not the case here. The play is beautifully acted, two lovely performances are given by Miss Jessica Tandy and Miss Joyce Bland, and there is some first-class playing by a very large cast.

At the same time I do not advise Miss Christa Winsloe who wrote the play, Miss Barbara Burnham who translated it, and Miss Leontine Sagan who produced it—I do not advise these ladies to dramatise *Eric: or Little by Little*, for if they do they will doubtless find themselves marched little by little to the police-station.

1933

February 20

Lunched with Lionel Fielden and Cecil Madden, both of the B.B.C. Fielden told me of a lively bit of dialogue at a dinner-party an evening or two ago.

A BRIGADIER. There must always be righteous wars.

FIELDEN. What in your opinion, sir, would be a righteous war?

BRIGADIER. Damn it, a war to prevent naked savages raping one's womenfolk!

FIELDEN. The first time a naked savage lays a finger on Mrs Culverin I give you my word, General, I'll enlist!

True story: The Mayor of some Lancashire town being presented with a pair of statues for the Town Hall remarked after inspecting the nude figures: "Art is art, and nothing can be done to prevent it. But there is the Mayoress's decency to be considered!"

March 6

Spent the morning with Dame Madge Kendal, who will be 84 in a
week's time. The old lady was in tremendous fettle and looking as
imposing as ever. With the exception of Queen Victoria she must be
the greatest English public monument since Boadicea. Her voice was
ringing and full, her gestures magnificent and her sense of humour
quite unimpaired. I took with me a little silver basket of camellias
and forget-me-nots, like one of her old bonnets. The object of the visit
was to arrange for her appearance in my new series of broadcast
talks: "Stars in their Courses". I wanted her to do *The Likeness of the
Night*, to which she objected that there are no good speeches for her.
The same with the old comedies, and as for the *Lady of Lyons*, it appears
the effect is visual and depends on her play of shoulder. The real
reason is that the old lady insists upon playing Rosalind, in which I
am told she was always not *bad* but something different, *not Rosalind*.
A young man called to tune the piano, and Dame Madge didn't object.
I did, and strongly, saying I didn't hear her voice often enough to have
so great a pleasure spoiled. We got on like two houses on fire. Apropos
of the Queen she said: "That's a good woman. I used to read to her
grandmother, the old Duchess of Cambridge."

March 8

Lunched with Charles Laughton, who asks my advice as to whether
he shall join the Old Vic. with Flora Robson.* Won't play Falstaff,
whom he hates. "I had to throw too many of his kind out of our hotel
when I was sixteen." Is making a Henry VIII picture and intends to
show him not as a phallus with a crown but as the morbid, introspective
fellow he actually was.

October 4

Listened in to the D minor Brahms Concerto, played by Solomon.
Enjoyed it very much in spite of passing railways trains and motors
changing gear uphill, and until in the middle of the last movement
the batteries ran out. This was my first acquaintance with the work.
Which only shows how shockingly uneducated I am. Only last week
I visited the Tate Gallery for the first time!!!! The best picture, in my
view, was Millais's "Christ in the House of His Parents", not because

---

* He did after making *The Private Life of Henry VIII*. "I went to the Old Vic. to
learn to speak," he explained at the time. His great ambition had always been to
play Macbeth, but unfortunately it proved a failure. "In tackling Macbeth, Laughton
for the first time in his career was in a position where he could not play Laughton,"
his biographer, Kurt Singer, has explained. *Ed.*

of the subject but because I was brought up on Holman Hunt's "The Hireling Shepherd" and Madox Brown's "Work" in the Manchester Art Gallery. Also Millais's "Autumn Leaves", though I loathe the anecdotal stuff. (By the way, is "The Hireling Shepherd" Hunt or Brown?) [Hunt.] The picture I liked next best was Degas's "Sur la Plage", and there was a charming Utrillo. There was a typical James Pryde, about somebody being buried in a grave dug in the floor of a bedroom and at the foot of a four-poster with a tester forty feet high. The Whistlers seemed to me to be becoming merely pretty. The trousers on Chatterton as he lies dead are a lovely blue, and Landseer's "The Bay Mare" is shoved away in a corner. But all this is no reason why my new house-parlourman should always arrange to let the batteries on the wireless run down whenever I am here! To make up for this he arranges flowers better than Fantin Latour could paint them. His name is Caddick, he comes from Cannock, and is a rattling good nurse. When I am nervy he doesn't rattle me. Was with the *Sign of the Cross* on tour for some years and played Romans and Christians impartially. I asked him if it was a No. 4 company and he said it would have been if there had been three others.

December 21

Mill's Circus at Olympia. Usual circus, usual luncheon, usual speech by Lord Lonsdale on the absence of cruelty. I should like to be let into the secret of how a forest-bred lion is peacefully persuaded to park his royal person on a yard of red plush on the top of a flight of steps and sit up and beg like a poodle.

1934

May 1

There are some little things in this newspaper world of ours which irritate me to the point when I do not know whether to laugh or cry. One of these is the craven attitude taken up towards advertisers. During the war a little east-coast resort, well known for its snobbery, did not allow wounded soldiers on its promenade. A great newspaper suppressed my reference to this grotesque piece of nonsense because it was afraid of offending one or two of that stinking little hole's hotels advertising in its columns.

Another thing is the absurd jealousy among papers. They are so afraid of advertising a rival that they will not even call the *News of the World* Golf Tournament by its right name if they can avoid it. Even more idiotic is the mania for self-advertisement, which will not boggle at such a sentence as: "The outbreak of war on August 4th, 1914, which, as readers will remember, was announced in *The Daily Blare* . . ."

I never hope to persuade newspapers to believe that a piece of writing is a piece of writing and should be paragraphed as the author wrote it. The view taken is that no reader can take in more than an inch without a break. But there is one folly which drives me to frenzy and against which I have fought for years and am still fighting. This is the mania for putting numbers into figures so that you find this kind of thing:

> Since the span of human life is 3 score years and 10, we do well to remember the poet's advice:

> In delay there lies no plenty;
> Then come kiss me, sweet and 20.

The lines, of course, are from 12*th Night*! Good shorthand and all right in a Diary but hellish in a piece of considered writing.

EGO 2

August 1934–June 1936

September 12 *Wednesday*

Received this from Edith Sitwell:

> *Rue Saint-Dominique,*
> *Paris VIIe.*
> 11*th September, 1934.*

DEAR MR AGATE,

I should have written to you much sooner, but no letters were forwarded to me as I was motoring about France. Before that, I was at Brides-les-Bains, a scene of much desolation, and the temporary haunt of people who have eaten so much that nature has supervened, and driven them to this desert where they can eat nothing. Here, my brother Osbert and I were much afflicted by the conversation of a Swiss lady who babbled of D. H. Lawrence and Aldous Huxley. Eventually, she asked me if I wrote under my own name, and if she ought to have heard of me. This annoyed me—it shows how conceited I am—and I replied: "I do, and you could not have heard of me. But my brother writes under the name of Clemence Dane." Unfortunately, the news spread like wildfire, and the Swiss lady, clasping her hands and turning up her eyes, kept on saying: "How *great* she is, your Dane! She is great as your Barrie! She is great as your Galsworthy, or your Walpole!" Told everybody. So that Osbert, looking very angry, sat surrounded by quite a little court of admirers of *Will Shakespeare*. He was perfectly furious, especially when photographers tried to take snapshots of him for the English newspapers. On one occasion, to my unconcealed delight, the Swiss lady, who was the high priestess of his admirers, spoke of him as the Great Dane. She is going to marry an Englishman and live in England, so there will be an awful scandal—especially as I have told her that *Will Shakespeare* was the result of automatic writing, and that Osbert wrote it in his sleep and must not be questioned about it as the doctor says the shock will be too much for his brain if he finds he has written it. This was because she wanted him to give a reading. I told her a lot about "literary life" in England. Oh, a lot! I have never met Miss Dane, but hear on all sides that she is a delightful woman, so I hope this scandal will not touch her too nearly.

Yours sincerely,

EDITH SITWELL

September 27 Thursday

Called on Dame Madge Kendal. She talked of her father, "who, if he had lived, would now be nearly a hundred", obviously forgetting that she herself is eighty-five. A bundle of majesty still. Some of the things she said to-day: Apropos of to-day's players: "My dear Mr Agate, you must not ask me to be impressed by any modern young actress. I saw Ristori! When the executioner bound Marie Antoinette's hands behind her and cut off her curls, the tears used to roll down Ristori's face as she said: 'Louis loved my curls.' To do this in full view of the public, Mr Agate, is acting."

"Ristori was a greater actress than Sarah because she had no sex-appeal."

"I once heard Sarah recite *Les Deux Pigeons* in a drawing-room. I watched not Sarah but the audience, and whatever it was she made the pigeons say and do, the effect on the audience was improper."

"The greatest of all was Rachel, whose life I daresay you have read." (I did not point out that I had written it!) "My father used to say that Rachel hardly ever made a gesture and would recite fifty lines of Racine or Corneille without one. But that on the rare occasions when she did make a gesture it swept everybody out of the theatre."

Apropos of *Josephine*: "There is nobody living to-day who could play Napoleon except, possibly, Cedric Hardwicke. He would be able to play him in a little way."

"S—— (I have forgotten the name Dame Madge said) was an actor of the old school. When, as Virginia, I embraced him as Virginius I used to take his temples in my two hands. Once this caused his toupet to rise and leave a gap. But he covered his head with his toga, and the audience perceived nothing. At the end he used to take my hair, which was long enough for me to sit on, and wrap it round the handle of his dagger before plunging the blade into my back."

She then recited some Wordsworth, and insisted on escorting me to the door herself.

1935

January 29 Tuesday

With some inconsiderable exceptions the reviews [of *Ego*] are the handsomest lot I have ever seen and far beyond anything I could possibly have hoped for. Incomparably the finest, of course, is Rebecca West's. This is a masterpiece of wit, writing and criticism. As she may never reprint it and as it ought not to be lost, here it is:

Our Mr Agate, the *Sunday Times* Mr Agate, the world's Mr Agate, is one of those people who create an impression of having strayed into life out of art. He is no larger than life, but certainly twice as natural. He has the concentrated and exaggerated aspect of a Falstaff or a Don Quixote, sharply focused to present its essentials to the human attention within the narrow limits of a work of art: he does not meander along with neutral tints, the damped down traits of those of us who are unframed save by seventy years or so and the whole of terrestrial space.

He is as recognisable as Mr Pickwick. When he appears in his evening clothes at the Ivy, anthropologists would have much ado to find a tribe of savages so unsophisticated that they did not instantly recognise that here was a dramatic critic. When he goes forth with his golf clubs or about his business with his trotting ponies he glows with a healthy tan, which is not, in fact, like the skin of any person who lives an out-of-door life, but which is exactly like the make-up of an actor playing the part of a person who lives an out-of-door life. His conversation falls into lines, his parleys with his friends divide themselves into scenes.

When his friends speak of James Agate and how charming he is without saying who he is by, it seems an example of that contempt for authorship reprehensible in many theatres, which are covered with the names of the stars in electric lights and posters covered with Press comments, but which omit to mention the name of the author who wrote the play.

That this impression of Mr Agate is no mere fantasy is proven by *Ego*, his truly extraordinary autobiography. It is well known that Pirandello and Mr Agate are not soul-mates, but this book presents a situation without parallel save in *Six Characters in Search of an Author*. For it tells a story that cannot possibly be true in the world of fact.

It is not that Mr Agate is telling lies; plainly, the facts he describes are the only and the only veridical facts about Mr Agate. But all the same, they cannot exist in this real world. They are inconsistent, they depend on no causal principle, people simply would not let them happen.

The obvious explanation is that Mr Agate is a character in the mind of a good but careless writer, who has made a lot of notes for the novel in which he intends him to figure, but who has just let the stuff pile up uncollated. This alone can be the reason why Mr Agate's family, firmly embedded in Lancashire, should habitually converse in adept French. It cannot really be a consequence of Mr Agate's grandmother having been in France as a governess, in which situation she became engaged to Guizot [French statesman and historian], but failed to marry him because she fell victim to a spinal disease which forced her to recline on a mattress, in which, doubtless for old times' sake, the resourceful girl secreted secret correspondence between Louis Philippe and her lover.

It really will not do. The explanation must be some scribbled note: "Whole family speak French fluently. Invent reason why." And it is odd that Mr Agate should complain about the governess-Guizot legend that "I have never believed a word of the story, and the dates do not fit", for he has written novels himself and should know the stage when an ultimately quite consistent story reads as "Grandmother went France governess—engaged great man—Guizot? Guizeau?—engagement broken off because bedridden by illness—bedridden woman secret agent—hides letters in mattress?—check dates." Mr Agate can console himself by reflecting that his grandmother and possibly all the circumstances of his tangled life will be all right in the typescript.

But really there is a great deal of work to be done on the notes. The author might have settled where his hero is to live. One of the most curious features in this record is the number of houses Mr Agate seems to inhabit. The only reason that with all his competing interests he continues to be a dramatic critic seems to be that a certain number of theatres must lie on the intersecting routes between his homes. "Lives Barnet? Bloomsbury? Westcliff? Bayswater?"

The desperate confusion that rages in his unsettled mind on this matter is mirrored in a wonderful sentence which can serve as a sample of this uniquely mad and charming book: "I have proved to myself *on paper* that three houses with only one tenanted one are as cheap as two houses fully inhabited." And there we come on the fringe of the most astounding unreal reality in Mr Agate's autobiography: his financial condition. This is sheer delirium. His accounts of his pecuniary affairs are more elaborate than anything in literature save Balzac's *César Birotteau*, but César was a more real personality than Mr Agate, and his budgets are humanly possible. Mr Agate's are not. Money flows in at the door to reward his remarkable industry, and on the hall floor turns to writs, and they have to be paid out in income-tax, with which, however, he seems to buy champagne and ponies in large quantities. Someone must have scribbled "Agate. Rich? Poor? Has Bentley because he loves comfort (comic stuff). No. Mustn't have too much money. Picks Bentley up for nothing. Must have money to enable him to show his gusto for living. No, mustn't have money, much too Bohemian. Settle all this later."

February 2 Saturday

Motored to Worthing. Leo in great form. Noting some workmen tinkering at a good Georgian building Leo said "Business as usual during the deteriorations". Also told me a story of X——, a well-known pianist and teacher suspected of flirting, and worse, with his pupils. An irate mother called one day and said to the maid who opened the door, "Is Mr. X—— giving my daughter a lesson?" The maid drew her apron across her nose and said: "Not now 'e ain't, mum. I can 'ear the piano."

Went for a stroll on the front and noted that all the women looked like Cicely Courtneidge in 'Arringay mood. Stood for some time leaning over a rail while Leo tried to quote Homer and keep his hat on simultaneously.

Lunched at Warne's Hotel, where the food even at half past two was excellent. Taking up the bill of fare Leo said: "Are we going to eat or tell our pasts, James? I'm in my most veracious mood." I said, "Do you spell that with an 'o' or an 'e'?"

Later Leo was seized by a sudden attack of pianism, owing to the discovery that the hotel piano was in tune. He made a terrific onslaught on Bach's Chromatic Fantasia and Fugue followed by Chopin's F minor Fantaisie. Both very fine, and listening to him I felt like a very small King of Bavaria. To turn on the wireless is one thing; to be played to alone is another. Leo reminded me that I once gave him the piano score of a Mozart Piano Concerto, with my name on it and the date 1890. This shows that I must have played or at any rate studied the work at the age of thirteen!! This afternoon Leo made the hotel rock, but not so dangerously as Charlie Openshaw says Westminster Abbey is rocking owing to Dickens turning in his grave at his and Ethel Dickens's adaptation of *Great Expectations* shortly to be produced with Martin-Harvey as Magwitch.

Dined at the Royal Albion. In the smoke-room before dinner Leo had a talk with, but did not introduce me to, a youngish very well-groomed man-about-town. After he had gone Leo said: "I was once asked to settle a dispute as to whether that fellow had been at Eton or Harrow. I answered, truthfully, that I couldn't decide the point, as when I first knew him he was third footman to Lord B." He went on. "I stood in the dock with him in 1902 on the charge of resisting the police outside the old Spaten Buffet in Piccadilly Circus."

During dinner the band, or some of it, played "Softly awakes my Heart," arranged for solo violin with a modicum of piano. When it was over, Leo called the head-waiter and said, "Kindly ask them to play the Ninth Symphony."

February 3 *Sunday*

I feel I ought to say what Leo looks like. He is sixty, middle-sized, with a bullet-shaped head cropped close, and extremely short-sighted. This makes him screw up his eyes, thus increasing the resemblance to an india-rubber doll whose expression changes at will. He invariably says the wrong thing, but deliberately and at the top of his voice. A gormandiser without a palate. Extremely untidy, and I remember that one day after he tried to cook for me I found stumps of asparagus sticking to the bottoms of the chairs. Yet this apparently warped and twisted creature is possessed of a greater kindness of heart, if he likes you, than almost anybody I know, though affection with him generally takes the form of bickering. A great reader with a wonderful, unprecise memory. A brilliant musician *manqué*—largely because he has always gone out of his way to annoy people who have tried to help him. If I had to put him in three words I should say—a Jewish Dr. Johnson.

It is a unique sight to see this odd creature ambling along a London street with his head on one side and pouring out invective to which Ernest Fenton impassively listens. Fenton is over six feet and looks like a vicious Renaissance cardinal out of a play by John Ford. Both are a bit of the 'nineties which has unaccountably survived.

February 4 *Monday*

Amusing post-bag. A young woman in County Down sends me a play which begins with the heroine cantering up an avenue on a chestnut mare. Also a letter from Winifred Graham hoping I don't mind her using my surname for a leading character in her sixty-third novel, *Hallowmas Abbey*. In the end Agate, who is a villain, sets the Abbey on fire and is consumed, and the book ends with the owner thanking God the haunted Abbey is in ashes and selling the site for a crematorium!

In Desmond MacCarthy's lovely book *Experience*—it's a bad title but the stuff is as readable as pie-crust is eatable—I came across a passage which, If I had known of it before, would have gone on to the front page of *Ego*. Desmond is discussing the fatal propensity of biographers, critics and moralists to judge people and things by the wrong standards:

> One who wrote of Bulwer-Lytton complained that in relation to his troublesome wife he did not behave like a gentleman. The standard applied must have been severe. I know what happened. The critic was comparing Lytton's behaviour with that of men who would never have got in such a predicament with their wives at all. Biographers, critics and moralists are always doing that. Has a man got into debt? His behaviour in that trying circumstance is compared with the hypothetical behaviour of, say, a man like Franklin, who would never have got into debt. Does a passion make hay of a man's life? His struggles are dubbed feeble by his biographer because Cromwell would have got the impulses under. Does another write a play on a theme which Ibsen would never have chosen? He is hauled over the coals for not conducting his plot with Ibsen's consistency.

The sentence would have been exactly right for *Ego*. In the essay on Chess there is another extremely interesting passage:

I am told that in the abstract world of mathematics, the methods of one man will reveal his individuality to fellow-mathematicians as clearly as a writer's style reveals him to literary men. It is the same in chess. True, you and I, reader, are unlikely, when playing over a match between, say, Lasker and Rubinstein, to detect in the moves of the former a magnificently deep vascular temperament, or in those of his adversary the refined tranquillity of an ascetic artist, diffident but of great integrity. But let us not be too much surprised if in the Q-Kt3, QR-B1, etc. etc. of Schlechter's game with John, Réti sees "a love of Nature" and "the grace and airiness of Viennese music".

I know exactly what Desmond means. I too have to keep a check upon myself less I fall into the mistake of dismissing Réti's "grace and airiness of Viennese music" as nonsense. Only the other day I was praising Neville Cardus for describing Woolley's batting in terms of Meredith's:

Lovely are the curves of the white owl sweeping
Wavy in the dusk lit by one large star.

I praised him still more for his justification of the seeming absurdity:

I admit, O reader, that an innings by Woolley has nothing to do with owls and dusk and starlight. I am trying to describe an experience of the fancy; I am talking of the cadences, of dying falls common to all the beauty of the world. My argument, in a word, is concerned not with Woolley, the Kent cricketer, but with that essence of his batsmanship which will live on, after his cricket is done with, after his runs and his averages have been totted up and found much the same as those of many other players.

February 10 *Sunday*

In the evening dined at Stanley Rubinstein's. Also present, Benno [Moiseiwitch] and his wife, Mark, [Hambourg] and sonsy Irene Scharrer. Just as dinner started, Backhaus in the Brahms B flat Concerto came through on the wireless from Berlin. This was great fun, the others all playing detective and listening eagerly, but quite without hope, for a wrong note. Mark said he didn't think Backhaus had ever played a wrong note in his entire career, while Benno observed that he had never known him cheat to the extent of leaving out a right one!

What with the concerto and the clatter of knives and forks and Mark shouting to everybody to keep quiet, the room was pandemonium, rising to its height when in the bubbling *coda* this convocation of politic pianists joined hands and did Backhaus the honour of singing the *coda* with him.

José Levy came in after dinner and we played bridge at a shilling a hundred. By some queer chance I cut Mark almost every rubber, and he held yarborough after yarborough, one hand having nothing higher than the eight of Clubs. I held 150 aces four times and 100 honours five times, and magnificent cards all the evening, with the result that I lost only seven bob.

In the cab going home Mark said Anton Rubinstein was far and away the greatest pianist he had ever heard, though he thought Liszt might have been greater. Thinking that modern pianoforte playing must have advanced like billiards—i.e. Roberts was first-class in his day but not a patch on Lindrum—I asked whether Rubinstein would have been up to all the modern difficulties and Mark said Yes, undoubtedly. Noted how extraordinarily fresh the air was outside his house in Regent's Park, and Mark said it is always like that. Drank a glass of brandy with him in a corner of the dining room between a Raphael and an attributed Giorgione!

March 13 *Wednesday*

Geoffrey Whitworth has written to invite me to join the General Committee of the Shakespeare Memorial National theatre. I sent back a very loud and positive No, but said that I was perfectly willing to be on the Executive Committee. General Committees are a mere pretext for getting nothing done. The bigger and more representative the Committee, the less likelihood is there of anything happening. In my view, London doesn't desire or feel the need for a National Theatre, for if it insisted on having one in the way in which it has insisted on the stadiums at Wembley, Highbury and Stamford Bridge, it would have one. Besides, the existing Committee with its £150,000 has quite enough money to run a theatre. What it wants the remaining £350,000 for is the building. This is crazy. Having got a white elephant is no reason for building a rose-pink marble stable to house it in. If the Committee doesn't want to hire or buy an existing theatre—and some beautiful theatres are tó be had—it should, in my opinion, give the money to the Old Vic. If it cannot do this by law, then let it move Parliament to alter that law. Even altruism has its time limit, and to say that the £150,000 cannot be handed over to the Old Vic. and must await a National Theatre proper, is like endowing pigs with aviation costumes against the time when they are going to fly. I am satisfied that the Old Vic. can supply London with all the Shakespeare it has ever wanted or is going to want, and obviously the extra £150,000 would enable that admirably managed theatre to compete in the market for acting talent.

March 25 *Monday*

Russell Thorndike told us at the Savage to-night how as a boy he met Irving. Thorndike was a chorister at St. George's Chapel, Windsor, becoming head of the Decani and Queen Victoria's last solo boy; indeed he sang a Spohr solo at the funeral service at St. George's. After the service Sir Walter Parratt asked him if there was anyone among the Kings and Queens present whom he would like to meet. Thorndike pointed to Irving. Parratt, being very friendly with Irving, at once made the introduction.

I give Irving's words as nearly as possible as Russell repeated them. "You are a star to-day my boy, and I am very glad to have supported you. I hear you want to be an actor. If you ever do, remember this: be very sparing with your make-up. Use only as much as is absolutely necessary. God and the devil have written lines on your face that will help you to show the good qualities that are in you as well as the bad. Don't cover them up. Do you understand?" Little Thorndike, feeling that it would be becoming in him not to understand so great a man too readily, replied: "I'm afraid I don't sir!" Whereupon Irving resumed: "Well, my boy, there are only two ways of portraying a character on the stage. Either you can try to turn yourself into that person—which is impossible—or, and this is the way to act, you can take that person and turn him into yourself. That is how I do it!"

April 3 Wednesday

First night of *The Old Ladies*, the play made by Rodney Ackland out of Hugh's [Walpole] novel. A huge success and very fine acting by Mary Jerrold, Jean Cadell, and Edith Evans. Not more than a pin between any of them. Heard a good story. It appears that at the first rehearsal Hugh went up to Edith and said: "I hope you like the novel." Edith is said to have looked him full in the face and blurted out: "Oh! Is it from a book?" Lilian Braithwaite would have said this if she knew the novel by heart. Was given supper at the Savoy by a charming old lady, a Mrs Jefferson, who is as keen on a good hunter as Agatha Payne was on Miss Beringer's piece of amber. Believes there is nothing in the world worth living for except hunting. And at seventy, too! Martita Hunt, George Howe and a great-grandson of Coventry Patmore were the other guests.

April 4 Thursday

Here is Morgan's [Charles Morgan. See Concise Biographies] notice in *The Times* of *The Old Ladies*. I think it is the best bit of dramatic criticism since Montague. When Charles is in his best form he has us all whacked. *The Times* is happy to have a critic who is, when not insisting that sow's ears shall be silk purses, indisputably first-rate:

The lodgings of the three old ladies are in a draughty, dilapidated house in Polchester. By virtue of Motley's extremely skilful design the bleak little hall, the rickety staircase, and the three bed-sitting-rooms all lie open to view. Each room describes its inhabitant. In the foreground, on the level of the hall, is the cheerful neatness of Mrs. Amorest, a pink-cheeked widow with the gentle self-assurance of an easy conscience and a courageous, simple mind. In the curve of the staircase is the pale, indeterminate gentility of Miss Beringer, a timid creature whom life has starved and who responds to Mrs Amorest's neighbourly kindness not with warmth, for no warmth is left in her, but with an agitated, chattering gratitude at which a part of the audience laughed until even they perceived the icy tragedy of it. And on the first floor, at the back, is a room dripping with highly coloured shawls and fringes in the midst of which, telling the cards of her gypsy ancestors, Mrs Payne sits in her rocking chair, a sprawling woman like a fierce and raddled toad.

Mrs Amorest invites the others to a little party on Christmas Eve. Out of her poverty she has bought them presents and on the table has set up a tiny glittering Christmas tree. Miss Beringer is delighted, and Miss Jean Cadell, brilliantly discovering a school-girl's excitement in this old hunted woman, chatters and giggles and hesitates until one's heart would break. Miss Mary Jerrold, the hostess, calm and plump and wistful, is meanwhile drawing a portrait less spectacular, but in its nature more endearing and in its restraints as subtle. And down the stairs, supporting on the banisters her monstrous weight, comes Mrs Payne. Mrs Amorest, not being afflicted by nervous imagination, treats her with the tolerant affection that she lavishes on all the world, but poor Miss Beringer is with reason terrified. Mrs Payne says little or nothing. Colour and glitter arouse in her a silencing lust. Her black sodden eyes glare at the Christmas tree; her head becomes fixed, her bloated body seems to swell and loosen, her hands are flaccidly covetous. When at last the party is over and, on her way upstairs, she is shown the piece of carved and glowing amber that is Miss Beringer's dearest possession, her longing is directed towards it and her implacable cruelty towards its owner. The story of the play has still to be told—how Mrs Payne won the amber by a process of mental torture that drove Miss Beringer to collapse and death—but, in a sense, it is all told when Miss Edith Evans first sees the object of her desire. Her back is towards us; she is powerless to act with her face; but the wrench of that gross body, the horrible greed of the uplifted arm and hand are enough. The theme of menace and suffering is stated; what follows is a poignant elabora-tion of it. That the play is comfortable, no one need pretend; its life's blood is cruelty and terror, and they are not comfortable things; but its life is abundant, its impact continuous, and its performances, orchestrated by Mr Gielgud, collectively flawless. And Miss Evans's own performance is something more. It is creative and cumulative—a slow nightmare of *macabre* genius. The body, the eyes, the hands are terrible enough, but the mouth wears the very shape and colour of the mind's disease. The whole figure, in its stained and mountainous velvets, is like some insane doll that increases continuously in physical stature and spiritual decay.

May 7 Tuesday

Have been reading Dame Ethel Smyth's good little book on Beecham. [*Beecham and Pharaoh*.] Years ago I was lunching at the Waldorf, having vaguely noticed that at the table behind me was a party of ill-kempt, unwashable as distinct from unwashed, ragamuffins whom I took to be members of an orchestra. Suddenly I heard a silky, purring voice say: "Gentlemen, you may take it from me that Brahms never wrote anything that mattered." Without looking round I said loudly: "Nonsense, Sir Thomas!" Instantly the voice resumed: "Gentlemen, you may take it from me that with the exception of 4 symphonies, 4 concertos, 200 songs and a vast quantity of chamber music, Brahms never wrote anything that mattered!" It was in my father's dining room that my brother Edward persuaded Beecham to give his first concert in Manchester. Delius's *Sea Drift* was in the programme. The attendance in the Free Trade Hall was under 200.

Dame Ethel devotes the second half of her book to her adventures in Egypt, including the laying-out of a 9-hole golf course in the Nubian desert and her investigation into the nature of a hermaphrodite. But she does not say whether the hermaphrodite played golf, or what was its handicap!

May 28 Tuesday

The Marie Tempest matinee [arranged by the *Daily Telegraph* to celebrate Marie Tempest's Golden Jubilee] took place this afternoon at Drury Lane. Here is what I said about her over the wireless to-night:

> I am not going to waste words in giving a list of Marie Tempest's triumphs throughout fifty years. Besides you all know what they are. Nor can I hope to tell you how she looked in a dress of rose-pink silk shot with silver, the sort that Sargent painted.
>
> There are two points I want to make, a little point and a big point. The little point is this—if we were writing to, say, a cultured and intelligent foreigner, how should we describe our great English comédienne? I think we should say that Marie Tempest is an actress. By this I mean that there is no corner of the globe where she could be mistaken for anything else. In Paris, Berlin, Budapest, Sydney, Chicago—all over the world—she would be recognised as an actress. She is not one of these intellectual players who have to deliver themselves of some world-redemptive gospel in order to make it worth anybody's while to listen to them. She can very nearly do without a play, and Heaven knows that some-times she has had to!

She is mistress of all the forgotten arts of the stage—the art of walking, talking, and wearing clothes. She is mistress of the forgotten art of being a lady—an art almost entirely lost in these days. Marie Tempest is an actress of wit; and if that quality had not been in the world she would have invented it.

Her technique from her earliest musical-comedy days has always been perfect, and to her certainty in the matters of poise, balance, rhythm, and attack must be added her mastery of youth. Age is one of the lawful attributes of the tragic actor or actress; we expect some measure of old age from an Irving and a Ristori, a Geneviève Ward and a Macklin. These are the high priests and priestesses of the temple, and it is expected of them that they should be within measurable distance of the mysteries they interpret. And we are not surprised when they are.

But the business of a comédienne is to hold the years at arm's length. Which brings me to my second and big point. Marie Tempest's triumph is not only to be a famous actress or to be and look young at seventy. Her peculiar distinction is to have brought a talent to the stage, to have disciplined that talent through all the degrees of accomplishment which culminate in greatness, to have appreciated and kept before her that major quality of proportion, and to have followed the profession of actress with as much zeal and fervour as Florence Nightingale followed that of nurse or Grace Darling that of life-saver at sea. For any talent has to be nursed, and the theatrical seas can be stormy indeed!

This, then, is a moral quality, and one of the greatest. It has been my business for a good many years to record the artistic triumphs of this great little lady. To-day my privilege is to do honour to a precious talent not one grain of which has been spilt or squandered.

Further, it is a talent which is not yet garnered. I don't know what in words she has said to Mr Graham Browne, her husband and partner through so many years. But I know that her thoughts were Browning's when he wrote:

Grow old along with me!
The best is yet to be.

Mary went through it all with perfect aplomb. The King and Queen were there, but all George Bishop's art and craft failed with old Madge Kendal, besought in vain to bestow on the affair the august sanction of her bonnet. Hayden Coffin didn't show up either. Of all the two hundred and fifty actors who took part in the masque the one I admired most was John Gielgud. I wonder whether John is a *great* actor. His grace and poise are remarkable, and his voice would melt the entire Inland Revenue. Perhaps he is a great actor in the making. It occurred to me this afternoon that I have never seen a great *young* actor. Sarah, Réjane, Duse, Madge Kendal, Ellen Terry, Irving, Coquelin, Guitry père, Wyndham, Hare, even Forbes-Robertson, who was forty-four when he played Hamlet, were all old or getting on when I first saw them. Does this mean that I instinctively regard age as an essential quality in great acting? It is handsome of me to record the query, and I sincerely hope the Bergnerites don't get hold of it!

May 29 *Wednesday*

The Daily Express asked me to do an impression of the Rattenbury Trial at the Old Bailey. The facts were very simple and hardly disputed. Mrs Rattenbury, aged thirty-eight, wife of an architect aged sixty-seven, had been the mistress of her eighteen-year-old chauffeur named Stoner. Somebody had hit the husband over the head with a mallet, both of them having at one time or another taken the blame on themselves.

It was all very like the three French major novelists. The way in which the woman debauched the boy so that he slept with her every night with her six-year-old son in the room, and the husband who had his own bedroom remaining cynically indifferent—all this was pure Balzac. In the box Mrs Rattenbury looked and talked exactly as I have always imagined Emma Bovary looked and talked. Pure Flaubert. And last there was that part of her evidence in which she described how, trying to bring her husband round, she first accidentally trod on his false teeth and then tried to put them back into his mouth so that he could speak to her. This was pure Zola. The sordidness of the whole thing was relieved by one thing and one only. This was when Counsel asked Mrs Rattenbury what her first thought had been when her lover got into bed that night and told her what he had done. She replied: "My first thought was to protect him." This is the kind of thing which Balzac would have called sublime, and it is odd that, so far as I saw, not a single newspaper reported it.

All the time I was sitting there, there was something at the back of my mind which gave a picture of the woman in the dock better than the parallel with Emma. I couldn't think what it was, but on getting home told Jock, who found what I was looking for in my old *Manchester Guardian* cutting-book. The passage is part of a notice by Montague:

> The Lady Ellingham of the play is animated by Mrs Campbell into one of the women whom she acts as a class rather than individually—so that her acting almost seems like an argument, a theory of femininity, like Matthew Arnold's about "things that live and move Mined by the fever of the soul." Her Lady Ellingham seems, behind all that she directly says, to be asserting the title of a certain temperament to more of the good things of the emotional world than it commonly gets: the appealing lassitude, the troubled and plaintive tenderness all seem like changing modes following some one quest.

The general opinion appears to be that the woman will get off.

May 30 *Thursday*

Took Denys Blakelock to supper. He confessed to a *bon mot* at my expense. Asked whether I was going to the first night of *Acropolis* he had said: "Sure, I met him this afternoon coming away from his crammer's!" Promises to invite me home to lunch with his people as soon as I can satisfy him that I am "vicarage-trained".

May 31 *Friday*

Mrs Rattenbury acquitted and Stoner condemned to death. The second must not happen. If I had been on the jury I would have stuck out for a verdict of manslaughter, bad though that would have been in law, because there is no certainty that the recommendation to mercy, made in this case, will be given effect to. Such a recommendation should automatically mean that the man will not hang. In its account of the last scene *The Daily Sketch* has this cryptic sentence: "A mere boy, but it may be that he behaved as a man behaves." What a rum thing is the mind! This trial has moved me immensely, probably because I saw part of it, while the dreaful affair at Quetta makes no impression. The 20000 said to have perished in that earthquake might be flies. I see no remedy for this; one can't order one's feelings, and to pretend something different is merely hypocrisy. I suppose one could just shut up and perhaps ought to. Meanwhile the Rattenbury verdict, happening in the afternoon, has given an immense fillip to Emlyn Williams's *Night Must Fall*, a good, highly imaginative play about a murder in an Essex bungalow.

June 5 *Wednesday*

As we were setting off in the car the newspapers came out with the placard: "Mrs Rattenbury Stabbed and Drowned." [Mrs Rattenbury stabbed herself six times on the bank of a river and toppled in, drowning herself.] Reggie Arkell said this was the most dramatic thing he had seen in the streets since "Titanic Sinking". The two things in this kind which have shocked me most have been the arrest of Crippen, about which I read on the pier at Llandudno—I can still point out the exact plank on which I stood—and the newspaper placard announcing the death of Marie Lloyd. I remember how this rooted me to the pavement in Tottenham Court Road.

September 5 Thursday

At the theatre last night Peter Page showed me a cutting from a gossip column:

> Seen at a house party, Claire Luce curled up in an onion bed eating 'em raw and reading Kant's *Critique of Pure Reason.*

"It's true," said Peter. "It happened at my place last Sunday. Claire called me across to the onion bed, waved her book at me and said in her rich American accent: 'Peter, I don't get this guy. If what he calls the thing in itself really is the thing in itself, it kinda queers Plato's definition of the absolute!' "

September 25 Wednesday

Lunched at the Ivy with Curt Dehn, my lawyer, who asked the name of the man lunching opposite. I said, "John Gielgud." Dehn said, "It's a rum sort of head. The profile's Roman Emperor, but the rest is still at Eton." He told me that in Hamburg, and indeed other parts of Germany, whenever two friends part after a conversation in which politics have cropped up, it is not unusual for one to say to the other: *"Sie haben auch was gesagt!"* [You have also said something.] This is one of the most sinister things I ever heard.

September 30 Monday

The *Daily Express* blows the gaff this morning about Madge Kendal and her children, who get nothing from this Roman matron's estate except the income from £5000 under their father's will. In an interview one of the daughters speaks of her mother's "ungovernable temper". This is putting it mildly, for all actors know that in the theatre she was a virago unchained. There is a dreadful story about Madge K. and an ingénue shivering in the wings prior to making a first appearance. Madge strode up to the child, and tearing a wreath from her head together with a handful of curls said in an awful voice: "You are supposed to be the vicar's daughter. How dare you attempt to go on my stage looking like the village whore?" I think it was Courtenay Thorpe who told me this. He had a tremendous admiration for her as an artist. But her bosom in family matters was of stone, and it was this quality which in one play at least enabled her to reach the heights of a great tragic actress. Other actresses in *The Likeness of the Night*, when they said "Go back!" to the mistress about to touch the wife's hand, would have contrived a certain frostiness; Mrs. Kendal put an Ice Age between the pair. She inspired terror because, *au fond*, she was terrible. Madge Kendal was a Fury in human guise. That was nature; her pathos and her comedy, both irresistible, were art. Only fools will argue whether they would have preferred a better mother and a worse actress.

A cloud no bigger than a man's hand has appeared on the horizon. Jock, who is on three days' holiday, writes that Ivor Brown [see Concise Biographies] is insistently recommending him as his successor on *The Manchester Guardian*, the change to take place at once. (It seems that Ivor wants to cut down his work a little.) Jock writes that he will agree to anything that doesn't mean abandoning me entirely.

October 8 *Tuesday*

An idle day, which means that I have overlooked an article. Shall occupy it in setting down something about actors and acting, since after all that is probably what most people read me for. As I have written elsewhere all I have to say of the players of my youth and in view of that vow to say no more about Sarah I shall jot down some recollections of my father's table-talk. When I was a boy we had a Sunday dinner-table to absent oneself from which was an unheard-of thing. At dessert my father would hold forth about all the great actors and actresses he had seen. The list began with Macready, of whom he had no very great opinion; he was too cold. Phelps was a great name, together with the Younger Mathews. Fechter, too, he thought a brilliant actor, and I who had already read George Henry Lewes to Fechter's detriment had some difficulty in restraining my tongue. Then there was a great deal of talk about Fanny Kemble, and Helen Faucit, and especially about Modjeska, an exquisite Polish actress who was a beautiful Juliet. In 1881 Modjeska appeared in Manchester in *Frou-frou*, and W. T. Arnold wrote in the *M.G.* as follows: "The opening of the fourth act was touchingly played with a kind of sad dignity which suited the part. The scene with Sartorys was moving and powerful and the death scene in the fifth act touching. Its great merit was the continued thought for the child at the dying woman's feet. Sarah Bernhardt forgot him too soon." I was only four years old when this appeared, and not a noticeably better dramatic critic than some of my young colleagues to-day. Also I did not see Modjeska, though when years later I saw Sarah play Frou-frou, Arnold seemed to me to have committed rank lèse-majesté.

Three names were continually on my father's lips—those of Alfred Wigan, Barry Sullivan, and "Little" Robson. The critics of the past treated Wigan rather shabbily, and the best thing I have ever been able to find about him is Henry Morley's: "Mr Wigan has been for many years quietly and steadily advancing in the public esteem as a careful and conscientious actor, who understands the art to be an intellectual one, and so pursues it." But that, considering that it was written in

1853, says a great deal more than it appears to do on the surface. About Barry Sullivan my father always said that he was the last of the great actors, and could and did tear a passion to tatters without being ridiculous—which cannot be said of to-day's actor who is much more likely to be ridiculous without tearing a passion to anything approaching tatters. But the best intimation of Barry Sullivan's quality came to me not from my father but from Courtenay Thorpe, that fine intellectual actor of the 'nineties. Thorpe, as a young man, was walking with Barry Sullivan in Westminster. The great actor was explaining to him a point in his Hamlet, and neither of them noticed that they had arrived at a scene of congestion, cordons of police, and all that goes with the opening of Parliament. They began to cross the road and were stopped by a bobby. Whereupon Barry with a magnificent gesture not only spiritually waved but physically put the policeman on one side and continued his dissertation as though Parliament, and even the Monarchy, didn't exist.

On the subject of Robson my father was inexhaustible, declaring him to be very nearly the best actor he had ever set eyes on. Of this great little comedian and burlesque tragedian—he was no bigger in stature than Garrick—much has fortunately been recorded. Clement Scott has written of him: "The only strictly serious part that I ever saw Robson play was Desmarets in *Plot and Passion*, a performance never to be forgotten; but his burlesque was on the very borderline of tragedy. Such intensity he had, such power of sudden contrast, such quick changes from seriousness to fun, that he electrified one. In an instant he had the whole audience in his grasp, and communicated to them his magnetic personality. . . . He was a very little man, but in his inspired moments he became a giant. He seemed to swell and grow before our eyes. When he lifted himself up, his rage was awful; when he wept, the whole house sobbed in sympathy."

Still more illuminating is a little-known account by George Augustus Sala:

In *The Yellow Dwarf* Robson was the jaundiced embodiment of a spirit of Oriental evil; crafty, malevolent, greedy, insatiate—full of mockery, mimicry, lubricity, spite—an Afrit, a Djinn, a Ghoul, a spawn of Sheitan. How that monstrous orange-tawny head grinned and wagged! How those flaps of ears were projected forwards, like unto those of a dog! How balefully those atrabilious eyes glistened! You laughed, and yet you shuddered. He spoke in mere doggerel and slang. He sang trumpery songs to negro melodies. He danced the Lancashire clog hornpipe; he rattled out puns and conundrums; yet did he contrive to infuse into all this mummery and buffoonery, into this salmagundi of the incongruous and the outré, an unmistakably tragic element—an element of depth and strength and passion, and almost of sublimity. The mountebank became inspired. The Jack Pudding suddenly drew the cothurnus over his clogs. You were awe-stricken by the intensity, the vehemence he threw into the mean balderdash of the ballad-monger. These qualities were even more apparent in his subsequent personation of Medea, in Robert Brough's parody of the Franco-Italian tragedy. The love, the hate, the scorn of the abandoned wife of Jason, the diabolic loathing in which she held Creusa, the tigerish affection with which she regarded the children whom she is afterwards to slay—all these were portrayed by Robson, through the medium, be it always remembered, of doggerel and slang, with astonishing force and vigour. The original Medea, the great Ristori herself, came to see Robson and was delighted with and amazed at him. She scarcely understood two words of English, but the actor's genius struck her home through the bull's-hide target of an unknown tongue. *"Uomo straordinario!"* she went away saying.

I have quoted thus much about Robson because I have a relic of him. This is the tobacco-box he used in *The Porter's Knot*. A letter goes with the box, dated February 12th, 1908, and written by Mrs Emily Combes. The letter says: "Dear Mr Tree, On the chance that you may collect theatrical relics, I am sending you the old 'baccy' box used by the late Frederick Robson in *The Porter's Knot*, in the hope that you will do me the favour to accept it. It was given to Alfred Bryan the artist, by the widow of F. R. who gave it to my husband." The box was presented to me by the writer's nephew. I rank it third in what must be the smallest collection of theatrical relics in the country. The first two are a knife found under the floor of Shakespeare's house at the time of its restoration, and Henry Irving's press-cutting scissors. Seymour Hicks gave me these, and I like his story that Irving whenever he used the scissors to cut out the notice of some famous critic would snarl: "What does he know about it?" My fourth and fifth treasures are two photographs of Irving and Ellen Terry which, in their present frames, hung for twenty-five years on either side of Irving's dressing-table at the Lyceum. When Irving died his valet gave them to Lady Martin-Harvey, and she very kindly gave them to me.

My father was the most severe of critics and would come home after a performance of Irving's saying that the man had so many faults that he oughtn't to be on the stage at all! Yet at heart he admired him tremendously though he always said that Macaire was his best performance.

About Ellen Terry he held the opinion that she was the most exquisite of all human creatures, but not a great actress. Of all English actresses he placed Mrs Kendal first, one of her greatest feats in his opinion being to have turned her husband from a stick into a tolerably competent comedian. He had considerable admiration for Hare and Wyndham, and a strictly limited appreciation of the Bancrofts. But his view about Tree as a serious actor was that he ought to be whipped! Indeed I remember his taking me to see Tree and Mrs Patrick Campbell in *Fédora* at the Haymarket and telling me afterwards that the age of the professional actor was gone, and that all I had seen that evening was a couple of talented amateurs!

My own conscious playgoing began just about the time that the English Drama was undergoing one of its many re-births. I mean, of course, the first night of Pinero's *The Second Mrs Tanqueray* in 1893, which is not very noticeably short of fifty years ago. Elsewhere I have named my theatrical gods of that period. Has the reader noticed the omission to make very much of Duse? Here undoubtedly the actress's nationality has stood in the way of my admiring her. I have always avoided setting up to be a judge of any player speaking a language of which I don't know enough to order a mutton chop. But that the English have never understood Italian has not prevented them from hailing the Italian actress as a world-genius. According to Maurice Baring, who can speak anything from Russian to Choctaw, Arthur Symons, who could translate Dante standing on his head, Shaw, who could lecture to Venetians in their own language on the function of drains in a water-logged city, and the omniscient Walkley, whose beard could laugh in any language it liked—according to all these, Duse was an undeniably great actress. Personally I never trusted my own opinion about her because, as I have already said, I know no Italian except the names of some of the arias in Mozart's operas. In consequence I was never able to tell whether, when Duse came on waving her lovely hands and looking like the back of the kitchen grate, she was bewailing the coldness of the cold mutton at lunch or proposing to enter a nunnery! Also she affected me exactly in the way in which she affected Max Beerbohm. Some of to-day's young people may not know Max's dramatic criticisms by heart, and therefore I shall remind them of this: "Am I overwhelmed by the personality of Duse? Of course, I ought to be—there can be no question of that. But the wretched fact remains that I am not. True, I see power and nobility in her face: and the little shrill soft voice, which is in such strange contrast with it, has a certain charm for me. I admire, too, her movements, full of grace and strength. But my prevailing emotion is hostile to her. I cannot surrender myself, and see in her the 'incarnate woman-hood' and 'the very spirit of the world's tears' and all those other things which other critics see in her. My prevailing impression is that of a great egoistic force; of a woman overriding, with an air of sombre unconcern, plays, mimes, critics and public. In a man I would admire this tremendous egoism very much indeed. In a woman it only makes me uncomfortable. I dislike it. I resent it."

October 9 *Wednesday*

Lunch with Alexander Korda who to my enormous astonishment turns out to be a man of great culture and distinction of mind. We talked about a lot of things including the Goncourts' novels which, he says, "are not so good as we thought when we were young men." He insists that I shall help with his new film of *Cyrano de Bergerac* and for the reason that his Hungarian nationality prevents him from detecting the finer shades of English verse. In the end I agree to do what he wants, and I hope my incursion into films will continue as pleasantly as it has begun.

In the evening go to the Reinhardt film of *A Midsummer Night's Dream*, in which Shakespeare is alleged to make his first appearance on the screen. He doesn't!

October 10 *Thursday*

The law in America appears to be even more of a h'ass than it is in this country. I quote the following from *The Manchester Guardian:*

> Hauptmann appealed from the jury's verdict on the ground that the emotional atmosphere of the courtroom was prejudicial to his case and that no evidence had been advanced that he had committed a felony in addition to being responsible for the child's death. In New Jersey the death sentence is only possible when a prisoner is found guilty of murder rather than of homicide, and a conviction for murder is only possible if the prosecution proves either premeditation or that the victim died during the commission of a felony. To establish this felony the State alleged that when Hauptmann kidnapped the infant he also stole its sleeping suit. Ordinarily the theft of such a suit would be petty larceny, but if a theft involves unlawful entry it automatically becomes a felony.

In future, kidnappers will have to pinch the kids naked. Which means that they will die of pneumonia!

October 11 *Friday*

Spend a busy day interviewing young actors for the part of Christian in *Cyrano*. What is wanted is a Henry Ainley at the age of eighteen, and this is not easy. There are a fair number of good-lookers, but unfortunately when they have the right degree of unsophistication they speak like shop-assistants, and when they speak fair English they look like gigolos. One of them, Robert Eddison, seems to me to fill the bill as far as looks, boyishness, charm, and a cultivated voice go. But, alas, he is six foot three, and his face, though an agreeable mask, is too small for his body and I am afraid would not carry a wig!

In the evening took Jock to the first night of James Bridie's *The Black Eye*, for which I had suggested that he should write a practice dramatic criticism in way of being a dress-rehearsal for his *Manchester Guardian* job which starts next week. He was to write a notice in exactly the same time he will have for the paper, that is to say between the end of the play and twelve midnight. He left me at the theatre, after which I went to supper at the Savoy.

Got home at ten past one and sat down to see what I could do in an hour. Only I cheated, because there was all the ruminating over supper, and in addition I took two hours, if you count getting up out of bed three times in order to add finishing touches!

October 12 *Saturday*

Jock's article arrived with the midnight postmark showing he kept his word. Excellent, though bearing slight traces of stage-fright. He confessed this morning to having been momentarily tempted to return to Scotland for good by the midnight train. But he can teach me nothing about fright, for I suffered from it in Manchester for ten years, *and never got any better*. Never once throughout the whole of those ten years did I go to a play without something written in advance, which I used or not according to circumstances. The difficulty, of course, is that of trying too hard and attempting too much. It takes pretty nearly the whole of fifty minutes merely to write the number of words it takes to make half-a-column, never mind the four-fold job of telling the reader about the play as news, fulfilling the critical function, using the right words, and—last infirmity of noble mind—putting something of yourself into the whole thing. Writers either have this gift or they haven't and a man is not the worse critic for not possessing it. Montague and Walkley had this gift absolutely, and so to-day have Charles Morgan and Ivor Brown. But I know one very distinguished critic, the possessor of an exquisite mind and whose weekly outpourings are pure joy, who has been tried at this nocturnal job and spent his hour gaping like a fish at a blank sheet of paper. If Jock fails, which he may very well do, it won't be a failure in criticism or artistry. It will simply mean that he lacks a facility often denied the best brains and granted to the most commonplace. The reason I didn't altogether fail on *The Manchester Guardian* was that I sedulously collected the London criticisms of each new play as it appeared and so knew what it was about before it came to Manchester. From these I prepared my advance notices, and, further, provincial papers go to press an hour later than the London ones. I therefore had two hours, and not one, for the task—an immense difference.

However, Jock's first attempt was very much better than I expected, though not so good as it would have been if the time-threat had been removed. Bits of it are very good indeed:

> One went to the new play hoping at last for Mr Bridie's rounded, complete thing, a play with a "total gesture". Alas, no! It was evident early in the evening that he was going to make even more

little gestures than usual, one gesture per scene and the whole totalling nothing.

Also:

> Mr Morland Graham's appearance was all too short; he perfectly suggested the typical north-country father extremely nervous of allowing his heart to get nearer his sleeve than his elbow, so to speak.

Also:

> The moral of the whole thing, if it is a whole thing, is so trite than I cannot remember it.

These are not only good criticisms, but tellingly delivered, and only once does Jock go off into his preciosity as when he says that Shaw was in the audience, each particular hair of his beard *candid* with approbation! He justifies this nonsense by saying that he is using "candid" in its pristine sense, whereupon we trot out Webster. Jock claims a win on the strength of the quotation from Dryden:

> The box receives all black: but, poured from thence,
> The stones come candid forth, the hue of innocence.

Whereupon I point to a small word in italics which he disingenuously overlooks. The word is *obs*! A great argument follows. He is to write this week about *Romeo and Juliet*, and I ask him if he thinks the *M.G.* will allow him to call this "the world's greatest venereal tragedy".

He tells me that the moment he had posted his stuff last night all sorts of witty things came bubbling up in his mind. I told him therefore to sign his articles "E. d'E.," and when people ask what it stands for to tell them "Esprit d'Escalier"!

October 13 *Sunday*

Came across an old story of Sarah which I had quite forgotten. Landing at New Orleans she hailed a taxi and said to the astonished driver "A la forêt vierge!" using, I suppose, very much the same accent and gesture with which, in *L'Aiglon*, she would say: "J'empoigne la crinière. Alea jacta est!" The "r's" in "forêt" and "vierge" deep down in the throat, something between rutting tigress and strangled dove.

October 17 *Thursday*

Gielgud's production to-night of *Romeo and Juliet* puts Jock on his mettle and me as well. Taking a line through Juliet's punning speech:

I am not I, unless I wipe Jock's eye!

October 18 *Friday*

The boy in a great stew this morning because his notice is not in the London Edition of *The Manchester Guardian*. I say that this often happens with a longish article, and Ivor Brown confirms on the telephone. A. D. insufficiently assured, however, and I spend the day dictating to a lone, lorn creetur who could give points to Mrs Gummidge. Other people have had their articles turned down, but he feels it more than most!

In the meantime am vastly jealous of Darlington's grand article in the *Telegraph* in which he says that Edith Evans's Nurse is "as earthy as a potato, as slow as a cart-horse, and as cunning as a badger!"

In the evening dined at Claridge's with Korda and Charles Laughton and attended the first conference on the new *Cyrano* film. Also present two other people whose names I did not catch, but whom I took to be a Czecho-Slovakian secretary and an English publicity man. Found myself running hopelessly counter to Charles, who was in his ultra-highbrow mood and objected to any and every version of *Cyrano* which did not combine all Rostand's wit and all Rostand's poetry. I felt like suggesting that he should dig up and commission Congreve, but had the sense to keep my mouth shut. This went on for a long time and Korda kept his temper throughout, merely telling Charles that when he is being filmed whether he thinks about "dramatic fluidity" or cream cheese doesn't matter, as it's the photographer who counts! Nothing whatever was arrived at and we broke up at 11.30, good temper being more or less restored. Charles, who is a great baby as well as a genius, delightedly showed us the mechanical arrangements for Cyrano's cock-a-hoop bearing which are to enable him to give all his attention to Cyrano's crowing. He is to have the heels of his shoes shaved and the soles raised, and illustrated this by means of two books which Korda threw on the floor. One was Lytton Strachey, and the other Eisenstein!

Apropos of an actress for Roxane, at bare mention of whom I shrieked in protest, Korda said: "But I shall only let her loose for ten seconds at a time." Cedric Hardwicke told me the other day that film-producers, landed with a dud film-star, will pay huge sums to an actor with a stage reputation. The idea is that contiguity with a genuine player will give the film-dud the air of being a player also; the public sees a lot of polished playing and can't remember who did it. Korda told us of two friends of his youth, inhabitants of the little Hungarian village in which he was born. One was a man of sixty who wore a long smock of the kind we see in Russian plays. He was the village idiot, and his mania took the form of going up to strangers, lifting his smock and saying: "This is what I've got!" Korda added thoughtfully: "He

had the face of a saint," and Charles said quickly: "That's what saints
are like!"

His other friend was an older idiot who wore no fewer than five
hundred neckties and had his pockets stuffed with thousands of
envelopes to which he always referred as "my deeds". You could not
make him happier than by giving him an old envelope which he would
add to his store. "He died at the age of eighty-seven," said Korda,
"much respected!"

October 19 *Saturday*

Here is Jock's article which appeared this morning—the first serious
and, with the exception of a few lines about a silly play, the first article
he has written for *The Manchester Guardian*:

> Mr John Gielgud's production of *Romeo and Juliet* was triumphantly
> launched at the New Theatre last night. He has taken this tragedy
> of mischance and produced it almost, in the geometrical sense, as
> far as it will go. He has, produced it, as Hamlet would have
> reformed—he has produced it "altogether". The play was already a
> masterpiece of compression: it has been compressed further
> without cutting, but with the use of an ingenious double stage,
> which is successful once one has accepted the convention whereby
> the same cubicle is Capulet's loggia, a tavern, a friar's cell, a
> chemist's shop, and Tybalt's grave. Once again, Mr Gielgud has
> engaged for his designs the clever and resourceful young ladies
> called Motley. The setting is discreetly adaptable to the play's swift
> progress so that there are no waits and but one interval. Thus is
> the tragedy's note which is impetuousness emphasised.
>
> Many of the costumes are delightful and all of them have that
> bright new laundered cleanness which one has long had to accept
> in stage sixteenth century. The action is thoroughly well ordered,
> the duels have their right spirit of hot nights and the mad blood
> stirring. The pace is throughout impassioned, and in the charnel-
> house conclusion is that "glooming peace" noticed by the much-
> awakened Prince.
>
> There remain the players. Mr Gielgud to begin with was his own
> Mercutio and produced him at least as well as anybody or anything
> else. The part was spoken with rare virtuosity. Pater has said that
> the greatest art tends to escape into the condition of music. It was
> so last night. With this actor's delivering of the Queen Mab lines
> they became a scherzo, the words fluttering from Mercutio's
> brain as lightly as the elfin vision that they drew. Even the death
> scene, following hard upon, and made the more poignant by the
> vitality with which this Mercutio had been sketched, was hardly
> more moving than the famous speech. Miss Evans was heavenly
> as the Nurse, playing with great humour and immense vocal range,
> and endowing the unvenerable bawd with an apple's hard sweetness.
>
> But then this play should belong not to these two stars but to

that pair of star-crossed lovers. Mr Laurence Olivier and Miss Peggy Ashcroft would perhaps have been happier in their tragedy with a less formidable backing. Miss Ashcroft's Juliet was charming at the least but never more than touching at the most. In the great solo scene Juliet is aflame with her deep-down desires; Miss Ashcroft showed only the trembling surfaces. Mr Olivier began with the advantage of looking like a handsome young Italian, which is much. As the evening wore on, too, Mr Olivier reached expectation, then proceeded to surpass it. The part is notoriously difficult and all the great chances are given to the heroine.

Greeted at Mantua with news of his wife's death, Romeo has but a single line to indicate first grief and then resignation: "Is it e'en so? Then I defy thee, stars." He must go on instantly to talk of hiring horses and then with hardly a break proceed to enumerate the contents of the apothecary's shop. Mr Olivier was best of all at this triple hurdle, giving the big line the correct significance and isolation. His fault is a marked deficiency in poetry.

Some of the lesser parts were exceptionally well played, the lesser the better. Peter was comically individualised by Mr George Devine, and there was a goodly drawing by Mr Alec Guinness of the Apothecary. But why does the last always have Romeo's poison in his pocket ready to hand? And, incidentally, why does Shakespeare make him fuss so much at being paid? Perhaps in Mantua the chemists were not cash.

November 9 Saturday

A hell of a week, of which I remember:

1. Broadcasting about Sybil [Dame Sybil Thorndike], and on the theme that if she is great enough to be a Dame she must remain a *grande dame*. The point is not that S. should resist characters like Pinero's Lady Orreyed, but something much more subtle. If she went outside herself on such occasions I should have nothing to say. But there was a time when, although utterly free from any vulgarity of mind, S. had certain provicial elegances, mouth-twistings, arm-wavings and the like, *to which she returns for her comedy*. It is this that I find deplorable—the renewal of something long and success-fully put behind her. Her performances in *Advertising April* and *Madame Plays Nap* left me *bouche béante*, and here it is again.

2. After broadcasting, dinner at Isola Bella with Maurice Healy, a most amusing cove, brilliant talker, and author of this fine epigram:

> To the Memory of the 29th Division.
> We failed; but, when the sacrifice is needed,
> Fail you as nobly. We shall have succeeded.*

* This presumably refers to the Gallipoli Campaign. *Ed.*

A grand meal—oysters, minute steak, and toasted cheese—and the talk best of all. Moray McLaren in fine Scots form, while M. H., who began talking in English, finished up in Arthur Sinclair's richest brogue.

3. The Opening Lunch of the *S.T.* Book Exhibition. Rose Macaulay, coming up to me and saying: "Sir, a bone to pick with you," and me countering with the Hamlet-like: "Madam, a whole skeleton!"

4. Talking at the Exhibition with Sybil Thorndike in the chair. Charming to me, and looking and behaving like some female seraph, exactly what Coleridge meant by "a man all light".

5. Supper with James Bone at the Café Royal. J. B. in tremendous fettle. Stories about George Mair coming into the newly decorated Savoy Hotel, all white paint and panelling, and saying "This place would be exactly like the Berengaria *if only it were a bit steadier!*" About T. W. H. Crosland refusing tea at one of Lady Londonderry's political fêtes, ordering a bottle of whisky from the footman, writing his name on the label and putting it on the drawing room mantelpiece for his private use. About the late Sir Edward Hulton, who had in his library twelve sumptuously bound volumes lettered "Grand National Shakespeare".

6. A first-rate concert on my new wireless, *which works!* B.B.C. Symphony Orchestra, Hamilton Harty conducting:

> Strauss's *Don Juan*
> Chopin *Concerto No. 1* (Hofmann)
> William Walton's *1st Symphony*.

Why do pianists so seldom play the Chopin *Concerto*, which is lovely? Fascinated by the Walton, though one must not hear too much of this new stuff. Matisse & Co. make one look at Constable a shade patronisingly, and I'm not going to risk listening to Beethoven with amused contempt.

7. Swopping my old Dunlop and cheque for ten guineas against the best of the new Dunlops in the show at the Redfern Galleries, the portrait of a wistful little boy.

8. Hearing Richard Hearne, the amazing acrobat in the new Henson show, tell Duggie Furber that he couldn't stay late at the Savage Club unless he 'phoned his mother. Everybody admired this.

9. Agreeing with Jock that in comparison with Rosalind's pure flame Juliet is a man-struck little besom.

10. Being told by Ion Swinley that as the result of my article on the speaking of Shakespeare's verse, Lilian Baylis is arranging for young actors to have their vowels opened at least once a week.

December 6 Friday

Lunched at the Savage with James Heddle, my first editor on the

Manchester Daily Dispatch and managing editor of the Hulton group of papers for twenty years. Full, as usual, of stories about T. W. H. Crosland, that gaunt wolf of journalism and talented poet, who is now so utterly forgotten. Yet this, I think, should be remembered. It is the epitaph he composed for himself:

Epitaph

If men should say aught of me
After I die:
Say there were many things he might have bought
And did not buy.
Unhonoured by his fellows he grew old,
And trod the path to Hell.
But there were many things he might have sold,
And did not sell.

Crosland lived in a flat built like a railway carriage, and the view from the three rooms was the same—a railway line and a primitive urinal. He threw money away, and if a waiter interrupted a story to bring change would send tray and money flying. (It was generally somebody else's money.) Crosland had an appearance rather like Dr Johnson's, but there the likeness ended. "I had the melancholy pleasure of paying for his funeral," Jimmie said.

December 30 *Monday*

End of my valedictory wireless talk tonight:

This is the last talk of the present series and whether they are to be renewed or not is one of the things which lie in the lap of the New Year. It may be that the time is at hand when the screen will finally swallow the theatre, in which case I do not see how film criticism can help swallowing dramatic criticism. Now I have read some film critics, and I gather from them that the screen is producing great actors and actresses at the rate of three a fortnight. Irvings and Bernhardts, it appears, are tumbling over each other, and every morning a new Ellen Terry or Réjane rises with the lark. Now, listeners, I am not going to have any truck with any of this pestiferous nonsense. I may be out of date. Bright young critics are arising who never saw, and cannot even spell the names of the actors and actresses who were great in my day. Whether the era now dawning will want to have any truck with me I neither know nor care. I intend to have no truck with it. All around me young critics, even in the theatre, are being kind to players who, in the days before the film existed, would have been told to get off the boards and go and learn their job. The honest thing, of course, would be to retire, or go and put my head in the gas oven. But while I have plenty of moral courage, which is the easy sort, I have too little of the other and shall continue to write for bread. Yet I cannot hope wholly to escape the blight which is creeping over the age, and I have no doubt that I am on the verge of writing twaddle as contemptible as that of the youngest film critic. For this reason, while there are still some vestiges of sanity about me, I have composed my epitaph. This, then, be the verse you grave for me:

> Though
> In his declining years
> He used the words
> Great, First-Class, Pre-Eminent
> Indiscriminately
> Like everybody else
> JAMES AGATE
> At his unclouded best
> Remembering what great acting was
> Allowed no second-rate player
> To get past him.

December 31 *Tuesday*

Here are two views of Ireland and the Irish. The first is the Dedication to *The Impossible Irish* by one Tom Penhaligon:

This book is flung in the face of the Irish—a fighting race who never won a battle, a race of politicians who cannot govern themselves, a race of writers without a great one of native strain, an island who have yet to man a fleet for war, for commerce or for the fishing banks and to learn how to build ships, a pious race excelling in blasphemy, who feel most wronged by those they have first injured, who sing of love and practise fratricide, preach freedom and enact suppression, a race of democrats who sweat the poor, have a harp for an emblem and no musicians, revelled on foreign gold and cringed without it, whose earlier history is myth and murder, whose later, murder, whose tongue is silver and whose heart is black, a race skilled in idleness, talented in hate, inventive only in slander, whose land is a breeding-ground of modern reaction and the cradle of western crime.

Then this, by one Louis MacNeice, a Belfast poet and St. John Ervine's fellow-townsman:

Therefore I resign, good-bye the chequered and the quiet hills,
The gaudily-striped Atlantic, the linen-mills
That swallow the shawled file, the black moor where half
A turf-stack stands like a ruined cenotaph;
Good-bye your hens running in and out of the white house,
Your absent-minded goats along the road, your black cows,
Your greyhounds and your hunters beautifully bred,
Your drums and your dolled-up virgins and your ignorant dead.

Grand invective, and real poetry!
My work this year:

Sunday Times	. .	100 000 words
The Tatler	. .	60 000 ,,
Pseudonym No. 1*	. .	60 000 ,,
Pseudonym No. 2	. .	85 000 ,,
Daily Express	. .	80 000 ,,
B.B.C.	. .	50 000 ,,
Ego	. .	100 000 ,,
Odd Articles	. .	20,000 ,,
		555 000 ,,

Compare Arnold Bennett in 1908: "I have never worked so hard
as this year . . . total words 423 000." If I include *Kingdoms for Horses*
(45 000 words) I can bring the grand total up to 600 000 words. But
this would be cheating as it is only old stuff worked up. In addition
have visited between 100 and 150 plays, 50 films, glanced at 500 books
and more or less read 200. As these average 100 000 words each my
eye this year must have taken in twenty million words. I am half-
inclined to disbelieve these astronomical figures, and will base my claim
to an industrious year on the amount I have *written*. Here the calcula-
tion is precise. I have churned out, and Jock has taken down 455 000
words, while, *with my own hand and in my spare time*, I have written
100 000 words of Diary.

1936

January 3 *Friday*

The people who bore me with letters have started the year well.
The pest has twelve varieties:

(1) It sends samples of its dramatic criticism, and will I (*a*)
appoint it as my deputy, or (b) find it a job on some other
paper.
(2) It has a lot of old theatre-programmes, and will I buy them?
As often as not, these are forwarded and turn out to concern
nothing earlier than Herbert Tree's Shakespearean productions.

* Agate wrote for several years under a variety of pseudonyms of which the main
ones were Richard Prentis in *John o' London's Weekly*, George Warrington in
Country Life and Sir Topaz in *Eve*. Alan Dent tells how Ralph Richardson once
boasted that he had discovered 'a better critic than your Jimmy'. It turned out to be
George Warrington! *Ed.*

(3)   It submits a novel already rejected by forty publishers, and will I read it and say why?

(4)   It owns a complete edition, all but one volume, of an illustrated Shakespeare printed in the 'forties, and will I say what this is worth?

(5)   As it inhabits Widnes or Wednesbury it doesn't get much chance of going to the theatre, and will I say what it ought to visit in London next Easter when it is coming up?

(6)   It is a lady who says that her brother was at school with me, and will I therefore help her niece, now an assistant in a book-shop in Leamington, to find a typist's job in Fleet Street, beginning, say as editor's secretary?

(7)   It wants to know whether I reviewed a book called, it thinks, *Father India*, and published about eighteen months ago, and what was the proper title and the publisher and the price, and what did I think of it?

(8)   It is the president of the Isle of Thanet Thespians, a list of whose productions it encloses, and do I think it foolhardy to attempt *King Lear* next season?

(9)   It says it met me at the first night of *Mary Rose*, and will I see it, please, as it has something to say that it can't say in a letter. This is always marked "Urgent and personal".

(10) It is obviously an ardent spinster and it wants to know whether I agree with her that Dame Sybil Thorndike in *Saint Joan* is . . . (some seven pages of closely written script).

(11) It is a doddering old actor who begins by saying that, having played with Alfred Wigan, it knows I shall be interested in a great number of pages containing nothing of the slightest possible moment.

(12) It writes from Thurso or Thirlmere to tell me what ought to be my views on current successes, and how I ought to express them.

Have devised this formula to be sent to each and all:

"MR JAMES AGATE REGRETS THAT HE HAS NO TIME TO BOTHER ABOUT THE ENCLOSED IN WHICH HE HAS BEEN GREATLY INTERESTED"

January 18 *Saturday*

Kipling died early this morning. *Many Inventions* and *Life's Handicap* contain stories as good as anything by Maupassant, whom I have read in his entirety. I do not know enough of the short stories of Tchehov to justify comparison. As a boy I was a great Kipling fan. I remember, in 1898 when he was desperately ill in New York, making a solemn vow that if he died I would wear a black tie for the rest of my life!

One minute before midnight last night the dance music on the wireless was faded out and an announcer came to the microphone to broadcast news of the King's illness. Not the attack of bronchial catarrh which matters, but "signs of cardiac weakness which must be regarded with some disquiet". Four doctors at Sandringham.

Two lighter moments in a bad week. One was when I mentioned some self-advertising woman and Jock said acidly: "She retired from private life forty years ago!" The other was Noel's *Hands Across the Sea*, a really witty half-hour playlet. They gave me a box so that I could have the corridor to cough in, and I went in my thickest suit, buttoned up to the chin.

January 20 *Monday*

Fred Leigh's boy has got hold of a copy of *The Times* for November 7th, 1805. The paper consists of four small sheets only, and as it was printed in the days when people read with their minds instead of their eyes there are, of course, no pictures. It begins with one sober column of advertisements and then launches straight away into the *London Gazette*. Beneath a heading taking up less than one inch of space, this gives Collingwood's despatches containing the first account of the Battle of Trafalgar and the death of Nelson. The account goes on for three columns and then turns the page. The second page is entirely taken up with extracts from the foreign Press, after which there are two dignified leading articles, from the second of which I cull:

> No ebullitions of popular transport, no demonstrations of public joy, marked this great and important event. The honest and manly feeling of the people appeared as it should have done; they felt an inward satisfaction at the triumph of their favourite arms; they mourned with all the sincerity and poignancy of domestic grief, their Hero slain.

Fancy any modern newspaper holding that the honest and manly feelings of a people can be expressed except through the medium of streamers and paper caps, crowds, piano-accordions and Trafalgar Square!

Yet the age was not wholly unalive to expediency. One of the advertisements announces the publication that day of an engraving of Hoppner's picture of Lord Nelson, while the dramatic critic tells the reader:

> After the Comedy of *She Would and She Would Not*, in which Miss Smith acted Hypolita with admirable spirit, the Proprietors of this Theatre, ever alive to the national glory, produced a hasty but elegant compliment to the memory of Lord Nelson.

January 21 *Tuesday*

Yesterday was a moving day indoors. At 5.30 the wireless announced: "The condition of His Majesty the King shows diminishing strength." At 9.25 came the statement: "The King's life is moving peacefully towards its close." Heard afterwards that the Queen drafted this. At 10 o'clock there was a five-minutes' service beginning with the 23rd Psalm. Then every quarter of an hour the repetition of the last message. One couldn't read or do anything, so George Mathew and I sat and talked. News that the King was dead came through at 12.15.

January 22 *Wednesday*

Every flag was at half-mast yesterday except Buckingham Palace where there was no flag at all, there being no sovereign. The town like a Sunday; all theatres and cinemas closed and all public functions abandoned. Dined quietly at the Langham with Moray McLaren and Rose-Troup, and at 9.30 went across to Broadcasting House to hear the Prime Minister. Very good and well-delivered. Moray said the speech was for all Europe as well as England—"Hitler and the boys will be listening." When Baldwin spoke of the Prince of Wales and his tremendous responsibilities there came into his voice, or I thought so, just a hint of the Lord Chief Justice, of *Henry IV*, Part 2 Act V, Sc. 2.

EGO 3

August 1936—July 1938

August 17 *Monday*

I shall never be a really *first class* critic owing to my inability to wrap things up. I must blurt them out. This morning I cut the following out of Neville Cardus's *Manchester Guardian* notice about Henry Lytton:

> Old men with long memories have been known to maintain that Lytton was not as great a comic actor in the Savoy operas as Grossmith was, or George Thorne. The truth is that Lytton could never be estimated purely and simply as an actor. There was indeed a touch about him of the inspired amateur; that is to say, he usually seemed able to win his audience without the help of the tricks of the footlights. On or off stage he was the least theatrical of men; his art was indeed nothing but his nature. . . . In private life Lytton was very much as he was on the stage—he required only to dress himself for his parts and 'taste' them rather than present them in the technical gadgets of the theatre. In Jack Point he did, to some length, emulate a definitely histrionic art, and in the death scene his own personality was submerged by an emotional current of no little strength. Yet even here the expression was naïve, not of the green-room's sophisticated texture. The great thing about Lytton was that you loved him first and then, by taking thought, admired the very absence of those technical adornments which are three parts of the equipment of most comic actors.

The truth is that Lytton was a poor actor; in my view he could not hold a candle to C. H. Workman, who played his parts in the provinces. Ernest Fenton, who was with him in *The Princess of Kensington*, *The Earl and the Girl*, and *The Talk of the Town*, said yesterday, "Lytton was like some small prehistoric bird hopping about the stage. He did it all by a catch in the voice, which he used for the humorous, the amorous, and the pathetic. This trick was always the same and pleased the audience, which knew exactly what to expect."

By the oddest chance, and going into the Savage Club about eleven o'clock to-night I met Cardus.

J. A. Look here, Cardus, What would happen to a batsman who lacked those technical adornments which are three parts of the equipment of most cricketers?
N. C. Bowled all over his bloody wicket, old boy!

August 30 *Sunday*

Here is a paragraph from Rebecca West's article in to-day's *S.T.* on the latest Brontë book:

> If Emily looked blankly past the curates it was because her spirit was keeping a tryst with Heathcliff. There was a dignity in her which would keep her from being responsible for any such tableau as quaint as that which Monsieur Héger presents throughout the ages, looking downward from the branches of a tall tree, waiting till the implacable little tigress-governess should go home and he can come down and return to his undistinguished hearth. But she never does go home. Immortality has seen to that. He is eternally treed, eternally entirely in the right and entirely ridiculous.

What a joy this woman is!

September 5 *Saturday*

Neville Cardus told Jock of a momentous occasion when he was on the mat before C. P. Scott for using the phrase, "from whence". He pleaded that precedents were to be found in Smollett and Fielding. Scott said, "Neither Mr Smollett nor Mr Fielding would have used it twice in my paper."

September 27 *Sunday*

Lunched to-day at Lord Kemsley's at Farnham Royal. I suppose it will take years to stop thinking of him as Gomer Berry. Not quite so many ex-viceroys present as usual—just an Irish peer, Sir John and Lady Reith, Herbert Morgan, and the family. Somebody asking me whether I listened in much, I replied "Only after the B.B.C. has closed down". I explained the apparent rudeness of this by alleging the superiority of German wireless, which, at one o'clock in the morning, can send out such a programme as one I heard last week—Mozart piano concerto, Beethoven string quartet, and the *Coriolan* overture. Reith explained that this was not the regular German programme, which, like ours, closes down round about twelve. The programme I heard was their equivalent to our Empire broadcast, which starts about the same time. And, just as listeners within 150 miles of Daventry cannot hear our Empire broadcasts, so J. R. said, Germans within 150 miles of Berlin could not have heard that programme, whose equivalent in musical value we too are sending out. I denied this strenuously, being totally unable to credit the B.B.C. with so much musical imagination. In any case why should Cape Town and Sydney get better stuff than we do? Reith said the Germans' great idea is propaganda, and that they think nothing of putting on the Berlin Philharmonic at midnight. I said I was sure the English notion of classical music at midnight would turn out to be a scratch orchestra and the *Poet and Peasant*, *Light Cavalry*, and *Mireille* overtures. Afterwards we got more friendly. I told Lord K. that the *Sunday Times* ought to promote broadcasting to the same rank as books, music, and the theatre, and give it a weekly *critical* article. Reith backed me up quite fiercely, and we agreed upon Filson Young as the ideal man for the job. F. Y.'s interests are very wide, and he can write equally well about church organs and flying. He has great culture and writes beautifully. The fact that many people dislike him is unimportant.

I drove Herbert Morgan back to town. Passing through Slough, he made an admirable remark: "I have always held that if one has an income of five thousand a year, four thousand should be considered as pocket-money."

October 2 *Friday*

Gate Theatre for Leslie and Sewell Stokes's play about Oscar Wilde. Found it very moving. Robert Morley, who played O. W., differentiated very cleverly between the overblown peony which was Oscar in the witness-box and the bedraggled rhododendron he became in the dock. I shall long remember that Awful Face, and how the body seemed to have lost a couple of stone. The play's total gesture, as Montague would say, is to point the peculiar tragedy of the homosexual, which is that of the tight-rope walker preserving his balance by prodigies of skill and poise and knowing that the rope may snap at any moment.

October 4 *Sunday*

An orgy of sound. Thought I would like to go to a last night at the Proms. Sallied forth with George Mathew and found an incredible programme. *Merry Wives* overture. Good. "Ritorna Vincitor" from *Aïda*. Unutterable muck. Saint-Saëns's Piano Concerto No. 2. Utterable muck. Bach Chaconne done for full orchestra by Casella. But why at this concert? *Songs of Travel*. R. L. S. and Vaughan Williams pretending to like soggy crusts. "Bread I dip in the river—There's the life for a man like me." Holst's *Planets*. All right. Interval. *British Sea-songs* arr. Wood. Korbay's fine song about Mohac's Field, after which a lot of baritone stuff like a Saturday night at the Savage Club. Finally Elgar's *Pomp and Circumstance* No. 1, taken at breakneck speed, as though H. W. was impatient to get to the Closing Scene. Left the hall in a violent state of musical indigestion, the result of listening to a band on a pier without any pier. All the same, it would be dishonest not to admit that I was moved when "Tom Bowling" was played as a 'cello solo.

Rather better concert today. Drive in Richmond Park with George Mathew in the morning, returning for lunch at the Café Royal. (G. M. "Is it middle-class to talk about food?" J. A. "Yes. But it's a mark of exquisite breeding to write about it.") The programme at the Palladium announces Rachmaninoff's Piano Concerto No. 2 and Tschaikowsky's Fifth Symphony. As these don't need listening to I fill myself up with roast beef and a bottle of cheap wine. About half-way through the Concerto I fall into something that isn't quite sleep. And then a wonderful thing happens. The nerves temporarily cease their turmoil—in plain English, chuck it. It is the one hour's respite I have had this week.

October 6 Tuesday

Joseph Hone's *Life of George Moore* reminds me of my youthful phases. There was the Meredith phase and the Kipling phase. I had a phaselet for Henry James, and I can remember where the tram was going to on the top of which I first fell for Jane Austen. But none of these was quite so violent as the George Moore phase, which, while it lasted, was very violent indeed. Here was somebody who was tremendously *au fait* with Manet, Monet, Renoir, Pissarro, Sisley, Courbet, and so on. To listen to him, Moore lived in the bosoms of these painters' wives and mistresses, while the painters themselves exhibited no work which had not obtained Moore's approval. We now know that half of what he wrote about his life in Paris was false in fact and all of it wrong in implication; Moore's idea of an artist was that he could tell any lies that suited his purpose. There is a good deal of nonsense in *Confessions of a Young Man*, but nonsense which to a young reader was intoxicating—passages about how it had been worthwhile to throw ten thousand virgins to the Roman lions if it provided Giorgione with a subject. Yes, it seemed a very brave old world when seen through Manet's bock and Moore's absinthe. Later on one became more seriously indebted to Moore. I owe my enthusiasm for Balzac to his essay on that little-known short novel *La Vieille Fille*. Everybody reads *Madame Bovary*, but I think I should never have gone on to *L'Education Sentimentale* if it had not been for a blazing article in the short-lived

Cosmopolis. To this day I remember how Moore first quoted the famous passage about the funeral of M. Dambreuse and then went on to say something like this: "Once a year the six or seven awakened spirits of Paris assemble under the lime-trees in the Champs-Élysées to read this passage aloud to one another by the light of the moon."

November 30 *Monday*

On going into the Café Royal late heard that the Crystal Palace had been burned down. The waiters had gone on to the roof to see the blaze. One said, "Every bit of it is practically missing." The tape was so excited that it became incoherent, and we read, "The vicinity of the tower was pushed away by onlookers."

December 4 *Friday*

> What dire offence from amorous causes springs,
> What mighty contests rise from trivial things!

And what little things flow from great! Am told today that owing to this affair of the King's marriage the big bookshops are completely deserted. I understand this. Why spend seven-and-sixpence on romance when you can get reality for a penny?

Determined not to let major preoccupation disturb the noisy tenor of my way, I did some much-needed shopping, and ordered three new suits, twelve new shirts, six new dress-shirts, and lots of ties, socks, handkerchiefs, etc. Shall do the shoes and hats tomorrow. Cannot put up any longer with the loop'd and window'd raggedness in which I've been going about for the past six months. Took Edith Shackleton and Jock to lunch at the Ivy. Edith said two lovely things: "There should be better work in the world for a man than to write little books about Nature." And: "*Peter Pan* is a charming play for children. It is not a rule of conduct for a great nation." Jock said about the crisis that we ought to look upon it as one of the histories of Shakespeare.

December 9 *Wednesday*

Waste! Waste! Waste! The secretary's cry which ends Granville-Barker's tragedy brings down the curtain on this one also. What of the King himself? "Dispute it like a man," says Malcolm to Macduff in his extremity. And Macduff answers, "I shall do so; but I must also feel it as a man." If I write of this matter as a dramatic critic, it is because I feel it as a dramatic critic. Therefore I see the King as an actor in a world drama echoing Antony's

Fall not a tear, I say; one of them rates
All that is won and lost: give me a kiss;
Even this repays me.

December 11 *Friday*

So far as I am concerned, the King abdicated when the news was
announced over the wireless at six o'clock last night. The ceremony,
for such it was, was moving. Baldwin came out of it very well. It
entirely cleared my mind of any possible doubts as to the way in which
this thing ought to be looked at. I see the affair now in terms not of
Shakespeare's Antony but of Wells's Mr Polly, who, when Destiny
tried to bully him, stood up to Destiny:

> Man comes into life to seek and find his sufficient beauty, to
> serve it, to win and increase it, to fight for it, to face anything and
> bear anything for it, counting death as nothing so long as the
> dying eyes still turn to it. And fear and dullness and indolence and
> appetite, which indeed are no more than fear's three crippled
> brothers, who make ambushes and creep by night, are against him,
> to delay him, to hold him off, to hamper and beguile and kill him
> in that quest.

History will record that Edward VIII found the Kingship of England
to be insufficient beauty.

December 12 *Saturday*

After the fall of the curtain at the Old Vic St Denis, the producer of
The Witch of Edmonton, said, "It is a pleasure to work with Miss Edith
Evans, who is a great actress. She is a great actress in a great way."
What else is this but a restatement of the first sentence in G. H. Lewes's
essay on Edmund Kean: "The greatest artist is he who is greatest in the
highest reaches of his art."
Then how about the quality which Frederick Myers said was
characteristic of Homer—"the sense of an effortless and absolute
sublimity"? I suggest that the player who possesses this quality at
once passes into the strict and narrow rank of great actors. There is no
doubt that Edith Evans ranks as a great comic actress. Is she a great
actress in the sense of effortless and absolute sublimity? If not, is it
only because the sublime has not come her way? In any case, as Barrie's
Cinderella said about the love-letter, "it's a very near thing".

December 18 *Friday*

Home about two, and found I couldn't sleep, which is very rare with me. Turned on the light and read, rather guiltily, John Bailey's *Shorter Boswell*. I have often felt that I should like to abridge Dickens (deleting the sticky passages), so that the novels might be brought home to readers with very little time. I really cannot see greater vandalism here than in making gramophone records of excerpts out of operas for people who haven't time for Covent Garden. Would I take the story out of *Madame Bovary* and leave only the style? No, but I'm sure I could shorten *L'Education Sentimentale* without anybody being the wiser, or sensibly poorer. The people who would kick up most fuss are, of course, those who have never read the book and don't intend to.

December 27 Sunday

Lunched at Colville Hall, where Peter Page had collected one of those parties whose very incongruity makes their success. C. R. W. Nevinson, the painter, and his wife; Princess Troubetzkoy and her brother; Mrs Akers-Douglas; and a delightful Belgian whose name I didn't catch. Also a young American journalist setting out to conquer London on his charm and enough money to last a fortnight. I wished him well and promised to do all I can to help him, with a mental reservation about lending him money. We played, for no stakes, a highly complicated game called "Monopoly" or some such name. All about real estate. The game was interrupted, as somebody's dog got lost. Wherefore the party, me excepted, set out to scour Essex in the dark. They returned two hours later without the dog and minus two of the guests, who had also got lost. As we didn't finish the game nobody won, and indeed I gleaned no idea of what constituted winning.

Nevinson told us a good story about when he had double pneumonia. A publicity fiend rang up, and as the nurse was out of the room C. R. W. answered the 'phone, which was by his bedside. "Has he gone yet?" said a voice. "No," said C. R. W. "Give us a scoop when he does," said the voice, and rang off.

1937

January 21 Thursday

Dined last night at Scott's with Clifford Bax, Meum Stewart, and a Mrs Blanche, an artist. Best potted shrimps and talk I have tasted for a long time. Went back to C. B.'s flat in Albany and stayed till very late. They took me up to see some of the lady's paintings—women bisected lengthways and grafted on to halves of violoncellos; wicker dummies fully crinolined, but with a punch-ball for head and boxing-gloves for hands; cornucopias spilling ladies' gloves—the whole done in salmon

pink, and *très* Regency. Asked if I liked it, I said it affected me like
Sitwellian poetry. Asked if I liked Sitwellian poetry, I said it affected
me like Alban Berg's music, and was no further harried. Clifford showed
me his Sims picture, which he says he understands, as he knows the
next world intimately. Was quite positive about the smallest details.
Long talk about Buddhism. Clifford offered to put on a gramophone
record of somebody dead speaking at a spiritualist séance. As it was
two o'clock I flatly refused to hear it. Happening to mention having
read some new theory, according to which Cause and Effect, not directly
connected, rotate round one another like spots on a rapidly revolving
cone and result in no more than a confluence of probabilities, I said
this would mess up one's notions of morality. Clifford said, "Some of
us have done that already, James."

January 26 Tuesday

Arthur Price, who murdered William Terris's at the stage door of the
Adelphi Theatre forty years ago, died in Broadmoor Asylum yesterday.

January 28 Thursday

The Musical unanimity of London is something to marvel at.
Either everybody is banging and scraping away or there isn't a note to
be heard. Tonight, for example, there wasn't a sound, except at the
Philharmonic for a Mozart-Beecham programme, all seats of course,
sold long before I knew what the week's plays would be. I just managed
to squeeze into Sadler's Wells for *The Barber*. They were the last seats
in the house, or I couldn't have made any use of my free evening.
Glad I went, because it gave me the opportunity to be gorgeously
rude to the *Times* critic for the stuff he recently wrote about *Salome*.
Still worse is the unanimity about rare works. Either you are not given
the chance to hear *Les Troyens* at all, or they have simultaneous
Sunday performances at the Albert and Queen's Halls, while at the
Palladium somebody else does the *Symphonie Fantastique*. After which
Berlioz is allowed to sleep for seventeen years.

February 6 Saturday

Seymour Hicks rang up to ask if I will join the Garrick Club. O
vision entrancing! How all the other passions fleet to air!

February 12 Friday

Eddie Marsh, retiring after forty years of being Private Secretary to Everybody, becomes Sir Edward. Any millionaire can be a Maecenas; Eddie has been that richer thing, an unmoneyed Maecenas.

February 14 *Sunday*

Lunched at Hove with Lord Alfred Douglas, whom I met for the first time. A very gracious and pleasant meal with A. D., obviously best side out. Plenty of lively talk and still more lively listening (me). I thought that after the War the old story would die down. But it doesn't. Sherard has just produced an enormous pail of whitewash, A. D.'s point here being that Wilde in Paris continued his devices more extravagantly than ever. Told me that A. J. A. Symons is to produce yet another book on O. W. this year, and that it is very well done and perfectly authenticated. He also told me that everything Wilde wrote after *Dorian Gray* and excepting *De Profundis* was written when A. D. was living in the same house with him, and generally in the same room, or else when he was a daily visitor: "He used to read bits of *The Importance of Being Earnest* as he wrote them down, now and again incorporating something I had said, when we would both roar with laughter." I came away with the notion that, as between Ross and Harris, there was precious little to choose. My impression of A. D. was that he has mellowed. I think I should like a little of him very much.

February 23 *Tuesday*

Seymour Hicks having written hinting at certain difficulties about my election to the Garrick, and Darlington, who was to have proposed me, corroborating, I dispatched this:

> 22 *Antrim Mansions, N.W.*3.
> *23rd February*, 1936.

DEAR SEYMOUR,

I gather from your letter and Darlington's that there is a considerable amount of opposition to my election. If at any time the Committee, being unanimous, should invite me to join the Club I shall be proud and happy to become a member.

But I have no intention of being snubbed by some worm-eaten old gentleman who would probably have blackballed Garrick himself. Nor do I intend to give some extremely bad actor a toothsome bit of revenge. After all, I haven't asked to join the Club! So let us drop the whole thing.

I will lunch with you with the greatest pleasure when ever and wherever you like, including the Garrick.

> Yours as before,
> JAMES AGATE

March 4 *Thursday*

A peculiarly murky morning.

9.0. John Gielgud, returned from America, wakes me up with a 'phone call, which, however, is not for me, but for Jock.

10.0. Jock arrives, early but quipless.

10.5. Open letters and find one from Seymour regretting my withdrawal from the Garrick, but admitting the existence of "one or two objectors who are not to be got over".

10.15. Consider books to take away for week-end reviewing—a lugubrious lot which includes *The Family Skeleton, Murder on Manoeuvres, Death Took a Greek God, Death at Screaming Pool,* and *The Dormouse Undertaker.*

1.30. Lunch with Sam Eckman of Metro-Goldwyn-Mayer, a delightful fellow whose idiosyncrasy is to drink a liqueur brandy and smoke a cigar immediately before lunch and without having had breakfast. As we sit down Sam says, "Is that a Garrick Club tie you're wearing, James? I'm dining there tonight. Are you?"

James replies that it isn't and he isn't.

March 27 *Saturday*

John Drinkwater's death was the result, it is thought, of a heart attack brought on by the excitement of the Boat Race. He was fifty-four. Drinkwater nothing common did or mean. But, like St John Ervine's Jane Clegg, he made everybody else feel common and mean. This must not be allowed to affect one's judgment of his work and influence on the English theatre. *Abraham Lincoln,* the play by which he will live, was very nearly stillborn. It is an old story now, but one which ought to be told whenever the theatre-going public in this country gets on its hind legs, boasts that it recognises the best whenever it sees it, and instances *Abraham Lincoln.* The facts are that for some time the piece played to almost no houses at all. It was taking £8 a performance when William J. Rea, who played the title-rôle, fell ill. Nigel Playfair let it be known through the Press that Drinkwater himself would step into the gap, and that night the house was crammed, the excellence of the play coming through even that performance, for Drinkwater was not a good actor. The result was that the house remained crowded even when Rea resumed his excellent portrait.

There is a passage in Whitman in which the poet describes a meeting with the President: "His look, *though abstracted,* happened to be directed steadily in my eye. He bowed and smiled, but far beneath his smile I noticed the expression I have alluded to." Rea caught this wonderfully well. His Lincoln had a trick of spiritual withdrawal, of communing in another place, which in the original must have been not a little irritating. After a time Drinkwater acquired something of the same sort. In the end Lincoln's nobility came to be something of a bee in the Drinkwater bonnet. On the other hand, this quality was of immense value to the English theatre, when in the years immediately after the War it stood in desperate need of re-ennobling. Plays like *Mary Stuart*, *Oliver Cromwell* and *Robert E. Lee* were at that time of extraordinary value.

March 31 *Wednesday*

From a letter:

> You have used a fine phrase of Hazlitt's—from that fine essay "The Fight"—without using quotation marks. The impression left on the average reader is that you are a much better writer than you really are; the reader familiar with Hazlitt is furious because you take his gems and flaunt them as your own!

My answer:

> You have raised the question which has been raised hundreds of times. You cite Montague. Infidel, I have you on the hip. Do you know C. E. M.'s *Dramatic Values?* There you will find him writing: "Mr Robey will come on the stage first as that veteran theme, the middle-aged toper in black, frockcoated, tieless and collarless, leering with imbecile knowingness, Stiggins and Bardolph and Ally Sloper in one, his face all bubukles and whelks and knobs and flames o'fire."
>
> No quotation marks here! Nor here: "The finely announced entry of Dalila shines like a good deed in a naughty world."
>
> Nor here: "Was this [Ibsen's *Ghosts*] the play that launched a thousand ships of critical fury?"
>
> Nor here: "Does it [Meredith's talk] all seem idle talk to you, froth for froth's sake, or the crackling of thorns under a pot, whereas life is real, life is earnest, and so on?"
>
> In none of these cases does Montague use inverted commas. He just takes it for granted that the reader is educated enough to know his Shakespeare, Marlowe, Bible and Longfellow.
>
> The principle is not to use commas in cases where people of education must know that you are quoting. One has to run the risk of wrongly impressing people without education because that is a lesser risk than offending the educated, who will be the bulk of your readers, by unnecessary quotation marks.
>
> I should not, for example, run the risk of insulting a reader's intelligence by putting commas round the statement that though Shaw's habit of standing on his head looks like madness, yet there is method in't. Curiously enough, Montague himself has a passage which exactly marks the dividing line: "It all brings us back to the Aristotelian conception of matter and form, and the unending process of wearing down your matter, making what you leave of it more and more perfectly organic, allowing none of it 'to lie in cold obstruction and to rot', but filling it all with aptness

for some function until—far off, divine event—nothing inorganic, no *mere* matter is left."

Here is perfect nicety. *Measure for Measure* is not a very familiar play, but everybody may be presumed to know his Tennyson.

April 7 Wednesday

A poor day.
(1) Gollancz turns down *Ego* 3.
(2) The Westminster turns down my Dreyfus play.
(3) Insurance company turns down J. A. on medical grounds.
I never expected (2) to come off, and (3) was mere impertinence on my part. But (1) is rather worrying. *Ego* sold over four thousand copies, and *Ego* 2 round about two thousand. There is no doubt that this figure would have been considerably larger if the Abdication had not knocked the book-trade endways. Gollancz makes the point that books "which are necessarily a repetition in manner if not in matter necessarily show diminishing returns."

April 8 Thursday

A better day.
(a) Sell *Ego* 3 to George Harrap, who doesn't beat about the bush ten seconds.
(b) Make a contract with the German authors of the Dreyfus play. As there are two of them and one of me, the shares are to be 60–40. Miss Fassett, of the London Play Company, who is handling all this, is still convinced we shall get a production somewhere, at some time or other. I don't believe it.
(c) Am telling myself that because an insurance company has turned one down is no reason for going about like somebody in a picture by John Collier.

April 9 Friday

In the car coming down to my bungalow at Thorpe Bay realised I had left my asthma stuff behind. Stopped at a small chemist's and bought some tablets. Said to Leo, "I just can't bear to run short of Acetylmethyldimethyloxamidphenylhydrazine."

April 18 Sunday

Last of the season's Sunday concerts at Queen's Hall. Took Julian Phillipson, who knows two tunes only—*I've Got You Under My Skin* and the big theme in the last movement of Sibelius No. 2. Mark

[Hambourg] came on to the platform with one stick and in his oldest suit, and got a great reception. I hate the people who don't like Mark; if they played bridge with him they would better understand his piano playing. Mark talks before, during, and after every hand, and when he forces himself to silence his mind continues to ferment; this is why he has *fortissimos* and *pianissimos*, but disdains *cantabile*. This afternoon he played Rubinstein's D minor Piano Concerto with admirable truculence in the first and third movements, and a laudable attempt at tenderness in the middle one. I now know that Brahms' Fourth Symphony is permanently too dry for me. I think I can get something out of the first three movements, but confess to finding the Passacaglia a bore. The programme says that the thirty-two variations show Brahms' "complete mastery of the technique of his art". A fat lot I care! Repeating a dull thing thirty-two times doesn't make it less dull.

MY AMERICAN VISIT

April 26 Monday

The *Sunday Times* has been dangling America before me! *Pour-parlers* are now finished, and I leave on the *Bremen* on Wednesday. The idea is to write about the New York scene, with the theatre as pivot. I was a little nervous about this until in Borrow's *Celebrated Trials*—my present bed-book—I came across this: "It is no easy thing to tell a story plainly and distinctly by mouth; but to tell one on paper is difficult indeed, so many snares lie in the way. People are afraid to put down what is common on paper; they seek to embellish their narratives, as they think, by philosophic speculations and reflections; they are anxious to shine, and people who are anxious to shine can never tell a plain story." Jumping at the tip, I have decided to treat the whole thing as diary.

April 27 Tuesday

A jolly doctor friend of mine comes with me. As B. [Ralph Baker] looks like a Jewish Traddles, I have asked the shipping company whether there will be any Nazi nonsense on board. The clerk replies that the company does not allow politics to interfere with business. An admirable Jewish maxim!

April 28 Wednesday

Alan Dent—*i.e.*, Jock—who is to hold the *Sunday Times* fort, makes me a platform offering of his own copy of *Le Voyage de M.*

Perrichon. Remembering Madame P.'s "Vous faites des phrases dans une gare," I refrain from effusiveness, merely recommending him while I am away to shine, but not outshine. Wanting to know how good a doctor B. is, I ask him during breakfast if he can do a tracheotomy. He replies, "Yes, if you've a penknife." A Baron Something, whose name I do not catch, but whom I take to be a Director of the N.D.L. Company, is extremely civil to both of us. The Southampton Sewage Works are gay with flower-beds and a bowling-green. Otherwise nothing of note until we go on board, to find the luggage snug in our cabins.

As we cast off the band strikes up *Eine Seefahrt die ist Lustig*. Lots of telegrams, and a letter from John Gielgud in his exquisite, absurdly tiny handwriting, telling me all the things I should do and the people I must meet: "The nicest person of all is Lillian Gish." The boat is about half full, with nobody on board I have ever heard of except Max Schmeling, the boxer. The food is excellent beyond belief. For lunch we have the most decorative hors-d'oeuvres, including a delicious, velvety herring known as "Swedish Appetiser", langouste, and a German family dish of chopped beef. A good bottle of Eitelsbacher Sonnenberg at 4 marks. Am struck not so much by the extreme attentiveness of the stewards as by their spick-and-spanness, and above all their noiselessness. This is dream waiting. The lazy man need never trouble his pockets; when he wants matches there is always a silent presence to put the box into his hand, like the ghost in the story. A band-box smartness pervades the ship. The lift-boys in their white uniforms suggest tap-dancers in a revue; the stewardesses have the rectitude of hospital nurses.

Leaving Cherbourg, we meet the *Queen Mary* coming in. She left Southampton two hours after us, but is faster by three knots. I ought to be able to calculate when she will catch us up, but even at school could never do this kind of sum. And now I have not the vaguest idea how to employ the time. I have put on an Elia-like quality of super-annuation. I am Retired Leisure. I am to be met with on trim decks. I grow into gentility perceptibly. I am like a dog which, having been on a leash for years, is suddenly liberated and has forgotten how to frisk.

April 29 *Thursday*

It is just untrue that on the first night out one doesn't dress for dinner. Nearly everybody dressed last night, including Schmeling, elegant as a prize-fighter can be who really wins prize-fights. Handsome is as handsome does is truer in the boxing ring than anywhere else. George Bishop, who is *persona grata* with everybody at sight, would by this time have made Schmeling promise to attend the Malvern Festival. If I get introduced to him I shan't bore him with questions about Braddock and Joe Louis. I shall ask him about Salzburg, and tell him as much as I can remember of Ernest Newman's views on Glyndebourne.

Lunch-time.

How these Germans eat! A man at the next table breakfasted off grape-fruit, haddock, a dish which the menu described as "Sauté'd chicken liver in claret with mushrooms", and fresh strawberries. At eleven o'clock they bring round soup and rich-looking delicatessen, after which you are supposed to be ready for lunch at twelve-thirty. At two o'clock they begin again with coffee and cakes, tea at four and the rest of the day is a thick-coming procession of kickshaws, with, at seven o'clock an eight-course dinner to relieve the monotony.

Just received a radio-telegram from Sam Eckman, the London head of Metro-Goldwyn-Mayer. "Hope Neptune will be as kind to you as you will be to us." That's just it. I have always found Americans enchanting, while rather boggling at their country. This is probably because it frightens me; I am afraid of its slang, efficiency, bustle and stark cruelty. No English critic would want to write, and no English editor consent to print, Robert Benchley's notice of a new play in the current number of the *New Yorker*: "There must have been a play called *Bet Your Life* which opened last week, for I have it on my list. However, as I can't find it anywhere in the advertisements and nobody seems to know anything about it now, we might as well let the whole matter drop." Against this my reason suggests that the American hurly-burly may conceal an inferiority complex. But does that help? What about mine? Can there be anything more dangerous to mutual under-standing than a clash of inferiority complexes?

And on what, pray, do I base my prejudices? On some Sunday-school Longfellow, sickly Hawthorne, priggish Emerson? A handful of modern novels, some plays, all the Hollywood nonsense? The only American book I have ever really liked is Louisa M. Alcott's *Little Women*. Or am I worried by the lack of great dramatic and singing poets? Walt Whitman has written sound sense about this. His first point is America's *material* preoccupation, which in any new country must come before the arts. His second point is about Shakespeare and Tennyson. He calls the plays "the very pomp and dazzle of the sunset" while the poetry is "feudalism's lush-ripening culmination and last honey of decay". Just before sailing I threw into my bag W. W.'s *Complete Prose*. "Meanwhile democracy (meaning American democracy) waits the coming of the bards in silence and in twilight—but 'tis the twilight of the dawn." A fine passage which ought to put the English visitor to the States on his guard against uppishness.

May 1 *Saturday*

Already foresee that I shall be defeated by America's sheer in-calculableness. Here is a paragraph from to-day's issue of the *Lloyd*

Post, published on board, being an item in the News Service wirelessed
from New Brunswick:

> Stopping Oak, Tennessee. After keeping silence for fifty-two days
> while Jackson Withlow starved himself to the verge of death, the
> Lord told the mountaineer Friday night to take a little wine for
> your stomach's sake and suggested orange juice as a chaser.

May 5 *Wednesday*

Went to *Babes in Arms* at the Shubert Theatre. This is a fresh
inventive musical comedy played by a sixteen-year-old cast headed by
Mitzi Green and Duke McHale. The girl is clever, and the boy is a
budding Richard Bird who can sing and dance as well as act. I enjoyed
every moment of this; the music by Hart and Rodgers is written in a
fascinating idiom which is theirs and nobody else's. Haunting! The
show cost comparatively little to stage—fifty-five thousand dollars
only—and could be put on in London for a quarter of that sum. But I
doubt whether it would be a profitable experiment. Seeing that it has
been put together with many brains, I foresee flattering notices and
empty houses. London likes its musical comedy to be solid, substantial,
and thick; *Babes in Arms* is airy and fanciful, and the scenery is of the
sketchiest. This is as it should be, since the whole notion is that a lot
of actors' orphans will be sent to work on the land if they don't make
good with a revue of their own concocting. The bill for the kids'
scenery is forty-two dollars, which Sam, son of the orphanage master,
puts up in return for 49 per cent. of the profits. "Just like the real thing."

I find myself at variance with New York opinion about its good things.
(The contemptible is the contemptible all the world over.) For example,
Clare Boothe's *The Women* is said by Benchley to be "pretty amusing".
I think it is more than that. At least, I was seated between two very fat
men on an intensely hot night in the densely packed Ethel Barrymore
Theatre, and watched and listened to the intoxicated full of my eyes
and ears. The piece is a venomous comedy on an old theme beautifully
summed up by this play's cook to the parlourmaid: "The man who can
think out an answer to that one about the husband who adores his wife
while making love to another woman is going to win that prize they're
always giving out in Sweden." The cast of thirty-five consists entirely
of women, each of whom makes you see her man as though she were a
Ruth Draper, which very nearly each is. The playing of these American
companies is superb, and I doubt very much whether we could match
this one individually or collectively. This is nonsense. I am in no doubt
at all; we hardly have the actresses, and certainly we haven't the team.

At least, if I were to present this in London I should want Norah
Howard, Marda Vanne, Marie Ney, Jean Cadell, Martita Hunt, Olga
Lindo, Margaret Rawlings, Isabel Jeans, Greer Garson, and twenty

more, including somebody who can suggest a discomfited giraffe. I
should also insist on thirty-five American producers, one to each actress
to give her the pace! Thirty-five Oliver Blakeneys would do fine. What
this play won't stand is your English leading lady laboriously making
her effects while the rest of the company yawns and looks on. Some of
the actresses who did magnificently to-night are Margalo Gillmore,
Ilka Chase, Adrienne Marden, and Phyllis Povah, although in fairness
I should give the whole cast. These women do not play themselves in;
they come on and there is your character, as sharp as if Rebecca West
had described her. The scenes include a sitting-room, a hairdresser's,
a boudoir, a dress-shop, an exercise parlour, a pantry, a nursing home,
an hotel bedroom at Reno, a bathroom, another bedroom, and the
ladies' room on the Casino Roof.

May 6 *Thursday*

Called on Mrs Patrick Campbell, who is living at a clean little hotel
in West 49th Street. Took her to lunch at a place she insisted was
called the Vendôme, but which turned out to be Voisin's. Didn't notice
what we ate or drank, and don't remember paying. Probably very
good. After lunch went for a drive across Washington Bridge. This
also I dare say is very nice, but my attention was entirely taken up by
Mrs Pat, who radiated quicksilver. Saw the *Hindenburg* nosing majesti-
cally between the skyscrapers on its way to Lakehurst, and had the
taxi turn round so as to follow it and get a better view. By the time we
had rounded a block it had disappeared, and we couldn't catch it
again. This made Mrs P. pretend it had never been there, and that I
needed psycho-analysing. I think I have never been in contact with a
mind so frivolous and at the same time so big. She talked a great deal
about "flight" in acting as being the first quality of a great actor. For
four hours I listened to chatter about everything, from Moses to
Schnabel. About the former: "He probably said to himself, 'Must
stop or I shall be getting silly'. That is why there are only ten com-
mandments." She described Schnabel's playing of Beethoven as being
"like the winds of the air and the waves of the sea, without shape."
As she said this I heard again the crooning of Mélisande.
Of a well-known English novelist: "He has never met a great actress.
No actress could be great in his presence. He has a worm in his brain.
He lives in hell and likes it." About an American actress: "She has a
Siamese forehead and mouth like a golosh." About another actress:
"She is the great lady of the American stage. Her voice is so beautiful
that you won't understand a word she says." About the same actress:
"She's such a nice woman. If you knew her you'd even admire her
acting." With a smile, about *Ego*: "I did so enjoy your book. Every-
thing that everybody writes in it is so good." About Washington
Bridge: "The world's greatest piece of architecture after *Hedda Gabler*."

About Hedda: "You have always been right. I never could play her because I could never get the Latin out of my blood. I have had Swedish masseuses who were ten times better Heddas." About herself: "Many people say I have an ugly mind. That isn't true. I say ugly things, which is different." And again: "My voice at least has not gone, and Brenda can always make me another face." About her future: "I don't think I want to return to London. They seem quite satisfied with Miss B." The whole of this was punctuated with stories of her white Pekinese, Moonbeam, and melodious altercations with the taxi-driver, who failed to convince her that a certain monument was not Grant's Tomb. About Sarah Bernhardt she said: "I toured with her for five months, sat on her bed till five o'clock in the morning, and never heard her say a word to which a child could not have listened." She told me how she dined with Sarah three nights before she died. Sarah was wearing a dress of pink Venetian velvet with long sleeves, sent for the occasion by Sacha Guitry. Knowing that she had not long to live, she sat there with a white face eating nothing and infinitely gracious. Her son Maurice was at the table, paralysed, and fed by his wife. At the end of the meal Sarah was carried upstairs in her chair; turning the bend of the staircase, she kissed one finger and held it out. Both knew they would not meet again.

When I got back to the hotel I found I was holding a velvet geranium which, on one of the altercations with the taxi-driver, had become detached from Mrs Pat's headgear. We had chattered and chunnered for four hours.

May 7 Friday

I had just written the foregoing when a terrific thunderstorm broke· Great crashes and a lot of lightning, which made me fear for the skyscrapers. These were said to be in no danger. I suppose it is that, the sides being sheer, the stuff shins down them without opposition. In spite of the torrents, it was unbearably hot, so I took off my clothes and lay on the bed.

At twenty to eight I went downstairs, and the middle-aged, motherly receptionist said, with a telephone to her ear, "Sakes alive, Mr Agate, my daughter has just called me to say she's heard on the radio that there's been an explosion in the *Hindenburg* with everybody killed."

Within a minute people were saying "Sabotage". Somebody in the lounge who appeared to know about these things said that normally the ship would have avoided the storm and delayed making her moorings, but that she couldn't afford to do this as she had to return to England last night with a full complement of passengers for the Coronation, and to pick up films. The special editions of the news-papers struck me as being slow in coming out, but the electric news-signs got busy at once and Times Square was almost impassable. I was intending to see Katherine Cornell, and there meet B., who had spent

the afternoon with his brother. As it was Cornell I particularly
wanted to see, and *Candida* has nothing important till the last act, I
delayed going, and listened to the radio's version of the disaster. I
noticed that the announcers were very careful to qualify each and every
statement, and to say that this was the nearest that could be guessed.
A grim touch of realism was given by the command to all owners of
motor-cars proceeding to Lakehurst to turn back and leave the road
clear for doctors and ambulances. There was also a stern order to
sightseers to keep away. New York is deeply moved by the tragedy,
and nobody can understand why hydrogen was used. It is thought
that if not lightning, then some electric friction in the air—supposing
there is such a thing—was the cause. If it wasn't then the disaster happening at the same time as the storm is an extravagant coincidence. I had
forgotten how short a play *Candida* is, with the result that I got there
in time to see the curtain descend upon a beautiful apparition bowing
more lavishly than ever Bernhardt acted.

Called for Maurice Evans after his show. He has made tremendously
good here, the view being taken that if he is not the best English-
speaking actor he will have to do till the next comes along. He told me
that Mrs Pat said after his first night, "I like it all except the honey-
coloured hair," and then, turning to an immaculate blonde, "I always
think fair hair destroys personality, don't you?" Wound up the evening
at the Cotton Club. This is the place to hear swing music as the negroes
like it. What I personally think about it doesn't matter; it stirs American
audiences to frenzy. Duke Ellington conducts, presuming conducting
is the word. A first-class cabaret follows. This takes place in a purplish
penumbra, in which the dancers, naked except for diamond girdle
and breastplate, are a twilit salmon-pink. They are extraordinarily
attractive. The principal star is one Ethel Waters, and her enthusiastic
reception argues talent. The Nicholas Brothers are here, tinier and
skinnier and cheekier than ever. The waiters share the general frenzy;
the very plates, as they are put before you, shimmy. Our waiter is a
magnificent fellow with blue-black hair; the chap at the next table is
pure ivory. A delightful little lady, like a drawing in sepia, persuades
me to buy two toy dogs on the plea that they come from Manchester,
though whether the English or the American Manchester she doesn't
say. We regale ourselves with broiled lamp chops, chickened rice, and
sausages with scrambled eggs. I drink half a bottle of champagne, the
other two insist on whisky—and the bill comes to five pounds. All that
was yesterday!

May 9 Sunday

Am writing this on the verandah of a builder's hut on the slope of a
hill overlooking the Croton Lakes, some forty miles from New York.
The Grenekers have motored us here. Mrs G. is a provocative little

creature and hair's-breadth image of the Bergner. Heavenly day. Apple-blossom and the décor of Viennese operette with Lea Seidl in the wings preparing to warble. There are five workmen, Italians from Trieste, though they prefer to call themselves Austrians. All are of an incredible *Gemütlichkeit*; the one named Rudi is the perfect Joe Gargery. The hillside belongs to Greneker, who has already built three houses on it, and is busy on a fourth. Or rather it is Mrs G. who is busy; she is architect, builder, engineer, plumber, decorator, and foreman of works. The land is terraced as in Provence, and one of the feats of this extraordinary little lady, as practical as she is fascinating, has been to make a road 800 feet long, 16 feet wide, and in places 20 feet deep, without any engineering training whatever. She builds, without plans, large airy rooms of sweet-smelling pine. I do a lot of scrambling, holding on by the scaffold-poles, and wonder what it is in the New York air that enables me to sit up till all hours of the night in an atmosphere which in London would make a horse dizzy, but here merely clears the brain.

Lunch in the open air consists of salami, raw Italian ham and cheese, followed by chicken soup, chicken and spinach, iced beer, coffee, and crème-de-menthe frappé. This was the workmen's meal, cooked by them and smelling so good that we jumped at the invitation to share it. Where it all comes from even the Grenekers don't know, as this is a wilderness apparently without hotels, restaurants or shops. We are an extraordinarily gay little party, and I feel I am nearer to American life than I have yet got. Mrs G., who as the day wears on becomes more and more like the Bergner, has the same child-like *mutinerie* masking colossal intelligence. She has invented finger-stalls with brushes at the end of them. These are for the use of painters, enabling them to work on their canvases with five or, I suppose, ten fingers at once. She combats the suggestion that this is painting *à la* Lewis Carroll by the statement that the method is psychologically and functionally more correct. I refrain from retorting that I shall look forward to listening to a painting by Mark Hambourg.

May 10 *Monday*

My meal is taken at a famous hotel. The lamb chop has the consistency of indiarubber. Nothing in America tastes of anything.

> Let beeves and home-bred kine partake
> The sweets of Burn-mill meadow,

occurs in, I think, *Yarrow Unvisited*. Let me revisit Yarrow, or even Barrow, and partake of home-bred beeves! Iced water to drink, or so it is proposed till J. A. puts in his little oar. Nobody else drinks anything, and it is explained to me that no American can take a drink during business hours for fear of being over-reached.

The other guests are Cedric Hardwicke, the English actor, and Winston Paul, the first man in America to make ice by electricity and therefore a millionaire. Our host is Eddie Dowling, lessee of the St James's Theatre and Maurice Evans's partner. Cedric has the idea of a floating deck halfway between New York and London on which to stage plays striking a compromise between their conscienceless professionalism and our own aspiring amateurism. According to Cedric the English are playwrights who cannot finish off plays, like trainers who can do everything with a horse except make it win, whereas the Americans are up to every dodge of putting plays together without being able to write them. The ice man is typical, I imagine, of all American millionaires; that is to say, his clothes make you wonder how often he can afford to lunch at sumptuous places like this. Hearing that I may be going to Philadelphia, he says he regrets he hasn't a place there, but will telegraph this afternoon, putting at my disposal a friend's apartment, car, and chauffeur. If, on the other hand, I have a mind to visit Idaho, he will be delighted to offer me the same facilities plus a ranch in the Rockies to which from time to time he runs down. A warning to me not to despise strange Americans, for I do not hear about the ice and the millions till later! Our host, Eddie, was originally a music-hall artist who toured England some years ago, without, as he himself admits, achieving any particular fame. His wife is Ray Dooley, who was at one time a partner in vaudeville with W. C. Fields—music-hall is music-hall all the world over. Eddie, who called me Jimmie at sight, is an infectious little man who looks like a member of the Lupino family. He takes to you, you take to him, and you are bosom friends before you sit down. He told me some astonishing things about Maurice Evans's success over here. How a total stranger to Maurice, having seen him in *Romeo and Juliet* and *St Helena*, wrote to him asking if he had another play and wanted money for it. If so, would he meet him in a bar? Maurice, having nothing better to do, turned up, and the man said, "I'm sorry, but since I wrote you I've engaged my capital elsewhere. Would twenty-five thousand dollars be any use, and what's the play?" Maurice stammered out "Shakespeare's *Richard II*." But the man did not blench, and, calling for pen and ink, wrote out a cheque then and there. Maurice then went round to most of the other managers and brokers, and in each case was politely bowed off the premises. At last he fell in with Dowling, who first enacted an amusing little comedy in which he pretended to be his own secretary, and so played Jorkins to his own Spenlow. Before the interview was over, the pretence was abandoned, and another twenty-five thousand dollars was forthcoming. When the time came to pay back the first twenty-five thousand dollars, the original philanthropist was asked what share of the profits to date he thought he ought to have. He replied that he hadn't been out for profit and would be satisfied with six per cent interest! The result is that our young actor is now a rich man. Maurice modestly told me as much himself, and added that he had a permanent offer from Hollywood at a thousand pounds a week, which he intended to go on turning down. Coming back from lunch, I was driven past the Waldorf-Astoria. This is a stone building as impressive as a Sibelius symphony, and I have a notion to try the cooking there.

At five o'clock George Jean Nathan called to take me out for cocktails. As I do not want to drink much—for what little drink there is in America is immensely potent—I order tea and crumpets, and get some very poor tea and very mean crumpets. The place is expensive, and I note one or two little ladies who look exactly like white toy poms. They are accompanied, and obviously of the highest respectability, though only Peter Arno could do justice to their utter inability to open their mouths, and, when they do, to produce anything resembling human speech. Amazing children.

Nathan has not changed. He still has the same delicate features and beautiful hands, the look of the fallen cherub, and the smile which breaks out when you say something malicious and he thinks of something to cap it. After a bit we are joined by Richard Watts, the dramatic critic of the *Herald-Tribune*, and I listen while they tell me about the greatness of Maurice Evans, who, I am rather shocked to find, is over here rated above Gielgud. From what these boys say, I judge that Maurice must have made enormous strides. For if we are to talk about greatness I begin, as always with first things, and must therefore contrast Maurice's baby-face with the august masks of Irving, Forbes-Robertson, Benson. A great actor must include the forbidding in his facial range: when I last saw Maurice he could do no better in this line than stave off with impudence.

Excursion, by Victor Wolfson, at the Vanderbilt Theatre, is a fantasy about a Coney Island steamer that put out to sea with all its passengers on board and found an island. When I woke up the steamer with its passengers was coming back. A mixture of *Outward Bound* and *The Passing of the Third Floor Back*. We could act this and probably will.

May 11 *Tuesday*

Lunch with the Drama League. The Leaguers contrive to be over-dressed and dowdy. Hardly a man to be seen, and none who dares to be heard. I sit between Peggy Wood, of *Bitter Sweet* fame, and the little lady who is Richard II's Queen. Peggy tells me that she is to play Portia again "in order to have a finger in the Shakespeare racket". Her view about Nathan is that it is not playing the game to make so much money out of a thing you despise, that thing being the theatre. Richard's Queen is the most appealing, sensitive little lady I have met in this continent. She has a Plantagenet coiffure and wears a frock of red silk on which the figure '83' is printed some hundred and fifty times. I ask what this means. Richard's Queen says she hasn't noticed it.

The object of the lunch is to present the medal for the year's best acting performance won in previous years by Katherine Cornell and Helen Hayes. This time it goes to Maurice, who turns up an hour and a quarter late! Among the celebrities present are Mrs Richard Mansfield, who, it appears gives readings from Shakespeare with her late husband's annotations, and Ruth St Denis, formerly a great dancer and now an exquisite figure with white hair and the first approach I have seen to anything one can call a manner. There is a lot of introducing from the chair, and each person as she is named stands up and bobs. I am introduced as the Dean of English Criticism! In the course of the speech-making we are told that Gielgud during the last week of *Hamlet* took eighteen thousand dollars and that Evans's run of *Richard II* up to date *averages* eighteen thousand. I am twitted with these figures, and asked what London can show against them. I speak for a good ten minutes, in the sort of a cathedral hush which befits a dean, the difficulty of praising Evans to his face being got over by the fact that the face is no longer there, its owner having grabbed his prize and gone. In the matter of figures I tell the League with a well-simulated air of conviction that if America will send us two Shakespearian actors as good as Gielgud and Evans we will . . . I don't need to finish the sentence. An American audience though dull-looking is quick-witted.

The rest of the afternoon is devoted to the censorship question, which has suddenly became acute, and in this way. The authorities, being disturbed by the prevalence of the strip-tease act, recently closed down all the burlesque theatres, and having done this, were seized with doubts about the legality of this proceeding. Accordingly something called the Dunnigan Bill has been rushed through both Houses, and now only awaits Governor Lehman's signature to become law. What the promoters of the Bill appear not to have realised is that giving a censor power over burlesque theatres makes him tsar of all other theatres. Here is what the *Tribune* says on the matter:

> The Bill would leave every serious production in New York under threat of instant decapitation if Mr Moss, or any machine politician who might later succeed him, or any pressure group which could get the ear of a licence commissioner or exploit the exigencies of any passing electoral campaign, should happen to feel that the production was 'immoral' or 'impure'. A single line or word or gesture could serve as the pretext for such an edict; while no real right to review is allowed, since the Bill prohibits a stay on appeal. The burlesque houses may have been indecent (if so, the courts were and are open for their suppression), but this Bill carries the question far beyond the matter of the burlesque houses. It makes it a question of preserving the integrity of the New York stage.

As one of the speakers at the luncheon to-day put it, "this Bill would degrade the New York stage to the level of the English". In every New York theatre tonight leaflets were distributed inviting the playgoer to petition Governor Lehman not to give his sanction to the Bill. B. signed one, but I refused, holding that as an Englishman I have no standing in the matter. I realise that B., and the wider culture of the Jews, has no sense of this limitation. It is important to recognise that the movement against the proposed censorship does not come from the burlesque houses. It has originated with and is backed by the most responsible and respectable theatrical elements. These include the Actors' Equity, the League of New York Theatres, the Theatrical Protective Union, the Drama Critics' Circle, and the Dramatists' Guild. But the question is not so simple as it sounds. Much was said at the luncheon about the political use of censorship. Here it is important to note the difference between the English and American connotation of the word 'political'. Over here the word has a sinister implication totally unknown to us. There was not the slightest objection to the strip-tease acts until the burlesque theatres brought them into Broadway and began to draw audiences away from the legitimate theatres and cinemas. Whereupon the vested interests began to have qualms on the score of decency. In England the objections to a censor are based on the potential asininity of whoever holds the office. In America it is feared that wealthy managements may attempt to get less powerful organisations censored out of existence. This and nothing else is the kernel of the battle.

Called on Helen Hayes and found her to be a very bright, extremely intelligent little woman full of an inner distinction which looks out through a pair of woebegone grey eyes set wide apart from the nose. We were not there very long, as Helen wanted to listen to Alexander Woollcott on the radio reading Edward VIII's abdication speech. She disapproved of Woollcott doing this eve-of-Coronation stunt, but intended to listen all the same.

May 12 *Wednesday*

Coronation Day. Cable from my sister May: "London is empty without you!" Claud Greneker rang up before breakfast to ask what I had thought of the proceedings, which here started at 5 a.m. It appears that Mrs Greneker is also a wireless expert and had connected up the whole show. G. sounded very weary, and I refrained from asking the poor man whether he had got up to listen or had been kept up.

Dined last night at Voisin's. Now that Mrs Patrick Campbell was not with me and I could give some attention to the food, I found I had discovered a restaurant which is the equal of anything in Paris. The service was both attentive and understanding, and the habitués looked as though they were accustomed to food. Attended première of *Orchids Preferred* at the Imperial Theatre. As my views of musical comedy are known, I shall reproduce what Brooks Atkinson of the *New York Times* says:

For the antiquarians it might be reported that the story, in its graceful and airy summer fashion, deals with the adventures of some amiable girl prostitutes. There is, of course, an ingénue who really doesn't know what her friends are up to and is much shocked when the hero, thinking she is no better than her companions, makes love to her. . . . Tastefulness is not one of the outstanding qualities of *Orchids Preferred*, but it isn't the vulgarity that is likely to bother you. It is the excessive tediousness of the proceedings that will probably send you screaming into the streets, or, preferably, into *Babes in Arms*, which is playing near by and will help you forget some of the horrors of this little spring catastrophe.

I have spent the whole morning writing, and this being Coronation Day propose to do no more work. Seeing New York is not all beer and skittles. I would rather say that it is very little beer and very fatiguing skittles. I am therefore going to take the afternoon off prior to attending the Coronation Ball tonight.

May 16 *Sunday*

To-day's *New York Times* weighs two ounces short of two pounds. It has 14 sections—New York news, general news, finance and business, editorials including letters and special articles, sport, society, book reviews, magazines, the news in pictures, drama and music, science (which includes aviation and motoring), real estate, classified advertisements, and pictures of the Coronation in rotogravure, 220 pages in all. Eight narrow columns to a page each containing some 800 words. The pictures and the classified advertisements take up 26 pages, leaving 194 pages. Cut this in half to allow for the unclassified advertisements, and the result is roughly 100 pages of 8 columns. This means 640,000 words per issue, or somewhere about the length of seven average-sized novels. The price is 10 cents, or roughly 5d. The *New York Herald-Tribune* weighs 1 lb. 10 oz., and is made up in similar fashion, but with a comic section in colour. Any attempt to read these papers as a whole must fail because it would take more than a week; you choose the section you want.

May 18 *Tuesday*

Seeing is believing. I have heard of tree-squatters, but never believed in them until this morning, when I saw Shipwreck Kelly, "The World's Champion Flagpole Sitter", perched high above a music-hall and now in the fourth day of a squat which is to run thirteen days, thirteen nights, thirteen hours, and thirteen minutes!

Lunch at a French open-air café, where a green hedge, half a dozen shrubs in tubs, and the accent of the waiters transport one into the Pyrenees. After lunch explore Radio City. It is a world in itself. Magnanimity's purest poetry, reducing it to the prose of the fact is a sorry business, though a little of it must be attempted. The underground part of it covers four blocks. The ground floor is Burlington Arcade in excelsis. I concentrate on the music-hall section; the entertainment here is a combination of stage and screen. First I am amazed at the foyer, easily ten times the size of the Empire's. The dominant decorative note is Ezra Winter's 60 × 30-foot mural: "Based on an Oregon Indian legend, this Shows the Upward March of Man toward the Golden Mountain where the Author of Life dwells beside the Fountain of Eternal Youth." (The prose is American.) The two twenty-nine foot chandeliers weigh two tons each. I am indebted for this and a mass of other information to the page-boy detailed to show us round, who looks as though he had come out of a Richard Strauss opera. All the ushers are men in livery, and there is a complete absence of the cow-girls, Quakeresses, little Miss Muffetts, who enliven our cinemas at home. We are taken through banqueting halls, kitchens, and into the Celebrity Room, where we sign the visitors' book. Presently we attain the Balcony, so high that looking down into the foyer is a giddy business. A panel slides back discreetly and we find ourselves in Radio City Music-hall, which is exactly like the interior of an airship hangar. What light there is filters through hundreds of slats. There are six thousand two hundred seats. The screen measures seventy feet by forty. The drop-curtain weighs three tons. A news-budget is in progress with the house in darkness. This over, the lights go up and we become aware of a symphony orchestra; I reflect that here is the concert hall of which Berlioz dreamt. The orchestra plays an overture with Beechamesque punctilio, while changes of lighting bathe the audience in a glow of tender dawn warming to wanton sunset. The band returns hydraulically to the place whence it came, having done great execution. A lady clad entirely in diamonds now goes through the motions of the haute école with the assistance of a dazzlingly white horse. This concluded, we arrive at the Rockettes. There are thirty-six of them. They are as good as the Tiller Girls. Then comes the new Fred Astaire–Ginger Rogers picture *Shall We Dance?* which imbecility I refrain from seeing. We emerge, having looked on something which is potentially the greatest show on earth. One says potentially, because a show needs an audience, and there do not seem to be more than a couple of hundred people present. But the place is so vast that these two hundred may actually be two thousand. If you can't see an orchestra of seventy players you can hardly expect to estimate the number of human dots scattered about the floors of this measureless cavern.

Dine with Nathan at the Colony, said to be New York's last word in cooking, but the first I have heard about this art. We eat Canapé Colony, which is crab meat on pastry with a bisque sauce, cold soup, a filet mignon Henri-Quatre, and a chocolate ice. To drink there is

Zeltinger 1931 and half a bottle of champagne, the brand of which I cannot see through the napkin. This place is firmly confident of itself, and the crowd too; both are justfied. Not as guest but as an observer of social conditions I ask the cost, and Nathan is forced to show me a bill of just over eight pounds.

Tobacco Road at the Forrest Theatre. This drama of Georgia's back of beyond is utterly and entirely American, and I am warned that I shall not make much of it. All the actors speak in undertones; it takes me half·an hour to hear, and another half-hour to understand what I hear. The nearest thing is the plays of Synge, except that there is no poetry, actual or implied; the humanity is as remote as the statues on Easter Island. Jeeter Lester is the owner of what was once a tobacco farm and now grows so little cotton that he and his family are starving. He is married to a wife of whom he says, "When she was young she was that ugly it didn't make sense." The play is a maze of frustration, incest, and decay. We are shown some home-made nuptials between a semi-idiot and a revivalist female who has become possessed of an automobile; the boy will not hear of a honeymoon because he wants to joy-ride! James Barton plays Jeeter rather in the manner of Joe Jackson, the English music-hall comedian in trouble with a bicycle. The audience rocks with laughter throughout, taking no notice of the grandmother who hobbles through the play without saying a word; she is the counterpart to Firs in Tchehov's *Cherry Orchard*. This extraordinary mixture of grim, sordid drama and riotous fooling has been running for four years.

Supper with Maurice Evans at Sardi's, the equivalent of Rules, after which we are escorted to Harlem. Except in the matter of complexions, Harlem looks exactly like Pimlico. We drink beer and eat mutton bones drenched with pepper in a resort called Moon-Glow. This is a dingy little cubby-hole crowded with darkies carrying on like a scene in a Cochran revue staged by Professor Stern. The waiters handle their platters after the manner of Salome. The heat is terrific, and the noise so great that I cannot hear a single word of a saucy song composed in my honour and bawled into my ear by a dusky gigolo. For some time B. has been trying to say something to me. But there's no opportunity of hearing what it is until about three o'clock, when he seizes a moment of comparative silence to yell: "You don't appear to be getting much golf." At four o'clock some idiotic drink restrictions come into play, and we make a move.

Lunched at a chop-house. Very comfortable and cheap. I appeared to have lunched twice to-day! This is not so, but due to writing and living a diary simultaneously. To-day's entry up to now was all about yesterday; with this lunch I catch up. In New York it is almost impossible to keep events from telescoping. This is due to the *slow* American hustle. I once had a horse that ran away at a walk. Here the hustle takes the form of not letting you alone; a continual, relentless buttonholing goes on all the time. B. has his hands full, less in making contacts we want than in avoiding those we don't want. It doesn't seem to occur to anybody that one may like occasionally to be left alone for five minutes, if only to think over what one has seen.

Went in blazing sunshine to the top of the Empire State Building and hated it. There is a glass cage in which I felt fairly safe, but anywhere near the parapet was impossible. Something sways, but whether it is you or the building is as moot a point as I know. The visibility to-day was charted at 25 miles, and for the first time I realised how small the island is and why the skyscrapers came into being. The view includes the Manhattan skyline seen from behind, the Statue of Liberty, the encircling Hudson with its scores of fussy little tugs, the *Normandie*, which has just arrived and looks, as the fellow in *Lear* says, "diminished to her cock", the great bridges, Central Park, the rule-made avenues and streets, rival monsters like the Chrysler Building and Radio City, and hundreds of lesser pinnacles in stone like marzipan. Perhaps Man is not so inferior to the ants after all. I am, of course, not surprised to find that none of the Americans I meet up here is a New-Yorker; no Londoner ever climbs the Monument. The people I talk to on the roof answer me in French, German, Swedish, Italian, Russian and broad Lancashire.

Once more on terra firma we went to the pictures and saw the Coronation and *Hindenburg* films. The shots of Queen Mary made a great impression, the people near me crying out, "Isn't she lovely?" But the whole film was received with the greatest enthusiasm. The *Hindenburg* picture included some of the evidence of Captain Rosedahl, the head of aviation at Lakehurst, who said that it was well known that airships generate electricity. This is discharged as soon as the landing-ropes touch earth, and members of the crew handling them before establishing contact have been known to suffer severe shocks. All this electricity runs wild in the immediate proximity of seven million cubic feet of extremely inflammable hydrogen! The Germans say they can't afford to buy helium, which can only be got from America, though here I am given another explanation. This is that German airships are not designed for helium. If they change their design they will be unfitted for hydrogen, which is the gas they must use in the event of war since they would not be able to get the other from America.

Dinner at the Grenekers' apartment, twenty-three stories high and overlooking Central Park. Down below there is a constant stream of motors, and four games of baseball are in progress in a space the size of the Oval, but grassless. I had asked to be given a typically American meal, as this is probably the only private house in New York in which I shall eat. The menu consisted of cream of mushroom soup, duck, asparagus, fresh rice, and for dessert a grape salad with hot cheese rolls. As a concession to British taste a bottle of Beaune.

The play to-night was *Yes, my Darling Daughter*. It is being played to packed houses, all of which endorse the maternal sanction to a young girl to behave as she likes.

May 19 *Wednesday*

Opening of the Renoir Exhibition at the Metropolitan Museum of Art. A large, well-dressed crowd possessing a distinction I have not met anywhere else. This magnificent collection of over sixty pictures has been got together through the courtesy of several other galleries and some twenty private owners, including Helen Hayes and Edward G. Robinson, the film actor. Here is the glorious *Déjeuner des Canotiers*, an amazing piece of sheer paint. About this Harry B. Wehle writes: "None of the girls or young men present is smiling, none is definitely flirting. A striped awning shields them from the sun, and they sit there over the remains of their luncheon, some of them chatting, one playing with a lap dog, others doing nothing whatever. Gentle breezes from the river seem to caress them—and they are completely happy. The picture is a hymn to youth and summer-time."

Here too is *By the Seashore*, a picture of a lady sitting in a basket-chair with a background of cliffs. But the loveliest canvas of all is *Le Bal à Bougival*, painted in 1883. A pen drawing for this picture is inscribed, "Elle valsait délicieusement abandonée entre les bras d'un blond aux allures de canotier." I came back to this picture half a dozen times. The grave innocence of the girl, the eyes wide apart like a kitten's, the swirl of the white dress, the red of the hat, the blue of her partner's rough suit, the animation of the scene which is yet not without melancholy—all this makes up a composition brilliant yet tender, like Sarah's playing in the first act of *La Dame aux Camélias*. Even when I got outside I went back to have one more look at a picture owned by the Museum of Fine Arts, Boston, and which is going to be one of my best excuses for returning to America next year.

The foyer of the Astor Hotel is as full of people coming and going as is Charing Cross Railway Station. We lunched with Milton Shubert, and I was asked a lot of questions about the English stage. I began to answer these with the freedom imparted by two thousand miles, when I saw B. making frantic signals for me to shut up. Nothing escapes him, whereas I in my simplicity had not recognised an interviewer. The room in which the meal happened was a combination of box-office, bookstall, flower-shop, and motor sales-room. The appearance of food was a surprise. Matinée of *Richard II*. A packed house and great enthusiasm for Maurice. I still have the impression that his features are too boyish for the conveyance of tragedy, though this view would be very unpopular here, and I do not give expression to it

In the evening *High Tor* at the Martin Beck Theatre. Defeat with heavy slaughter, and even B. routed. The difficulty is to see this play through American eyes, which I suppose one ought to do. As an Englishman I am now certain that it is high fudge interlarded with bleak, totally unfunny humour. But I am alive to the danger of regarding this as criticism. That a Japanese might not be tickled by the fun in *Juno and the Paycock* would be no criticism of Sean O'Casey's play.

The fact that B. and I sat glum while the audience roared its head off tells me that I am no closer to an American than a Japanese is to an Irishman. Renoir once said, "After all, if you are going in for oil-painting you may as well use oil-paint." If a poet is going to write a fantasy he may as well be fantastic I don't boggle about the fantasy part of this play—high-faluting is the same all the world over. It is the comic interludes which strike me as inexpressibly dreary. I can only suppose that they awake echoes in the American mind which escape me, though I can find no hint of them in the text. The production has *Theatre Arts Monthly* written all over it, and the play would probably do very well in London if cut in two and produced in two theatres—the guff at the Mercury and the larks at the Gate. Nothing in either text or production could prevent one from recognising a potentially very fine actor in Burgess Meredith. This young man has an immense amount of vigour and a tremendous honesty, and I guess that he represents pretty exactly what young America is thinking. He has a fine voice, an excellent presence, and an open countenance conveying a backwoods likeableness. I should very much like to see him in something other than the backwoods idiom, something to be spoken instead of snarled. But I am in no doubt about his acting powers.

Here is raised a question of vital interest in the American Theatre—how to keep its young actors. Meredith's success means that next year he will be entirely absorbed by Hollywood. As this process will be repeated in the case of every promising young player, the result can only be the complete dearth of grown-up players. The theatres are very much worried about this.

May 20 *Thursday*

New York declares against the proposed dramatic censorship. Here is Governor Lehman's decision:

> While fully appreciative of the high purpose of those supporting this bill and while warmly joining in the desire to maintain the theatre on a proper moral plane, it nevertheless seems to me that the specific provisions of this bill are too broad and too susceptible of abuse in administration.

Was given luncheon to-day by the critics. There were Brooks Atkinson of the *New York Times*, John Mason Brown of the *New York Post*, Burns Mantle of the *News*, Joseph Wood Krutch of the *Nation*, John Anderson of the *New York Journal*, and George Jean Nathan, who writes for all the other papers. Very jolly. They want to know who are the heads of the English stage, meaning the present-day Irving and Ellen Terry. I reply John Gielgud and Edith Evans, with a reservation in favour of Laurence Olivier as the most promising young actor. It appears that I am right about *High Tor*, which nevertheless was awarded the Drama Critics' Prize by a majority, Nathan voting against it; right about Burgess Meredith; wrong about Maurice Evans. But I gather that, generally speaking, first principles are the same here as in London. Atkinson is austere and Morganesque, Mason Brown is the New York Darlington, and Burns Mantle reminds me very much of Baughan. Krutch is the Ivor Brown, I cannot quite fit in Anderson, and Nathan is his mischievous self. Mason Brown says, "Nathan is a good game, but you've got to know the rules." Was told a lot of lovely stories, the best being the remark of the French lady at the six-day bicycle race: "Ah nuts, alors!"

Worked all afternoon, then taken for cocktails to the Fort Belvedere in West 55th Street, a newly opened bar lavishly decorated with frescoes of the Duke of Windsor, who if he wanted could be crowned King of America to-morrow, the Prince of Wales's feathers, and an escort of Life Guards. The wits congregate here. I asked one of them what he most wanted to see in England. He said, "Oxford." And the second thing? "Lady Oxford." Dined in logical sequence at the Queen Mary in East 58th Street. This is laid out shipwise with an illuminated model of the boat. Swedish hors-d'oeuvres are spread on a refectory table and you help youself. One plateful is a meal. B. had two platefuls, and but for my innate decency would have attempted a third. Decide to have an evening of real drama instead of make-believe. Arrange therefore to be taken to a night court in West 54th Street, where we have seats in the front row. The performance starts at 8.30; the décor is that of any English police-court. The players are almost as inaudible as English actors. Police, burly as all-in wrestlers, shepherd their prisoners with a kind of rough gentleness. The magistrate, who wears neither wig nor gown, is thirty-five, keen-faced, looks *fortiter in modo* and turns out to be *suaviter in re*. The offences have all been committed since five o'clock this afternoon. Men and youths accused of peddling without a licence. They carry their wares with them. One batch is eleven strong, all Italians. They are discharged with a caution. Street-betting cases, a string of fourteen vagrants, old, some of them with heads which look definitely imbecile, all indescribably filthy. Might be the inmates of one of Gorky's doss-houses. Pitiful. All are discharged. Most of these cases have taken less than a minute; the longest five minutes.

An old Jew, who should be a figure in Italian comedy, pleads that he was not begging but selling umbrellas. These, produced, are obviously unsaleable. Old Jew says they are saleable if it rains hard enough. Acquitted. A young man with the air of a shabby Narcissus pleads not guilty to a charge we cannot hear. A whispered colloquy between judge and prisoner, at the end of which the young man is told to go away and behave himself. There are no more prisoners at the moment, and an interval is taken. It is a Gilbertian court which waits for crime to be committed!

The shriek of a police-van as in the films. A young man has beaten up his wife for spending his wages on silk stockings. The magistrate tells the young man he is exceeding his authority. Will he promise no more beatings? Yes, if there is no more buying of stockings. A bargain is struck. Another young man is accused of violently assaulting his neighbour's wife! Will he desist? No, he will assault her again the moment he is out of this jam. She is a bitch, and has brought it on herself. The magistrate keeps him in cells till the morning, for his own protection. The neighbour seems wholly disinterested. The next is a drunk. "You're soused," says the magistrate. "I'm not sure you're not canned. Cells till morning." A voluble Japanese has refused to pay a taxi-driver $1.75. He has no money, but if he can go home on the subway he will return with the cash before the court rises. "But since you have no money how are you going to get the fare for the subway?" The Jap points to the taxi-driver: "He will lend it me!" The court dissolves in laughter, and the pair leave amicably. Another wait, then more peddlers, more vagrants, more drunks. It is twelve o'clock, and we go to supper. B. in his capacity as medical adviser sends me home soon after two. He insists on my having an early night, himself being all for another spot of Harlem's Moon-Glow.

May 21 *Friday*

B. is a fellow-traveller of genius. His latest notion is that while I am working he should look at the things which it would be disgraceful to leave New York without one of us having seen. This is splendid of him. Came in this morning to report that Shipwreck Kelly was still sitting on his pole; when he saw him he was eating the luncheon he had presumably taken out of the basket on which he sits.

Have come down to Coney Island in lovely weather, first calling for money in Wall Street, which to-day is distinctly livelier. Our chauffeur, who is second cousin to Kid Lewis, points out J. P. Morgan's home and library, the Law Courts, and Tombs Prison. The view from Manhattan Bridge is superb. To the left it might be the Thames. To the right is Brooklyn Bridge, beyond which we glimpse the Statue of Liberty. Behind us is still the Manhattan skyline, which keeps all its glamour. We proceed through slums, then suburbs which might be Tufnell Park. Then a long stretch of shady avenue, very like Bournemouth. Coney Island is like Southend Kursaal, only on a bigger scale. The season has not yet begun, and very few of the fun-fairs are functioning, though we manage to catch a glimpse of a Creature with a Human Head and the Legs of a Horse, and a Woman whose Body is Turning into Stone. We are introduced to Jack Johnson [Heavyweight Boxing Champion of the World 1908–15]. Lunch at the Half Moon Hotel, on a balcony overlooking the boardwalk, narrow sands, and a lazy sea. Nobody about. The hotel is vast, clean, and comfortable. On the walls is an exhibition of graphic prints and easel paintings, all very modern and I think good. I should like to buy Isabel Bate's *Push Carts—Bronx*, which I think Tommy Earp would approve. But I am told that nothing is for sale, the exhibits being the property of that part of the Government known as Works Progress Administration Federal Art Project. As B. is sunbathing and I am alone in the restaurant with 78 empty tables, this is a convenient opportunity to say something about the most important thing I have struck during my visit. Far and away the most important.

In January 1934 Maxwell Bodenheim, a poet from Greenwich Village, picketed Relief Headquarters with a board proclaiming, "Artists can starve as well as bricklayers." W.P.A., which stands for Works Progress Administration, promptly put Bodenheim in gaol, and three weeks later created the first Writers' Project. This means giving writers work at minimum rates in place of a dole. This was quickly followed by the Easel Project, for the benefit of artists. Next, with the establishment of the Federal Theatre, came the turn of the players and the studio employees generally. At the beginning this was run on more or less military lines by an ex-Army officer, Colonel Earle Boothe, who was in charge during the War of the Argonne Players in France.

In August 1935 the playwright Elmer Rice had the notion of making the undertaking aesthetic as well as benevolent. He enlisted the sympathies of Mrs Hallie Flanagan, organiser of the Experimental Theatre at Vassar. This lady 'pours tea at the White House', which is American slang for moving in the best society. So encouraged, the Government proceeded to pour out money, $6 000 000 being forthcoming between October 1935 and June 1936, which rate of subsidy still maintains. To-day the Federal Theatre has 200 active companies employing some 15 000 people. They perform anything and everything, from Shakespeare to Eliot, and have recently produced with great success *Murder in the Cathedral*, Marlowe's *Dr Faustus*, and the negro *Macbeth*. No living author receives more than $50.00 a week, while the actors get $23.00. The highest price of admission is 55 cents, and at least one-third of the audience is composed of people who have never seen a play before. The theatre plays to an audience of 15 000 000 people all over the United States, giving free performances in parks, hospitals, and schools. It has a research laboratory. This addition to the culture of the country during the last eighteen months has cost less than half the initial cost of a battleship. Brooks Atkinson of the *New York Times* tells me that it costs $50.00 a month to put a man on the dole, and that with all the overhead charges, rent, costume and scene-designing, lighting, and management, and transportation by truck, the Federal Theatre costs $110.00 per man per month. Whence he rightly argues that for the extra $60.00 a month something of extraordinary social value has been accomplished. The Broadway theatres take but little interest in the movement. One or two managers of tumble-down rented theatres "where the balcony rubs knees with the stalls" have profited by making lets. An unbiased opinion seems to be that whereas the Federal Theatre has time and money it lacks discipline. Actors returning to Broadway after a season at the Federal Theatre are said to need relicking into shape.

Now consider the Government and music. Here are a few facts: Music-teachers are giving free instruction every week to half a million persons in 260 project units. W.P.A. units have performed 4 915 works written by 1481 musicians living in this country. About 2 500 folk-tunes have been collected and transcribed by workers in a dozen regions. Three hundred and forty-nine copyists, arrangers, and librarians assigned to twenty-four projects in eighteen states are at work in libraries, universities, and project offices, and have turned out several hundred thousand music manuscripts and folios, which are to be made available as nuclei for public lending libraries. On April 1 of this year 13 310 men and women were on the Federal Music Project's rolls and were employed in 763 units, including 155 concert orchestras, 80 bands, 91 dance bands, 24 theatre and novelty orchestras, and 260 teaching projects, choral groups, opera units, chamber ensembles, and in other kinds of units. In New York City since the inauguration of the Project's programme 7 689 406 lessons have been given to children and adults unable to afford private instruction.

May 22 *Saturday*

Last night, directly we got back from Coney Island, we went to a concert given by the W.P.A. Federal Music Project at the Federal Music Theatre, West 54th Street. We saw an elegant theatre half full of a wholly attentive audience with its gaze fixed upon a stage bare as one thought only Russian stages can be bare. The band of thirty contained two women, one of whom was the leader. I thought it played about as well as the best English amateurs. Price of seats, 55, 35, and 25 cents. The programme was the following:

Fugal Concerto for Flute, Oboe, and String Orchestra, Opus 40, No. 2 ...	...	Gustav Holst
Serenade, Opus 7	...	Richard Strauss
Concerto Grosso for Strings and Piano	...	Albert Stoessel
Concerto in A minor for 'Cello and Orchestra, Opus 33, No. 1	...	Saint-Saens
Symphony No. 26, in E flat major ...	...	Mozart

The programme is annotated in the handsomest fashion. The note on the Strauss Serenade is strengthened by a quotation from our own Ernest Newman, though the annotator has wit enough of his own. Of the Holst piece he tells that "the little Concerto trots peacefully away until, suddenly getting up and scratching itself, it disappears in a trill for the two wind instruments and a rising pizzicato scale in an absurd rhythm."

From the concert we rushed to the Federal Theatre. It is difficult to understand, let alone explain, *Power*, by Arthur Arent, presented at the Ritz Theatre. Quite simply it is an attempt to stage the front page of a newspaper. *Power* is a plea for state ownership of the manufacture and supply of electricity. In form it is a revue, containing two acts and twenty scenes. The dialogue is bleaker than a Blue book, consisting almost entirely of statistics culled from private and governmental balance-sheets. Here is one scene. "Connecticut," a voice sings out. At once two actors come down centre as in the last scene of a panto-mime, line up, and chant, "Private ownership twenty cents," "Govern ment ownership five cents." Per unit per hour, or something of the sort. This is repeated twenty times with different states and different rates, till the stage is full. The background consists of changing film-shots of the power plant. There is music and dancing, and the whole thing exceeds in violence any tub-thumping the English know. It is propa-ganda sheer and unalloyed. It is malevolent, witty, sinister, laughable, destructive, and constructive all at the same time. The ushers are in Russian costume, and there is just a hint of Ogpu behind it all. But it is intensely vital, and I know nothing in England to match it. The house is crowded nightly by young people bursting with social consciousness. B. and I, who are totally indifferent to the price of electric light in New York or anywhere else, sit entranced. The acting is far and away the best we have seen in this country, and I am convinced that this movement is the most significant thing we have struck over here. In art, music, and drama it has shown itself tinglingly alive. Indeed, I cannot understand why the New York critics have said so little about it, since it is easily the highest cultural force in America, actual and potential, and they left us to stumble on it by accident. Perhaps it wasn't quite accident. We were looking for something of the sort and found it.

May 26 Wednesday

This has been our last day. We sail tomorrow literally at the earliest possible moment, one minute after midnight to-night. Farewell lunch at Passy's to Claud Greneker [Shubert's publicity manager]. I refuse to believe that he has had spies sitting next to us in the theatres to overhear and report our lightest whisper. I do not think he is as Machiavellian as people here try to make out. Yet when that slow, sweet smile of his subsides I see what they mean; the residue is something cut in lean grey stone. Everybody insists that in comparison with Shubert's intelligence organisation the Ogpu is sissy. I tell Greneker this; his smile is slower to come than usual and quicker to go. It is only proper to say that wherever we have been we have found him at our elbow. I think of him now as a combination of sheet-anchor, shepherd, and dragon—a mentor to whom we are infinitely obliged.

Next, packing. Have had to buy another trunk, which still leaves me with eight huge parcels. Tips are difficult. There is a Swedish valet who looks as though he had not seen a sixpence since leaving Stockholm. There are three foreign floor-waiters, but none so imbecile as to be untippable. Four lift-boys. Two of these are Welsh—one pines for Blaenau Festiniog, in which he was born, the other for the Rhondda Valley, which he has never seen. Both have kept their accent. Five bell-hops. (By the way, the bell-hop is a myth. These are no bells and nobody hops. Errands here are run slower than in England.) Two porters, one of whom does our motor-bargaining for us. The reception-ist, who will accept flowers. Macbeth's Three Witches, early risers who want to make our beds before we have got into them. That makes nineteen people to be tipped, twenty if we include the telephone girl. As a working rule we decide to give five dollars to any of those who smile at us, and ten to those who scowl. (Actually we got off with something under eighty dollars. This may seem excessive, but we got a lot done for it.)

Nathan called this afternoon to take me to tea with Lillian Gish. She came into the room looking exactly as she did in *Way Down East*. A sad, pinched little face, with woebegone eyes looking out from under a hat like a squashed Chinese pagoda. A trim, tiny figure very plainly dressed; the whole apparition strangely reminiscent of Vesta Tilley. Since she left films she has played Shakespeare, Tchehov, and Dumas *fils*: "I came from the theatre, and I am glad to go back to it." Nathan has a theory that acting has nothing to do with the film or the film with acting, and that the proper function of the screen is to exploit the exuberant vitality of the Robert Taylors and Loretta Youngs, and discard all players as soon as they cease to exuberate. He thinks Lillian was the last screen-actress. I talked a bit about her old pictures, and she seemed to like it. Anyhow she sat there silently, nodding like some grave flower.

May 27 *Thursday*

I think it was Wilde who said, "It is a terrible thing to part from people one has known a very short time." The same holds true of countries; though no truer, I suppose, of New York than of anywhere else. *Partir, c'est mourir un peu* was probably first said by Ulysses. Still, leaving New York is an emotional business. As B. was spending the last evening with his brother, I proposed to seek out the Stork Club, said to be the centre of the younger and rowdier fashionables—the kind of place to which in 1926 Evelyn Waugh's characters would have betaken their vile bodies. When it came to the point I couldn't face it,

and instead went for a last drive round Central Park, with a snack at
Tony's to finish with. Would have had another look at Harlem if I had
not paid off my guide. Left Tony's at 10.45, and was on the Hamburg-
Amerika liner *Deutschland* by eleven. This boat is half the size of the
Bremen and prettily done up in *rose tendre* and old gold. Full of Germans,
whereby frumpishness sets in again. If Schiaparelli herself dressed these
women they would revert to German before she got out of the room.
A great crowd to see us off and a great waving of handkerchiefs, which
begins at the first sign of departure and lasts till we actually move off.
It is stiflingly hot with that curious quality of steam-heat I shall always
associate with New York. This accounts for the mist, at first pierced
only by the Neon tower of the Empire State Building, and later by a
weak glimmer which is probably Radio City. Farther down the river
and leaving the docks the mist clears, and we see some of the lesser
skyscrapers, whose alternating panes of light and dark give them the
air of cosmic crossword puzzles. (For three weeks I have been wondering what familiar thing they are like.) Twenty minutes later we drop
the pilot—a bit of routine which the spotlight of the parent ship turns
into a shot from a film. And now New York begins to fade from my
consciousness. Or would do if B. were not whistling "Where or When"
from *Babes in Arms*, the first piece we saw and the one I enjoyed most,
musical comedy though it is! I think its sixteen-year-old naïveté gave
me some foretaste of this still new and still raw country.

June 18 *Friday*

Happy thought! Must write to Seymour Hicks telling him that my
American journey has made me eligible for blackballing at the
Travellers' Club as well as the Garrick.

June 19 *Saturday*

Barrie died early this morning. His was an irritating genius, which
never left one doubt either about the genius or the irritation. *Dear
Brutus* and *A Kiss for Cinderella* are pure gold. *Mary Rose* is enormously
helped by O'Neill's music, and I always succumb to it even when poorly
acted. I have come to hate *Peter Pan*. The ideal audience for this would
be a house composed entirely of married couples who have never had
any children, or parents who have lost them all. Barrie was a master of
plot and invention, though the informing spirit was always the same.
You could tell what a new play of his would be like, though not, as
the Scotch say, "what like it would be". His stuff could have been
written in any age; if its author had lived in the era of Waterloo he
would merely have put the characters in *Quality Street* back to the time
of Bannockburn. The theme of *The Boy David* would have been too

much for him at any time. You cannot bind the influences of Pleiades with baby-ribbons.

June 24 Thursday

Am invited to spend the week-end on Lord Kemsley's yacht. Ernest Fenton said, "Better be careful what you wear, James, or you'll look like something in charge of sea lions." Lord K.'s secretary 'phoned instructions this morning about a yachting-cap; I remember that Monty Shearman was furious with me for taking a bowler down the Loire!

Have composed the following costume: pair of white gaberdine trousers, cleaned, but originally very expensive, with double-breasted jacket to match, also cleaned. Not being new looks as if I was used to yachting. Blue double-breasted blazer from Moss Bros., in case the white is not correct. Had the brass buttons removed and black ones put on. Two pairs of *darned* white socks—a neat touch. New white buckskin shoes. White sweater, and, of course, the cap. Have plenty of soft white shirts which I wear with the stiff white collar. Navy blue tie. Am thinking of sleeping to-night in this rig-out so as to get accustomed to it. Irving always did this with a new suit of armour.

June 28 Monday

The whole thing was an enormous success. A lovely yacht—750 tons, with a crew of 28—and a charming passenger-list. It was a thrilling moment when we passed the *Berengaria*, a blaze of lights, waiting to take my first article to America. We left Southampton on Friday about seven. Lay off-shore for a few hours and started the serious business of yachting after I had retired to a state-room in white satin evoking Evelyn Laye. Got to Deauville about eleven o'clock on Saturday morning. Deauville was like a bit of Eastbourne out of sorts. The season had not begun, and the fashionable part of the town was empty. But of an absolute emptiness! The milords, accompanied by their miladies, marched in procession from the yacht, along the quay, round the front, and back to the yacht again without meeting so much as a cat. The summer flower is to the summer sweet, and perhaps the same applies to the characters in Debrett's entertaining romance. There was one ecstatic hour after lunch when Time stood still, everybody else had gone to the Casino, and I was allowed to read and doze in the miraculous afternoon light with the snowy sleeves of myrmidons insinuating whiskies and soda at my elbow and as noiselessly retrieving the empty goblets. In the evening the town woke up. There was a waiters' fête and a torch-light procession, a Saturnalia before the season's work of robbing the English begins. When I woke on Sunday morning we were well in the Seine, an extremely beautiful river. Coal-barges from Glasgow dipped to us; we exchanged friendly greetings with a German steamer; some French lads bathing from a skiff permitted themselves to chaff us, possibly not knowing how well-bred we were. All was as gay as possible. Went ashore at Caudebec, a sleepy village with an exquisite sixteenth-century church. Bought the usual souvenirs and showed a little kid of seven, Jacques Something and son of the hotel chef, over the yacht, which he said was "très beau." His self-possession and manners were perfect and he looked delightful sitting in solemn state in the launch with three ship's officers to escort him back. Ought to have gone to Rouen by car, but preferred to stay on deck playing bridge in an esctasy of sun and wind. The bridge was ecstatic also, as by tea-time Beverley Baxter and I had taken over 5000 points out of our host and Lord Bessborough. But pride goes before a fall, even on a yacht, and I shall never forget an unhappy rubber of 3700 points which Bax and I lost together, he at a pound a hundred and me at half a crown. We got back to Southampton at nine o'clock this morning, and I at once settled down to the dreary job of making a witty article out of a lot of witless books snored over on Saturday afternoon while the others were taking money from the croupiers at Deauville Casino. What the article will read like I don't know. Jock, to whom I have just finished dictating it, says it is all about the French quality of light, the lace-work of those old French masons, Lady Kemsley's talk and jewels, and the poise of Lady Maureen Stanley. The only time I felt out of my element was on the first night in the drawing-room after dinner when the talk was largely about "Squiffy's" eldest and "Snooty's" second. Reflecting that in all probability the allusion was to the issue of some Duke and Marquis, I felt the same awe that David Copperfield experienced at Mrs Water-brook's dinner-party.

Week-end closed with the happy thought of writing to Seymour suggesting that I am now elegible for blackballing by the Royal Yacht Squadron as well as by the Travellers' and Garrick Clubs.

July 6 *Tuesday*

While I was in America Brother Edward borrowed four shillings from Alan Dent, and presently started to repay the loan. First a postal order for a shilling, and then four three-halfpenny stamps. This is very like Edward. Jock wrote that these driblets were all nonsense, and that he would rather have the balance in the form of a quotation. This arrived by return:

> Take away but the pomps of death, the disguises, and solemn bugbears, and the actings by candlelight, and proper and fantastic ceremonies, the minstrels and the noise-makers, the women and

the weepers, the swoonings and the shriekings, the nurses and the physicians, the dark room and the ministers, the kindred and the watches, and then to die is easy, ready, and quitted from its troublesome circumstances. It is the same harmless thing that a poor shepherd suffered yesterday, or a maid-servant to-day; and at the same time in which you die in that very night a thousand creatures die with you, some wise men and many fools; and the wisdom of the first will not quit him, and the folly of the latter does not make him unable to die.

(From a sermon of Jeremy Taylor.)

Jock, realising that I am grabbing this superb thing for my diary, demands the half-crown which it cost him. This is like Jock. I immediately pay him, which is unlike me.

July 13 *Tuesday*

It seems that some fields can never be completely gleaned. To-day's *Manchester Guardian* has a story about Sarah Bernhardt which is new to me, and which, if I don't rescue it, will be lost for ever:

Some thirty years ago Sarah Bernhardt was playing at Manchester, and one afternoon she took a drive with a friend into the country. As they were passing a field they heard shouts and stopped the landau. Two local teams were playing a vigorous football match, and, it being a wet day, were smothered in mud. Sarah climbed up on to the seat and, clad from head to foot in white furs, watched the contest with eager interest. When it was over she climbed down and sank back on her cushions with a murmured: "J'adore ce cricket; c'est tellement Anglais."

July 31 *Saturday*

Blackpool with Leo Pavia, whose malice increases. Man is a creature of habit, and it is with genuine pleasure that I sit down at the same desk, in the same lounge, in the same hotel as last year and take up what is doubtless the same pen. I am certain about the ink-splash on the wall. I remember making it. I suppose it is the mark of the bounder to notice the hotel staff. Anyway I am glad it has not changed, except that the mite who attends to the lift is nearer heaven by the altitude of a chopine. But my room has been changed, and I am afraid that when I jumped out of bed this morning and pulled up the blind for a good stare at the weather I did not realise that the curtainless window reached to the floor and that I was wearing my shortest nightshirt. (I have never abided pyjamas.) Having gazed my fill, and wholly unconscious of the gathering crowd on the promenade below, I was beginning to shave

when the hall porter arrived with a policeman's compliments and would
the gent on the first-floor balcony state wot 'e thought 'e was up to.
I said that the gent sent half a crown and his compliments, and would
the officer kindly step up since the gent had a perfect *alibi*! No more was
heard of the matter, and I am changing my room for one that faces a
blank wall!

August 8 *Sunday*

So Lady Tree has gone. A kindly soul and a delicious wit. It is always
said that the line in Barrie's play apropos of boiler-scraping—"What
fun men have!"—was one of her dress-rehearsal impromptus. I
remember how, about to recite at a charity matinée, she advanced to a
gold chair, and, swathed in heliotrope tulle, said smilingly, "I want
you all to imagine I'm a plumber's mate!" In her early years her
extreme plainness was a handicap. In later life her face became her
fortune; it was that of a benevolent horse. In her old age she was an
admirable actress who made the most of a good part, and got a lot
that wasn't there out of a bad one.

August 9 *Monday*

Another great woman of the theatre, Miss Horniman, has died at
the age of 77. She was the pioneer of the repertory movement, and
foundress of the Gaiety Theatre, Manchester. The first time I saw her
was in 1907, at the Midland Theatre in that city. She had brought the
Irish Players over from the Abbey Theatre, Dublin, and the programme
consisted of Synge's *The Shadow of the Glen*, Yeats's *Cathleen ni
Houlihan*, and Lady Gregory's *Spreading the News*. I could not decide
which impressed me the more—the plays, or the plaque of opals in the
form of a dragon blazing on the corsage of a dress of rich green brocade
which swept the floor.

A lot of nonsense has been and will be written about Manchester's
failure to support the venture at the Gaiety Theatre. The truth of the
matter is that the Gaiety, after a brave start, let down Manchester
badly. At the beginning, with managers like Iden Payne, Basil Dean,
and Lewis Casson, and players like Miss Darragh, Sybil Thorndike,
and Henry Austin, all went grandly. Later, managers of lesser calibre
were engaged, the plays became steadily drearier, and the players more
purposefully amateur. Now, perhaps, it may be said that there never
was a Manchester school of drama, but only an odd dramatist or
two who happened to be born or to live in Manchester. Stanley
Houghton's *Hindle Wakes* was a bright flash in what turned out to be
a very small pan, and Harold Brighouse never followed up *Hobson's
Choice*. The only first-class work of the so-called Manchester school

was Allan Monkhouse's *Mary Broome*. But still the notion that there could be such a school persisted, as nobody knows better than I do. (I functioned as a dramatic critic on the staff of the *M.G.* all through this very period.) Time after time the curtain would go up on a Welsh dresser and a kitchen table with Sybil weeping in frustration. Sometimes the dresser would be to the left, sometimes to the right. But the table and Sybil were constant.

By an odd coincidence Ivor Brown says in an article in to-day's *M.G.*: "So far the British tradition has maintained the old, unfounded, unfair belief that the player is a rogue and the theatre an abode of sin." The belief may or may not be sound: it is the only one which has ever got the British public into the theatre. That, and plays about people in evening dress.

Now consider what happened at the Gaiety. By stripping the gold paint and all garish appurtenances, and substituting a décor of unrelieved white, the place was made as much like a schoolroom and as little like a theatre as possible. There was no drink licence, but only the horrid spectacle of intellectuals consuming cocoa. No orchestra, and in the intervals pale young men, who had not gone out to drink cocoa, nodded glumly to one another across Professor Herford's beard. Nobody wore evening dress, and when an actor must he wore it gauchely, with a shirt that wasn't too clean. The actresses' clothes made dressmakers weep. Over the whole place brooded a joylessness, an air of edification, the suggestion of a theatre-going that was a part of citizenship. The better halves of men already too good wrote letters to the papers saying how heartening it was on wet nights to see actresses in mackintoshes sitting in last trams and grasping umbrellas *like ordinary mortals*. The last three words spelled the Gaiety's doom. The great actress Rachel left behind her a letter protesting her inability, after mouthing five acts of Alexandrines about tigresses passion-starved in Byzantine deserts, to go home to lonely sandwiches in fifth-rate provincial hotels. The general idea of a great actress—a regrettable idea which I share and endorse—is that at the end of the play she is whirled away in veil and barouche to an assignation with a dissolute nobleman, preferably of the Renaissance. (She need not do this, but must be thought capable of it.) The so-called Manchester school demanded actresses of respectability rather than glamour, a quality with which Welsh dressers do not consort. Lacking glamour, and knowing that they lacked it, Miss Horniman's leading ladies cottoned on to soul. I remember a scene in a Galsworthy play in which an ultra-soulful creature used to go to the window, open it, and flap her arms like the wings of a fowl. When I asked what this grotesque nonsense was supposed to mean, the actress—who was quite well known—said sepulchrally, "It's the soul in the act of liberating itself."

The non-Jewish part of Manchester might have been gammoned with this sort of thing indefinitely. But the Jewish part—which ran the Hallé concerts and has always been the chief support of the Manchester theatre—was a cultured and travelled audience not to be taken in by the Liberal and Ruskinian doctrine of morality and citizenship as the basis of dramatic art. The Manchester Jews knew a dowdy actress when they saw one, and perfectly understood what Balzac meant by "l'honnête artiste, cette infâme médiocrité, ce coeur d'or, cette loyale vie, ce stupide dessinateur, ce brave garçon." They also knew that the basis of popular theatre-going five nights out of six must be that which Abel Hermant, in his devastating and utterly delightful *La Fameuse Comédienne*, calls "la pièce chaste, un peu cochonne, avec une pointe de sentiment." In short, while they were prepared to accept master-pieces of gloom, they declined to tolerate inferior work just because it was depressing.

August 21 Saturday

If this diary is really to help the social historian of the future in his reconstruction of the present, it must not omit this: Owing to hundreds of excited females saying good-bye to Robert Taylor, the film-star, the *Berengaria* was thirty minutes late in leaving New York last week. Two girls were found under the bed in Taylor's state-room. He shook hands with both, and one of them said, "I shall never wash this hand again!" This was telegraphed to, and printed in, a responsible English newspaper.

September 12 Sunday

Made a jaunt to Canterbury. I asked the verger if Becket was buried in the Cathedral. He replied, "He was. But in Henry the Eighth's time they dug the swine up and scattered the bones outside." I went away making a note of this extraordinary utterance.

September 14 Tuesday

Walked out of *Crazy Days* at the Shaftesbury. Is a critic ever justified in doing this? Shaw confesses to have done it, and I saw Walkley do it. But I think they were wrong, and that I am. I hold that the modern critic should imitate the poet Martial, who declined to leave the arena when the bear began to eat the slave alive: "These are my times. I must see them. I want to know my times."

September 19 Sunday

Edgar Jepson, a dapper little man who must be a hundred and

fifty, looks like a well-preserved thirty, and has a voice like unsweetened mint-sauce, has written a second book of memoirs which is even better than the first. Leo spent the day with me, and was enchanted when I read out the sentence, "Isidore Leo Pavia, the pupil of Leschetitzky, played Chopin better than all the others." In the same bundle for review was Shaw's *London Music* in 1888–1889 as *Heard by Corno di Bassetto*. I read Leo the passage about Essipoff, Leschetitzky's second wife. This runs:

> That lady's terrible precision and unfailing nerve; her cold contempt for difficulties; her miraculous speed, free from any appearance of haste; her grace and finesse, without a touch of anything as weak as tenderness; all these are subjects for awe rather than for criticism. When she played Chopin's waltz in A flat, it did not sound like Chopin: the ear could not follow the lightning play of her right hand. Yet she was not, like Rubenstein at that speed, excited and furious over it; she was cold as ice; one felt like Tartini on the celebrated occasion when he got the suggestion for his Trillo del Diavolo. Additional impressiveness was given to the performance by the fact that Madame Essipoff had no platform mannerisms or affections. When the applause reached the point at which an encore was inevitable, she walked to the pianoforte without wasting a second; shot at the audience, without a note of prelude, an exercise about 40 seconds long, and of satanic difficulty; and vanished as calmly as she had appeared. Truly an astonishing— almost a fearful player.

Leo said, "That's very well done. Essipoff used to give me my lesson when Leschetitzky was away on holiday. She was a hard, horrible, emotionless woman who never smiled and never praised. She was also a nymphomaniac; her husband, coming home unexpectedly, found her in bed with two pupils. He kicked her out and married the Countess Donamirska, who became his third wife. Leschetitzky had four wives in all. He was undersized, immensely vigorous sexually, and a brute, though on occasion generous."

September 24 *Friday*

My Dreyfus play is to be exhumed again! Have signed contract with Jack De Leon, who is to put it on at the "Q" Theatre on October 25th. Campbell Gullan produces, and we are now looking for a cast.

October 9 *Saturday*

A busy week. On Monday Campbell Gullan read the Dreyfus play to the nucleus of a company with great effect. When I first handled the German original I had in mind George Bealby for Zola, Austin Trevor for Esterhazy, and George Zucco for Picquart. But Bealby, alas! is dead, Zucco is in Hollywood, and Trevor engaged elsewhere. Actors who are not in an engagement are filming, and it has been the devil of a job to get anybody. Two bits of luck, however. William Devlin, who has already played Clemenceau with magnificent effect, will take on Zola, and Clarke-Smith has promised to do Esterhazy.

October 13 Wednesday

Somebody has sent me a copy of *L'Aurore* of Jan. 13, 1898, containing Zola's "*J'Accuse!*" letter. Bought in the streets of Paris that evening and preserved ever since. Am having this framed for exhibition in the theatre. Have seen no rehearsals, and have no idea how the play is getting on.

October 14 Thursday

Jock, who has been lunching with Neville Cardus, tells me this story. Some time in 1910 or thereabouts George Mair took Pavlova to supper at the Midland Hotel, Manchester, and afterwards showed her round the office of the *Manchester Guardian*, where she proceeded to dance a tarantella on his desk. This was interrupted by C. P. Scott coming in to see what the noise was about. The old martinet surveyed the shocking scene with beard bristling and eyes popping out of his head. Pavlova at once jumped down and threw her arms round C. P., saying, "Oh you *sveet* old man. I *lov* your white 'airs!" I believe that Cardus and Jock made this up between them. But I can vouch for the supper part of the story, as I was in the Midland that night and saw them.

October 19 Tuesday

The Zola film at the Carlton. The word 'Jew' is not mentioned and all question of anti-Semitism hushed up, Dreyfus's nationality and faith appearing for less than a second on some printed document.

October 21 Thursday

Jock, asking James Bone if he was obliged to review my Dreyfus play, received this answer in pitiless Scotch: "The *Manchester Guardian* is very much interested in the Dreyfus case. It is also interested in James Agate. Whether it is interested in the two in conjunction is another matter."

After Mary Manning's *Youth's the Season* . . .? comes Lady Long-
ford's *Anything but the Truth*. Both contain portraits of a Dublin
homosexual. Lionel Hale in to-day's *News Chronicle* says that this
trend, new to Irish drama, "marks the beginning of the Sodom-and-
Begorra School."

October 24 *Sunday*

Sydney Carroll on the treatment of the Dreyfus incident in the
Zola film: "The racial side of the struggle is not unduly emphasised"!
The exclamation mark is mine.

Spent the afternoon and evening at "Q" Theatre, where the dress-
rehearsal of *J'Accuse!* took six hours. Seven scenes and thirty-four
speaking parts. The big-part actors huddle in threes in dressing-rooms
the size of armchairs; the lesser fry dress in Gunnersbury. There are so
many props that it is impossible to get round the stage; even then half
of them are in the yard under a tarpaulin. Tomorrow it will, of course,
rain like hell. One actor had colic, another had displaced a cartilage,
a third had mislaid his false teeth. But Clarke-Smith and Devlin are
going to be grand, and there is a hair-raising performance of Maître
Labori by Gordon McLeod. The play is tremendous in outline; the
point is whether the audience will mind being a bit fogged over details
which I could only have clarified completely by throwing the facts
overboard. In the Zola film the clarification is such that one feels that
a police magistrate would have seen through the conspiracy in half
an hour.

October 26 *Tuesday*

It rained like hell and the play went magnificently. There wasn't a
cough throughout the entire evening and not only the acts but even
the curtains to the scenes were received with immense applause. I
think that what the audience liked most was the fact that here was
something for the players to get hold of. Devlin got every ounce of
effect out of Zola's rhetoric, and Rehfisch told me that Clarke-Smith's
Esterhazy was better than any he had had in Germany. The chief
amazement of the evening was brought about by the young actor who
played Anatole France. The character is not on the stage more than
three minutes, and in this short space Gabriel Toyne, without doing
anything that one could single out, not only put the author of *L'Île
des Penguins* before us, but re-created the whole atmosphere of literary
France at the end of the last century. I have never seen anything quite
so remarkable in its way, or heard a more enthusiastic outburst of
applause than he evoked. I don't suppose that any London manager
will pay the slightest attention to Toyne, all the same.

The notice I like best is A. E. Wilson's in the *Star*. This is probably because it is the most flattering:

> Mr Agate's task was to bring some clarity and coherence into this extraordinary tangle of lies, deception, forgery, intrigue, false patriotism and fanaticism, and without interfering with the natural elements of the Dreyfus case, to bring into relief the characters and qualities expected in stirring drama. The task is well accomplished. Zola, with his passionate, crusading zeal—more concerned, perhaps, with the abstract cause of truth and liberty than with the prisoner of Devil's Island—is the hero and very magnificently does William Devlin play the part, particularly in his appearance in the Law Courts. Here he delivers his famous indictment with the shattering vehemence of an inspired champion. The effect is electric. . . .

October 31 *Sunday*

Ivor Brown, in the *Observer*, calls the play "baffling and chaotic". And again: "If you start with a complete knowledge of Parisian backstairs gossip in 1897 it may be lucid."

November 24 *Wednesday*

Lunched at Garrick Club with St John Ervine and Jimmie Horsnell. All of us much upset at the death of Lilian Baylis, whom Horsnell and I regard as having been of more importance to the culture of our time and the drama of the country as a whole than the entire crop of London managers since the War.

November 28 *Sunday*

Here is what I wrote in today's *S.T.* about Lilian Baylis:

> There was no nonsense about the Old Vic's manager, though "proprietor" was the word one used mentally. "Forthrightness, thy name is Baylis!" would have been a good motto for her. What I have to say about her will therefore be said forthrightly.
> Consult any of her portraits and you will see what flatterers described as a sardonic smile, this being a way of getting round the fact that the mouth was not in the middle of the face. But the mind was dead-centre. And that is the first, and the last, and very nearly the only thing to be said about Lilian Baylis. Though every stone in the building prated of her whereabouts, though the influence of her directing hand could be felt everywhere, though she ran the thing as thoroughly as a business, the owner was not much in evidence. Being the head and front of the whole affair, she did

not need to advertise the fact. She was too prominent to put herself forward.

She was short and odd to look at, she hung little gold chains over her rusty black dresses, and her speech was blunt. Yet she was wholly immovable. Indeed, I have always suspected that if another little, immovable Royal lady had still been alive to visit Lilian Baylis's theatre she would have sat in the box chosen by Lilian and taken tea when Lilian directed. For Lilian was the Old Vic's Queen.

As soon as she took up the reins of management in the Waterloo Road she resolved that through this dingy theatre, cheek by jowl with squalor, drink, bad language, smells, and all the concomitants of slumdom, should blow the great gale of Shakespeare. And for twenty-five years it has blown, reducing everything else in theatrical London, with here and there an honourable exception, to "piffle before the wind".

Lilian Baylis re-made that dramatist who at the beginning of the nineteenth century reigned at Drury Lane, but at the end of it had fallen before the scorn of time and *The Whip* of Arthur Collins. She made a new audience, and among the litter and refuse railed off something that was to become the holy ground of the London theatre. And as if that was not enough, she went on to rescue Sadler's Wells, where rude little boys were throwing stones at the ghost of Samuel Phelps.

Hers was and is a theatre for the people in the narrow sense, and the impulse to make it so undoubtedly sprang from the fact that she was of the people. It was and is the theatre of a people in the larger sense of the whole nation. She did for London what Frank Benson was doing for the provinces. Benson began in 1883. Baylis died last week. Their span gave England a National Theatre which has endured for more than fitfy years *and is in being*.

At the opening of the present season Lilian Baylis said: "I don't care a dash about the National Theatre. When I think of all the work that has been done by our three companies—drama, opera and ballet—I know *we* are the National Theatre!" That was a characteristic pronouncement, and only a fool would doubt its rightness. Our intrepid manager had one of the characteristics of the great artist; she did her greatest work when her difficulties were greatest. The roof might leak, there might be holes in the bank balance, but still she hammered away at presenting the complete cycle of Shakespeare's plays. If London has a Coopers' Guild, Lilian Baylis was its spiritual head. She achieved her object sometimes with the help of the best players, and sometimes with the help of the next best. She was obstinate yet fluid, and had the close secret of giving a stage producer his head and at the same time keeping him well in hand. It is an open secret that people did not make the journey to Waterloo to ecstasise over this actor or that producer. They came to see the plays of Shakespeare, and the spirit of Shakespeare, and the spirit of Shakespeare received them.

We shall not have done with Lilian Baylis when we leave the graveside and the trumpets have packed up. Or, rather, Lilian Baylis will not have done with us. As an impresario of Shakespeare she knew all about the haunting propensities of evil spirits, and now her good spirit is to haunt us. No jot of energy, no tittle of foresight, must be spared to keep the Old Vic and Sadler's Wells where they magnificently stand. You cannot fool all the people all the time. But you can inspire all of them all the time, and it is up to us to see that that granite spirit which was Baylis's is not whittled away either wilfully or carelessly.

The point, she would say, is not what she did when she was with us, but what we are going to do now that she has left us. What her spirit really wants to know is who is going to succeed her. A committee can draft a Parliamentary Bill; it cannot run a theatre like the Old Vic. Several names suggest themselves, but this is not the place to discuss them. The point I want to urge, because it is the one point which would satisfy Lilian, is that Amurath shall be succeeded by Amurath, and a strong woman by a man or woman equally strong. It is better to be strong and sometimes wrong than weak and occasionally right. Lilian Baylis may have had her weaknesses, though I never heard of any. The lasting things about her are her courage, her persistence, and her faith.

November 30 Tuesday

Yan Tan tethera pethera pimp, sethera lethera hovera bovera dik, yan-a-dik, tan-a-dik tethera-dik pethera-dik bumfit, yan-a-bumfit tan-a-bumfit tethera-bumfit pethera-bumfit figgit.

These, of course, are Cymric numerals still used by shepherds in counting sheep. I think of them whenever I hear Moiseiwitsch adding up the bridge score in Russian.

December 5 Sunday

Have just come in from lunching with Norman Haire, the psychiatrist, at his excitingly restored place at Hemel Hempstead, the other guest being a jolly young Australian journalist from the *D.E.* Name of Munday. (N. H. is an Australian.) Munday said that, down under, the newspaper reporter stands higher up in the social scale. (This is the first I ever heard of Australia possessing a social scale.) After lunch, in what used to be the tithe-barn, N. H. showed us some of the films he has taken, including a magnificent one of a bull-fight. He then told us a good deal about transvestists. It appears that these odd people—people are 'odd' when their peculiarities are not one's own—have an uncontrollable urge to put on the clothes of the other sex, not only in private, but in public. The urge, it seems, is as insistent as that compulsional neurosis which made Dr Johnson tap railings, and when I was a boy made me turn out the gas in my bedroom four times, in multiples of four; I suppose, I must often have turned the tap on and off thirty-two times. I did not go beyond because I would get sleepy, and the next multiple was sixty-four. N. H. said that 40 per cent of these transvestists are heterosexual, 40 per cent homosexual, while the remainder dress up for their own edification alone. These victims, addicts, or what you will, are not scallywags, but clergymen, schoolmasters, doctors, barristers, and big-businessmen who get worried by their infirmity and seek advice. It appears that for men to wear women's clothes in public, and for women to wear men's, is not a legal offence unless it is accompanied by an act likely to provoke a breach of the peace—which long-winded phrase conceals the homely 'importuning'. Now it is all very well for your Bishop, your Cabinet Minister or your O.M. to wave your curious bobby away with the grandiose "It's all right, officer, I suffer from transvestism." But what about your wretched little hairdresser, waiter, shop-assistant, who has the disease but doesn't know its name?

The talk then turned on Desmond MacCarthy's review of Laurence Housman's book about A. E. In the *S.T.* Desmond reprints the whole of the ballad about the young man whose hair was of a colour "nameless and abominable". After which he goes on:

> The implication is obvious. It is an indirect expression of sympathy with those who through congenital temperament are disposed to fall in love with their own sex, and a protest against the severity with which they are treated. Readers of Housman's poems must have often been struck by the frequency with which love is associated in them with crime and punishment. The young man who has to swing for some deed not unaccompanied by generous emotion; the intimate association of passion with disgrace, frustration, and ruth are recurring notes in *A Shropshire Lad* and *Last Poems*. These poems are transpositions of a fellow-feeling with moral outcasts.

I think Desmond would have made his point even better if he had quoted the poem now printed for the first time and beginning:

> Ask me no more, for fear I should reply;
> Others have held their tongues, and so can I.

Probably D. M. has felt it ridiculous that the popularity of the most widely read modern English poet should be based on a complete misunderstanding of what his poems are about. Turning up my notebooks, I find that Desmond in his review of *Last Poems* has this:

> It is strange, too, how often Housman saw the emblem of his own emotional life in an outcast, a youth condemned by other men to die in shame, and yet not strange once we suppose intense life came to him in the guise of "the love that dares not speak its name". His stoicism was of the head; it never steeled his heart, which remained tremulously, clamorously, helplessly sensitive. This was the clash, this the contradiction, that made and unmade

by turns so fine a poet; sometimes inclining him towards too soft a pessimism, sometimes resolving itself perfectly as in that immortal cry of weakness and remonstrance, "Be still, my soul, be still; the arms you bear are brittle." I risk a guess that no modern poem has been so often on the lips of those who otherwise were dumb in their distress.

Desmond was much praised for his courage in writing this. But in his case the courage is merely intellectual. The really plucky thing would be for some eminent critic, publicist, preacher, playwright, who has known what Housman felt to come forward and challenge the notion that the cure for this condition is gaol. Doubtless it would have been 'nicer' if the gods had not visited Housman with the rustic passion. Doubtless it would have been charming for everybody if he had married the daughter of a rural dean. In which case we should not have had the poems. And what, I should like to know, is the answer to that?

1938

January 9 Sunday

Scotland bound. The idea is to deliver four lectures to the good folk of Glasgow and a talk to the Women of Edinburgh. Take the relief train, which gets in $1\frac{1}{2}$ hours later. But it is also $1\frac{1}{2}$ hours emptier, which makes for comfort. Read Damon Runyon's new book right through, and afterwards play picquet with B., who wants to get back the twenty-five shillings he lost to me on the boat coming from New York. I win a further thirteen-and-sixpence.

January 10 Monday

First lecture, at Trinity Church, goes extremely well. Audience more alert than in England and gets my points before I make them. Am entertained to supper by one D. R. Anderson, who has with him A. C. Trotter, editor of the Scottish *Daily Express*, Robins Millar, author of the good play *Thunder in the Air*, young Neville Berry, who is Welsh, and the Rev. H. S. McClelland, Glasgow's *liaison* officer between Church and Stage. Can these Scots talk, or can they! They talk at, over, round, and through one, but never *to* one. Anderson's talk is as resistless as a glacier; you feel that a waistcoat button is in slow descent of the tablecloth. Had any member of this Scots quartet flourished fifty years ago Stevenson must have included him in his famous "Talk and Talkers".

Presently I throw myself into the conversational breach with a remark about James Bridie, and I hear this:

A. You'll no' deny there are dull passages in *Hamlet*?
Mc.C. Man, it's full of dull passages.
A. Were ye bored at any minute of Bridie's *Black Eye*?
Mc.C. Man, I was no' a wee bit bored.
A. Varra weel, then!

Which, of course, is the 1938 equivalent of "Whaur's your Wullie Shakespeare noo?"

January 11 *Tuesday*

Bridie gives me lunch at the Arts Club. I ask what Scots think of Barrie. He says, "When they revive one of his plays people go to it!"

Find the Paisley audience a bit sticky. Perhaps this is because the room is insufficiently lighted, which depresses me.

January 12 *Wednesday*

Lecture at Newlands more successful. Tell the taxi-driver to fill up car and self. When I ask what I owe him for drinks he says, "I didna' tak' a drink. I went insteed to your lecture. Some of it was no' bad." Thus does Scotch history repeat itself, it being some hundred and fifty years since the gallery-boy's "That's no' sae bad!" was hurled at Mrs Siddons.

January 13 *Thursday*

Hearing the country round Peebles is pretty—which Glasgow isn't— we take that road to Edinburgh, queen of capitals, which has all my allegiance. Being early, hang about to take a gander at our hostesses. B., who has got Runyon on the brain, says he will lay plenty of 6 to 5 these dames are such as will let a guy die of thirst. So encouraged, I suggest the local Good Time Charley's, where we have a couple of shots, and what with one thing and another, including the stewed veal and cold Edinburgh water, I get all mixed up in my address and say of an actress that, though she has plenty of poise and presence, she doesn't go off her hocks like a little mare I saw at Speir's. This gives offence to an old doll who looks like she has a good seat at the Coronation, and says in a crumpled voice she dislikes my address more than some- what. I do not say much in reply to the old tomato, as I hear the guy with her is the Kyle of Bute. Also I don't get my cheque, which is to be sent on to my address in London, owing, says B., to their figuring that I'm probably not James Agate at all.

January 15 *Saturday*

In the train. Have said good-bye to Scotland for the time being. We had lunch, I have written my diary for the week, and B. wants his revenge at picquet. He has it in his noggin to get back the thirteen and sixpence and a bit more to pay off the overhead around his joint, such as rent. A plague on this Runyonese! I must take a run-out powder on it.

January 28 *Friday*

Have made an arrangement with a doctor friend whereby every week I send him two of my review books against two of his free samples. This week while he is absorbing two nauseating novels I am imbibing Incretone, a preventive of senile decay, and Agocholine, "the most active cholagogue obtainable", whose function is drainage of the biliary tract. Next week he gets two dollops of fragrant bilge against cures for gout and gravel.

February 6 *Sunday*

Left Brighton about nine in brilliant sunshine, but at Sutton ran into a fog. St Martin's Church full for the Irving Memorial Service, which was impressive. In the procession to the statue I walked with Violet Vanbrugh, who has become the perfect Gainsborough, and Cochran, looking a little tired after his American trip. Crowd very quiet and respectful. I tried to find somebody to lunch with, but couldn't, so in a mood of some desolation had a solitary meal at the Café Royal.

And now, as Fielding says, for a hint of what we can do in the sublime: to wit, my article in to-day's *Sunday Times*:

> Hume having told Boswell that he was no more uneasy to think he should *not be* after this life, than that he *had not been* before he began to exist, Johnson thundered: "Sir, if he really thinks so, his perceptions are disturbed; he is mad. If he does not think so, he lies." If anybody thinks Irving was the greatest English actor of modern times and does not say so, he lies. If he does not think so, he is mad.
>
> That Irving would be laughed at to-day is the parrot-cry of hop-o'-my-thumbs. In 1893 he put on *Becket*, and it would be easy to say that in 1935 he would have put on *Murder in the Cathedral*. But I do not think this is true. Irving was undoubtedly influenced by Tennyson's prestige, and to encourage a rising dramatist was never any part of his business. I think in 1935 he would have revised the *old* play and snubbed young playwright and young actor. This may be uncomplimentary to Irving, but I think it is true.
>
> Mr Gordon Craig has said that, since it may be supposed some

day that Irving was either a bravura or a quietist actor, he had
better put it on record that he was neither, for the unshakeable
reason that Irving was a genius, and "a genius is both a quietist
and a bravurista". "I will speak daggers to her, but use none",
said Hamlet. Lots of middling actors can speak daggers: I have
never seen Irving's equal at looking them. To-day your player
comes on the stage with one look and keeps it, always with the
exception of Charles Laughton, who can pull his face about in the
way the street-merchant manipulates an india-rubber doll. But
Irving *made* faces, and when he made one it was in granite. I
have never forgotten, and to my dying day shall not forget, his
expression when as Dante he saw Ugolino starving in his tower.
He made faces for every part he played—macabre, jaunty, diabolical
faces. He had a pathetic face, a saintly face, and a regal one: "The
splendour falls on castle walls". He had faces for everybody, for
Mathias, Jingle, Louis XI, Dr Primrose, Corporal Brewster,
Shylock, Robespierre.

Yet people would tell you that he was "always Irving". And so
he was, if they meant that in every part Irving played there was a
hint of Mephistopheles. They said he never "acted". Nor did he
if by "acting" they meant pretending to be somebody else. Hear
Max: "Irving could not impersonate. His voice, face, figure, port,
were not transformable. But so fine was the personality to which
they belonged that none cried shame when this or that part had
to submit or be crushed by it. Intransformable, he was multi-
radiant, though. He had, in action, a keen sense of humour—of
sardonic, grotesque, fantastic humour. He had an incomparable
power for eeriness, for stirring a dim sense of mystery; and not
less masterly was he in evoking a sharp sense of horror. His
dignity was magnificent in purely philosophic or priestly gentleness,
or in the gaunt aloofness of philosopher or king. He could be
benign with a tinge of malevolence, and arrogant with an under-
current of sweetness. As philosopher or king, poet or prelate, he
was matchless. One felt that if Charles the Martyr, Dante, Wolsey,
were not precisely as he was, so much the worse for Wolsey, Dante,
Charles the Martyr".

Irving had more pathos than any player I have ever seen, and
whether this was an emanation of the soul or a trick of the larynx
does not seem to me to matter. Much has been written of the waves
of magnetism, or whatever you like to call it, which in *The Bells*
Irving sent over the footlights even before he had shaken the
snow off his coat. I would prefer to dwell upon the extraordinary
pathos with which Mathias suggested the man tormented and
conscience-stricken. For years nothing in the theatre haunted me
so much as that first act's unhappiness. It filled the theatre so that
there was nothing else left in the universe.

How would Irving have feared today? Could he *at any time*
have tackled Ibsen's Borkman, Strindberg's Adolph, Tchehov's
Vershinin? I think not. Put him in the dingy Russian uniform of
this last, and those three sisters, their visitors, and everybody in
the little town, even Moscow itself, would have disappeared and
left the world to darkness and Henry Irving. No; Irving is not

thinkable in the great plays of today. I even venture to hold that he was a Shakespearean actor only on condition that it was Irving's Shakespeare rather than Shakespeare's that was being performed. Comparing the piano concertos of Brahms with those of Beethoven, the staunch classicists of fifty years ago said that they were not concertos but symphonies with pianoforte obbligati. Irving knew nothing about providing an obbligato to Shakespeare or anybody; he insisted on being the entire bag of tricks.

Ellen Terry, who was a more radiant actress than Fanny Kemble and a wittier diarist than Fanny Burney, has left what are easily the best descriptions of the outer man and the inner artist: "I have never seen in living man, or picture, such distinction of bearing. A splendid figure, and his face very noble. A superb brow; rather small dark eyes which can at moments become immense; and hang like a bowl of dark liquid with light shining through; a most refined curving Roman nose, strong and delicate in line, and *cut clean* (as all his features); a smallish mouth and full of the most wonderful teeth, even at 55; lips most delicate and refined—firm, firm, firm—and with a rare smile of the most exquisite beauty and quite-not-to-be-described kind. His hair is superb; beautiful in 1867, when I first met him, when it was blue-black like a raven's wing, it is even more splendid now (1895), when it is liberally streaked with white."

Yet Irving could never have said of Ellen: "Look how our partner's rapt!" For she was not rapt. There was no moment when her critical percipience about him was not busy. She was not blinded by his genius as an actor to his defects as an artist: "He never admires the right thing." "Oddly enough, Henry was always attracted by fustian." And here are some bits found in a notebook after Ellen's death:

"His work, his work! He has always held his life and his death second to his work. When he dies, it will be because he is tired out. Now, double performances (Saturday mornings and evenings) oblige him to stimulate himself with wine, and at about midnight he looks like a corpse.

"He is a very *gentle* man, though not in the least a *tender* man.

"His illness has made him look queer. He is stouter, very grey, sly-looking, and more cautious than ever. Bother!

"A quite common young fellow in the company plays all the good parts which might befit Laurence, but H. I., thinking only of H. I., fancies L. an inch or so too tall to act with, so down goes L., and up goes himself!*

"He has terrified me once or twice by his exhaustion and feebleness. Then he appears grateful to us all, for we *all* give him *all*. But when he gets a little better, anything so icy, indifferent, and almost contemptuous, I never saw."

And all the time she is noting the extreme beauty of his hands, and how he always makes them up a gipsy brown.

---

* I once saw Laurence Irving and his father together. It was in Manchester, and the boy played Christian to the old man's Mathias. H. I. was quite right. His son was too tall for him. *J. A.*

My father, who was a great theatre-goer, would not allow that Irving was a tragedian at all. In his view Macready, Phelps, Fechter, Barry Sullivan, Salvini, were all better tragedians. On the other hand, he held that as Jingle; and in purely melodramatic rôles like Mathias and Dubosc, Irving was unapproachable. What, in my view, was the matter with Irving's Shylock was that it was neither Jewish nor foreign. Indeed, I used to have the impression that he never really studied Shylock, and that the trial scene was just Becket and Wolsey stuck together. But I now know that I was wrong. I realise now that Iriving's Shylock was a Sephardic Jew—that is, a Jew of Spanish-Portuguese descent, in contra-distinction to the Ashkenasic Jew of Eastern origin. It was this which accounted for Shylock's nobility and stiffness. I admit Irving's weakness as to legs and diction. Nor was the voice good, and Wilde wrote the purest bosh when he ended his sonnet to Irving:

Thou trumpet set for Shakespeare's lips to blow.

Truth to tell, that trumpet was much nearer the wry-necked fife. Yet I say that Irving's natural deficiencies and wiful faults became him better than his virtues and graces have become any other actor of my time. He was unescapably and without qualification the greatest male player that I ever saw. He possessed not more talent than any other player, but talent of a totally different order. When I first saw him he had turned fifty, and I like to think I had enough schoolboy wit to go about proclaiming:

              He above the rest,
In shape and gesture proudly eminent,
Stood like a tower; his form had not yet lost
All her original brightness, nor appeared
Less than archangel ruined, and th' excess
Of glory obscured.

The years passed, and

              deep on his front engraven
Deliberation sat and public care;
And princely counsel in his face yet shone,
Majestic though in ruin; sage he stood,
With Atlantean shoulders fit to bear
The weight of mightiest monarchies; his look
Drew audiences and attention still as night. . . .

And would again today! That is all that Milton and I have to say about Henry Irving.

February 10 *Thursday*

Sorting out my papers before the removal to Fairfax Road, which is now complete, I came across this letter:

Savage Club
1 *Carlton House Terrace, S.W.*1
9th April, 1936

DEAR MR AGATE,

Enclosed is a copy of the letter which George Bernard Shaw sent to George Alexander in answer to the invitation which had been sent to G. B. S. as a representative dramatic author to attend Irving's funeral in Westminster Abbey. C. Aubrey Smith would, if necessary, confirm its authenticity as he was present when I opened it. I have often quoted it, but it has never been published.

I, personally, destroyed the original in Adelphi Terrace soon after the funeral, when Lionel Belmore and I—in our youth— were looking for G. B. S. to 'tan' him.

Yours faithfully,
[Sd.] RALPH KIMPTON

And here is G. B. S.'s letter:

Adelphi Terrace
November 1905

MY DEAR ALEXANDER,

I return the ticket for the Irving funeral. Literature, alas, has no place in his death as it had no place in his life. Irving would turn in his coffin if I came, just as Shakespeare will turn in his coffin when Irving comes.

Yours very truly,
[Sd.] GEORGE BERNARD SHAW

This being too good to be lost, I wrote to G. B. S. asking his permission to publish, with the result that this morning Mrs Shaw rang me up and asked me to lunch. I went, primed with silence. Which was a good job, since from the moment I entered Whitehall Court to the moment of leaving it G. B. S. talked wittily, weightily, garrulously, informatively, charmingly. He has an odd way of not looking at anybody while he talks, sitting upright in a chair which is frail, spindly, and altogether beautiful like himself. I have no notion of what we ate or drank.

At the back of my mind was a letter I received this morning from Doris Thorne, Henry Arthur Jones's daughter, saying she wants to tell me "G. B. S.'s story of how it was entirely due to him that Irving was buried in Westminster Abbey!" Obviously, to hear from G. B. S.'s own lips how he arranged for the Abbey funeral and then declined to go to it must be a piece of Shavianism which any collector would want to bag. Going down to Whitehall, I had pondered what conversational fly to use. Needlessly. The old man landed himself before I had put the rod together; it was like picnicking on some delicious bank and leaving the fish to do the rest. What G. B. S. said went something like this, and if I paragraph it, it is only to mark the sense and not because there was ever anything like a pause:

"It's time somebody wrote an article to let the British public into the secret of that old humbug Irving. In his lifetime he was looked up to not only as an actor, but as a great figure of literature and what not, the fact being that he was entirely illiterate and didn't know Shakespeare's best lines from his worst. As a producer he was deplorable, and as a manager he was never any use to me. His principal merit was in making the public believe that a man who had none of the essential qualifications for an actor was a great actor. The reason that Irving when he first appeared in Dublin was hissed for three weeks was that Barry Sullivan had taught Dublin what to look for in an actor, and Irving was nothing like it. He had no voice, and, when you looked closely at him, no face. He set to work to make himself both, and there was never a moment when he wasn't studying how to impress himself on the public. He set about this as relentlessly as any Hitler or Mussolini.

"It was the fashion at that time for actor-managers to bribe critics, and Irving tried it on me by proposing to buy *The Man of Destiny*. As the best part was written to suit Ellen Terry I consented, only stipulating for a date, as it was a youthful work and I didn't want it producing in forty years' time as my latest. Irving hum'd and ha'd, and said there could always be a paragraph in the press. Dropping his voice, he said mysteriously, 'There's a man who does that sort of thing.' I said, 'Yes, I know him.' But he would make no promises, and presently I got a letter from Bram Stoker saying that while no date could be arranged I could always draw on account of royalties at any time I wanted. Shortly after this I went to see Irving's Richard III, and it seemed to me that something was wrong. At one point the house was electrified to hear Richard roar at Lady Anne, 'Get up-stage, woman!' In my article I said that Irving didn't seem to be answering his helm. A week later I met Bram Stoker, who asked why I had written so violently: 'Surely you knew the old man was drunk.' And do you know, my dear Mr Agate, it had not occurred to me. It is only fair to say that later on Harry Irving said he was glad I had written that article as it might do the old man some good and teach him to keep sober. Anyhow next day *The Man of Destiny* was returned to me with a note to say there was no further question of production. Most of the letters Irving sent out were written by his retinue. But I remember one in his own handwriting. The first sentence contained one of those simple grammatical errors which Queen Victoria used to make. The last sentence was 'For God's sake leave me alone.'

"The day after Irving died I got a letter from Lady Irving asking me to go and see her. She was an Irish woman, and"—with a twinkle— "the Irish are very good at living on hate. She said that General Booth and Dr Clifford were trying to arrange for an Abbey funeral, and that she was determined that her disgusting beast of a husband should not have any such honour thrust upon him. It appears that Irving had made a will leaving his property in three equal parts to his two sons and Mrs Aria, that he had not left her even his second-best bedstead, and that she intended to have her revenge. Would I help her to stop the Abbey funeral? I was terrified. I wanted an Abbey funeral, not for Irving's sake, but for the profession's, and I knew that she had only to send a postcard to Booth or Clifford to have the whole thing dropped and Irving cast into obloquy worse than Parnell's or Dilke's. So I went home and wrote her a long letter full of sympathy, at the end of which I said I felt bound to advise her as her lawyer would. I told her that when Irving caught a cold in Manchester and wanted to go to the seaside, the hat had to be sent round, that this sort of thing was always happening in the profession, and might at any time happen to Harry and Laurence. I went on: 'If this should happen, you, as the widow of a great actor buried in Westminster Abbey, have only to lift your little finger and you will get a civil pension. But if you are the widow of a worthless scoundrel you will get nothing.' That did the trick. Lady Irving withdrew her opposition and shortly after got her pension. I see no reason why the facts should not now be made known, though I would rather it was in a book than a newspaper article. You can also use my letter, which I had quite forgotten, but which I think is rather a good letter."

The talk throughout the meal was all about Irving, whose Charles I, G. B. S. said, was a wonderful mosaic. He said the moment when Charles went down on one knee and begged the soldier not to desert was one of the most moving things in the theatre. He said I had done the right thing about Irving in my broadcast talk, which encouraged me to ask whether, on the whole, he didn't think that Irving, who had begun as an illiterate humbug, had ended up as a magnificent actor. "I suppose you might say so," said G. B. S., "but he wasn't magnificent in the way Macready was." I asked how magnificent that had been. G. B. S. said, "I never saw Macready. But my father did, in *Coriolanus*, and when I asked him what he was like he said, 'Like a mad bull.' " Allan Monkhouse once wrote much the same thing about Benson's Coriolanus: "It is immensely spirited, and if he bellows like a bull it is one of Mr Meredith's 'bulls that walk the pastures with kingly flashing coats'."

February 11 *Friday*

Irving was a bit of a sadist and 'cunning past man's thought". Proof? His wire to Martin-Harvey on the first night of *The Only Way*: "Be bold and resolute." Was he hoping Jack would know the whole quotation?

February 17 *Thursday*

At supper at the Savoy Grill played one of my old games. What eleven guests, given *carte blanche* with everybody since Adam, would you ask to dinner?
For my list of guests I proposed:

> CHEOPS
> HANNIBAL
> BURBAGE
> THE CAPTAIN OF THE 'MARIE CELESTE'
> ELIZABETH'S ESSEX
> GILLES DE RAIS
> LE MARQUIS DE SADE
> CASANOVA
> BILLY THE KID
> SIR EDWARD MARSHALL-HALL
> SIR BERNARD SPILSBURY

The point is that the first four would solve the world's four greatest mysteries: how the Pyramids were built, the reason for the halt at Cannae, who wrote Shakespeare's plays, and what happened to that ship found in the middle of a dead-calm ocean with not a soul on board and the table laid for a meal. I would have included Mrs Wallace, the victim in the best of all murder cases, the Liverpool murder, but for the possibility that she was struck from behind and did not see her assailant. The choice of Essex is obvious. Billy the Kid was a Mexican bandit with more romance about him than your Chicago gangster.

April 10 *Sunday*

Good small party given by Herbert Morgan at the Reform Club. Not a burdensome amount to eat, but lashings of drink and talk. From which I cull:

> HUMBERT WOLFE. Dennis Wheatley told me his novels have been translated into every European language except one. I can't think which.
> PAMELA FRANKAU. English!

April 19 *Tuesday*

Spent Easter in Paris, where the best thing I heard was, "Men are held, *ma chère*, nót by our virtues, but by their vices." Also, this doubtless old story about Clemenceau, but new to me. It was his eightieth birthday, and the old man was strolling down the Champs-Élysées with a friend. A pretty girl passed them, and Clemenceau said, "Oh, to be seventy again!"

April 23 Saturday

Reading the Abbé Dimnet's *My New World*, I came across this:

> My companion, a Swede, knew interesting people in Paris and had been the guest of Madame Labori, the widow of Captain Dreyfus's famous counsel. It was still bad form in 1920 to draw people out, concerning the notorious affair, and consequently I refrained from asking questions. However, my room-mate once reverting to his conversations with Madame Labori, I asked him whether or not he had been able to infer the lady's own opinion of Dreyfus. The answer seemed interesting enough to be noted at once. Here it is: "Oh! Madame Labori told me that her husband always believed that Dreyfus was innocent of what he was accused of, but constantly dreaded that he might unexpectedly own up to something worse."

April 28 Thursday

It is a week since I saw Olivier's Coriolanus, and I cannot get his performance out of my head. There is a very good reason why *Coriolanus* is not a favourite play with the modern actor. The reason is that the modern actor cannot play Coriolanus. It is not a part to be lisped and babbled through. It requires every kind of grandeur, which means that it can only be played in the grand manner. Vocally Olivier's performance is magnificent; his voice is gaining strength and resonance, and his range of tone is now extraordinary. Physically it is admirable, containing one startling leap and a superb fall at the end. But I wish Larry would abandon that make-up like a Javanese mask and trust more to his own features, which are now buried beneath too much loam and plaster. And why doesn't he stop that clowning which he probably thinks is mordancy? There is not much of this in the present performance, but what there is is wholly bad, since it turns rage to naughtiness. It is not right that Coriolanus, whose dignity should be pauseless and whose whole point is his refusal to truckle to the mob, should play even to the Old Vic's gallery. But all the same, I feel that this is Larry's best performance to date, for it has a pathos I have not yet observed in him. The playing in the great scene with mother, wife, and son has great tenderness. The famous speech "I banish you!" is delivered not in the Kean way of "ungovernable passion," but with Phelps's "cold sublimity of disdain". The end is the full organ of acting, with all the stops out.

May 20 *Friday*

Cochran returned to the fray last night with a revue of great beauty and a personal triumph for Beatrice Lillie. In the interval some woman preceding me up the gangway bestrewed it with furs, laces, ribbons, and what-not. After my fifth retrieval I said, "Dear lady, you are behaving like Miss Lillie." She said, "Why not? I'm her sister!"

June 14 *Tuesday*

I have been formally invited by the Deutsche Akademie to attend a Festival on behalf of "the Art and Culture of the Contemporary German Theatre". The Festival will see the first performance of Richard Strauss's latest opera, *Der Friedenstag*, which, it is thought, will be a futher inducement to visit Munich. I have replied as follows:

DEAR DEUTSCHE AKADEMIE,

I am obliged to you for your invitation, which I must decline in the most emphatic manner possible.

My mother was educated in Germany, and I have been accustomed to hearing German from the cradle. All my life I have found my best friends among Germans. I have spent half my leisure time listening to German music. I immensely admire all that Germany has achieved since the War.

But I will not set foot in your country so long as you persecute Jews. We will not argue whether this is an offence before God; it is an abomination in the sight of man. I regret to have to write like this. But I feel deeply on the subject, as do hundreds of thousands of Englishmen who, like myself, have no drop of Jewish blood in their veins.

                                   Yours faithfully,
                                   JAMES AGATE

EGO 4

July 1938–June 1940

September 9 *Friday*

Sixty-one to-day. Jock keeps my birthday with his usual charm, wit, and unexpectedness. This is the fourth day he has shut himself up in his flat with the index to *Ego* 3, as the result of which I do not see him. But I hear from him. At eleven roses arrive. At three o'clock comes a record of Scriabin's Sonata No. 4 in F sharp major, Op.30. This is followed at seven by Antoine's *Mes Souvenirs sur le Théâtre-Libre*. I can see that this last gift is going to keep me up half the night.

September 10 *Saturday*

It does, and since nobody in England remembers—if, indeed, anybody ever knew—anything about that most gallant adventure, I shall reproduce the gist of the *Souvenirs* here.

In 1887 the French theatre is in the hands of Augier, Dumas, and Sardou. But the managers are getting anxious, for the triumvirate is showing signs of failing power. The battle for modernity, already won in the novel by the naturalists, in painting by the Impressionists, in music by the Wagnerites, is ready to invade the theatre. Who shall give the signal? The answer is an employee at a gas company, by the name of André Antoine. He begins by enlisting the sympathies of Zola, Léon Hennique, and Paul Alexis, each of whom gives him a play for production in a miserable cubby-hole in the Passage de l'Elysée-des-Beaux-Arts. The cubby-hole is the billiard-room at the back of a café, whose owner consents to light it with one gas jet from half-past eight to midnight on condition that each of the actors takes a consommation! Next, our employee goes to the office of the *Figaro* and demands to see the *courriériste des théâtres*. The gossip writer, shocked at the audacity of so miserable a scarecrow, receives him with disdain. Nevertheless next day he gives him half a column. In the meantime rehearsals have greatly intrigued Zola, and certainly Antoine knows what he is about when he arranges that one of the four pieces composing his programme shall be *Jacques Damour*, the dramatization by Hennique of a short story by the great writer, and which, as luck would have it, has just appeared in the *Figaro*. To the dress rehearsal Zola brings a number of friends, including Alphonse Daudet. The rehearsal ended, Antoine gives his arm to Daudet, limping a little in his descent of the *passage*. At a turning Daudet stops and, pointing to a window, says, "Antoine, I see ghosts in your street to-night! That is the house where I first met the trollop who became the heroine of *Sapho*." The first night is an enormous success. Zola, Daudet, Hennique, Chincholle, La Pommeraye, Denayrouze, of *La République Française*, and Aubry-Vézan, of *La Petite République*, are there. Next morning there is a magnificent article in the *Figaro*, by Henry Fouquier, concerning this "théâtriculet perdu au fond de Montmartre"! Now success follows success. Sarcey writes to apologise for non-attendance. He has been engaged at a conference at Lille, and for proof encloses his railway ticket. Porel, who has previously turned down *Jacques Damour*, announces that he will put the play on at the Odéon. All of which does not prevent the director of the gas company from regarding his employee "avec des yeux terribles"!

Now Antoine is in the middle of an advertising campaign at which Hercules would have boggled. He has written a little brochure and has persuaded some quixotic publisher to print two thousand copies. The idea is for Antoine to send a copy to each of the persons who subscribed for the recent performance of *Lohengrin*, got up by Lamoureux. To prevent these busy and wealthy people from confounding the brochure with the usual prospectus Antoine decides to write a letter to each—not a circular letter, but an individual appeal written by hand and running to four pages. As he has not enough money for stamps he delivers the appeals personally, at night, after the day's work. In fourteen days he writes and delivers thirteen hundred letters. Starting out on his postman's round at ten o'clock at night, he finishes at six in the morning. Since it is more important than ever, in view of the increasing ferocity of the gas company, that he should be at his work strictly on time he dare not trust himself to go to bed, which means that he goes to sleep standing. Swaying on his feet, it takes him five minutes to find the letter-box in which to drop his thirteen hundredth letter—addressed, incidentally, to the most wide-awake man in France, a certain Monsieur Clemenceau. How many answers is it reasonable to suppose Antoine receives? The reader has guessed right. Not one!

Nevertheless Antoine continues to rise in the world. With the help of the devoted Emile Paz, he rents a large studio with a staircase of its own. His theatre has two dozen subscribers, permitting him to pay something on account for rent and lighting. The invaluable Paz has found a furniture dealer who will hire out on credit three dozen chairs and some curtains. One of the stage properties is a divan on which Antoine sleeps at night, for though he is going up in the world artistically, he is still on the social ground floor. Or rather, he has no ground floor; he must sleep in the studio. And the gas company? Antoine has left it. Anybody inquiring for him at the office is to be told that he has *mal tourné*. Nevertheless for a penniless producer Antoine is doing pretty well. A certain Madame Aubernon de Nerville is in the habit of giving receptions. She has the notion of presenting, at one of these receptions, a performance of Henry Becque's *La Parisienne*, with Réjane. Will Antoine do her the kindness of playing the principal part opposite Réjane? And here is a charming cameo. Réjane is a little difficult, not with her fellow-player, but with her author. "Moi, je ne ferais pas ceci." Or, "Moi, je ne dirais pas ça." Becque solves the difficulty by putting his arm round Réjane's waist and waltzing her round the room.

From Réjane it is only a step to Bernhardt, who receives Antoine reclining on a *chaise longue*. From under the furs with which she is entirely covered she makes show of interest in the Théâtre-Libre, of which she has never heard. Antoine would make her realise how useful she can be to him, since she has a public which will follow her wherever she leads. And why not in the direction of his theatre? He reminds her of an article in which Mendès has just reproached her with taking no part in the battle for the new theatre. Sarah is not impressed. Antoine mentions a piece called *L'Abbesse de Jouarre*, in which the leading rôle has been played by a celebrated Italian actress, la Duse. At this moment an old lady appears from behind the *portière* which gives into the next room. Sarah, turning to her, asks her if she remembers this actress. The old lady replies, "Ah, oui! Ah, oui! La Duse, pas fameuse du reste."

Two years later. The date is January 12th, 1890. Antoine dines with Zola, who says to him, "You ought to have a look at an article by Jacques Saint-Cère about a Scandinavian author whose new piece has created an enormous sensation in Germany." Again Antoine wastes no time. Next day he writes to Saint-Cère, who tells him that the piece is a study on heredity by one Henrik Ibsen, and that it is called *Ghosts*. Three weeks later Zola promises to find somebody who knows Norwegian and will translate the piece. A fortnight later still a Monsieur Hessem, a fair-haired, shy, neurotic little person, turns up with a translation and a note from Zola saying the piece is "une curiosité sinon aussi retentissante que *La Puissance des Ténèbres*, du moins d'un intérêt aussi vif pour les lettrés." On March 15th Antoine, anxious to compare this translation with the original text, has recourse to one Rodolphe Darzens, who says, "I have a literary friend who travels in timber for a house at Le Havre, and who knows Norway like the back of his hand. If I ask him he will make me a word-for-word translation." Two days later comes the news that the Independent

Theatre of London has produced the play, and that the entire English Press has found it immoral and of a revolting obscenity. On April 20th Darzens brings along his literal translation, and Antoine finds a world of difference between this and Hessem's version. Darzens also brings with him a letter from Ibsen himself, authorising the use of Darzens' version. A month later the piece goes into rehearsal, and the first performance takes place on May 29th, 1890, with Antoine as Oswald. He writes, "For the majority of the audience the first shock of astonishment was succeeded by boredom, giving place towards the end of the play to extreme tension and the deepest emotion. I can only speak from hearsay; I underwent a new experience—that of not realising what was going on. From the beginning of the second act I remember nothing of the play or its effect on the public. For some time after the fall of the curtain I was unable to regain possession of myself. The piece makes a considerable noise despite the public's lack of understanding and Sarcey's jibes." But is Antoine discouraged? Not at all. He immediately puts *The Wild Duck* into rehearsal!

Four years later Antoine's debts threaten to overwhelm him. He goes to a banker, who makes him a present of 5 000 francs, which are, alas! a drop in the 100 000 franc ocean. The end of the book finds Antoine and his company stranded at Rome. Yet 1894 has not been an entirely unlucky year for him. In the early part of it he attends the guillotining of the anarchist Fortuné Henry. Originally it is Henry's intention to throw a bomb into the stalls of the Théâtre-Français. But the length of the queue prevents him from getting in. So Henry descends the Avenue de l'Opéra seeking an opportunity of getting rid of the bomb, which is still in his pocket. Proceeding along the boulevards, he comes to the Café Americain, where he recognises Antoine dining with Mendès and Pedro Gailhard. In gratitude for a pleasant evening spent at the Théâtre-Libre he refrains from throwing his bomb. Turning into the Rue Halévy, he gains the Gare Saint-Lazare, and annihilates several people taking their apéritif in the café of the Hotel Terminus.

October 9 *Sunday*

Came down to Brighton with Leo Pavia and Julian Phillipson. Leo in great form. Apropos of *Ego* 3, he said, "You needn't be afraid of actions for libel. Everybody in it is either dead or half-dead." For years Leo has been proclaiming how he too is in love with easeful death. The world events of the past fortnight having brought on his old heart trouble, I asked him why he should worry about the imminence of a consummation so devoutly to be wished. He said, "What I look forward to is not a violent death, but dying in the normal way, with my head in the gas-oven!"

November 1 Tuesday

No. 1 of my *Nouveaux Contes Scabreux*. The model, of course, is Villiers de l'Isle-Adam's *Nouveaux Contes Cruels*: At a banquet given to celebrate the award of the Order of Merit the octogenarian recipient makes a speech in which he boasts that he has always discarded his mistresses as soon as they arrived at the age of consent.

November 2 Wednesday

Southport fascinates me. It was here that I first saw *The School for Scandal*, wore my first London-made suit, and had my first semi-serious illness, a fierce attack of tonsillitis, not improved when the young and pretty night-nurse jumped into bed with me, starched cuffs and all, and stayed there. I was nineteen, and such a hellish little prig that next morning I begged the doctor to send her away! My lecture, on Bad Manners, took place in the Congregational Church. It went off fairly well, though I hadn't reckoned on delivering it from the pulpit. Audience composed of pigtailed schoolgirls, grinning schoolboys, and several hundred stolid burgesses with their wives.

November 5 Saturday

Motored to Windermere and decided that I am like Wordsworth, who, according to Miss Mitford, expected his admirers to "admire *en masse*—all, every page, every line, every word, every comma; to admire nothing else, and to admire all day long".

November 6 Sunday

Leo sat in the car for fifty miles without speaking, and with the face of a soured, elderly tart. Then he broke silence: "You know, of course, James, that my maternal grandmother and Sarah Bernhardt's mother were sisters. What you don't know is that one of my aunts was a *grande amoureuse* in the eighteenth-century connotation of that phrase. She died when she was nearly seventy, and left £69 000 to the ex-billiard-marker whom she had divorced and then re-married twenty years later!" I asked him what will happen to the Jews if and when neither Fascist nor Communist countries will harbour them, and the democratic countries do not easily tolerate them. Leo said, "There has always been somewhere for us to go; we have always been in the van of culture; we have always had our behinds kicked. There will *always* be somewhere for us to go; we shall *always* be in the van of culture; and we shall *always* have our behinds kicked." Later, in the lounge of a

Birmingham hotel, I met a strictly Aryan magnate. We agreed about
the absence of ventilation, the smallness of the writing-room, the
exorbitant price of everything. He said he was Sir Biggles Wade, or
some such name, and inquired mine. This meaning nothing to him, I
added, "Theatres." He said, "A long-haired fellah came into lunch
just now. Looked like a fiddler. Who would that be?" I said, "Probably
Paganini." He said, "Damned interesting!" And I reflected that there
will always be an English county for him to live in, that in the matter
of world culture he will always be in the rear, and that he left Eton and
Balliol in the tranquil consciousness that never again on this side of the
grave would he have his behind kicked.

November 25 Friday

Luncheon party at the Garrick to Hamish Hamilton, off to America.
Actually it was H. H.'s party, given to see himself off. A wonderfully
good host with a gift for blending guests. Clockwise: Hamish, Jock,
Jimmie Horsnell, Cyril Lakin, Lord Moore, Arthur Bryant, Ivor Brown,
J. B. Priestley, Harold Dearden, Frank Swinnerton, J. A., Eddie Marsh.
Eddie told us of a magnificent rebuke to a late-comer at a luncheon
party, the host being Lord Brougham and the guest a famous society
leader arriving half an hour late and pleading she had been buying a
chandelier. Lord B., looking straight ahead, said, "I once knew a man
who bought a chandelier *after* luncheon."

December 7 Wednesday

My boyhood's passion was cricket. (I still have a nightmare about
playing for Lancashire and missing catch after catch in the long field.)
A year or two ago I received a letter from K. J. Key, the Surrey crack
of those days. I wrote in reply that if he had sent me that or any letter
fifty years ago I should have dropped dead with ecstasy.

I told this to C. B. Fry, when I met him to-night at dinner at Clifford
Bax's. Clifford wanted to talk about fifteeenth-century Italy, Fry about
the theatre, and I about cricket. *We talked about cricket.* Fry, alluding
to man's universal desire to shine at something else, said: "I always
wanted to be a minor poet. I remember when I did my record long
jump saying to myself when I was in the air half-way, 'This may be
pretty good jumping. It's dashed poor minor poetry!' "

It was an exciting evening. To the great danger of some priceless
bric-à-brac the man who had been among the six best batsmen of his
time illustrated some of the strokes of the old masters, and some
modern failings. Pressed as to the world's greatest batsman, he declined to compare Grace, the giant English yeoman wielding a battle-
axe, with Ranjitsinhji, the princely master of the foil. But he definitely

thought Ranji the harder to get out, and in his mind the unspoken order seemed to be Ranji, Grace, Trumper, Bradman, Hobbs. He also said that the secret of Jessop's marvellous quickness lay in the fact that he was double-jointed all over. About the mentality of all cricketers: "If they were mice you wouldn't be able to teach them the way to their holes!" When I asked what bowler he had been most afraid of he replied, "Lockwood, of Surrey. He was a fast bowler with the flight of a slow one. No other man could ever deceive me with the same ball twice running. When Lockwood got me out I felt that, if I had the stroke all over again, the result must be the same!"

Fry also told us this extraordinary thing: On the day E. V. Lucas died Lady W——, who was lunching at Lord's, pointed to the door and said, "Look, there's E. V. going out!" Everybody looked, and there was nobody. She said afterwards that she saw E. V. quite clearly, and that he got smaller and smaller.

December 8 Thursday

At the little Etoile Restaurant in Charlotte Street to-day met Tommy Earp, who recited this poem which he had just written:

LAMENT FOR LORCA

Only the other day there was a poet in Spain
Whose poems were known from Vigo to Majorca,
For he was a Spanish poet, and his name was Lorca,
But he will not sing again.

When Granada fell to Franco and, they said, to God,
Murder ran in the street, and hate without reason,
To be a poet and to love Spain was treason,
Fruit for the firing-squad.

Better than those who shot him Lorca knew
The hearts of those who shot him, who were tipsy,
For his friends were peasant, bull-fighter, and gipsy,
And the Spain from which they grew.

Till men know their own hearts, and know their crimes,
There will be but death on the plains and on the mountains,
There will be no more singing by the fountains,
No end to these black times.

December 15 Thursday

Two more of my *Nouveaux Contes Scabreux*. All I can say about No. 2 is that the hero is a boastful fellow called Onanias. No. 3 is about an actress so much in love with her understudy that on the first night of the new play she feigns illness!

December 17 *Saturday*

Before going down to correct my proofs at the *S.T.* squeezed in a performance of the *Messiah*. Or, rather, Beecham squoze it in for me. I thought he over-Mozartified it. The soloists were not a patch on the singers of my youth—Albani, with a bosom like the prow of a battleship; Ada Crossley, an obvious victim to the inferiority complex common to contraltos; Edward Lloyd, with his waxed moustache and what I always took to be a wig: and that tottering old lion Santley, with the roar reduced to a bark and only the style left.

December 30 *Friday*

For years I have been trying to find the right place in which to say something wildly counter to received opinion. This is that after middle age only impermissible couplings are allowable. Elderly fribble and chorus-girl, matron and gigolo—these *liaisons* are not wholly disgusting, since youth has some part in them, even if it is compensated youth. But that a man in his sober sixties should contemplate relationship with the bouncing fifties revolts me.

December 31 *Saturday*

The year's work:

Sunday Times	.	.	.	100 000 words
Daily Express Reviews	.	.	80 000	,,
Daily Express Notes	.	.	25 000	,,
Tatler	.	.	.	60 000	,,
New York Herald-Tribune	.	10 000	,,
Pseudonym	.	.	.	85 000	,,
Ego 3	.	.	.	.	30 000	,,
Ego 4	.	.	.	.	30 000	,,
Odd articles	.	.	.	28 000	,,
			448 000	,,

The totals for previous years have been:

1935	.	555 000 words
1936	.	505 000	,,
1937	.	508 000	,,

I am dismayed at the falling off. However, since I made more money in 1938 than in any previous year—between five and six thousand pounds—I suppose it's all right!

1939

March 11 *Saturday*

Rachmaninoff recital at the Queen's Hall. The last word in piano-playing. The programme announced four Chopin studies, but I was conscious of a fifth—the expression on Moiseiwitsch's face! R. was the principal guest at the Savage Club dinner to-night, Benno presiding. As I was sitting in the angle of the T-table, within four feet of the chair, I had plenty of opportunity to study in Rachmaninoff that visual magnificence which comes naturally to great men like Irving and Chaliapin, to whose type this major artist belongs. It is an extraordinary mask, at once gentle and *farouche*, noble, melancholy, and sardonic. The result is composite—majestic indifference oddly united to the questing look of a French actor strolling the boulevards. When the lean figure rose to leave, everybody in the room stood up. Apart from royalty, this has happened before at the Savage only in the cases of Irving and Lord Roberts.

March 20 *Monday*

At the club nothing talked of except the war scare. Exactly like General Pirpleton in *Mr Pepys's Diary of the War*, or whatever it was called. Here is some of the gossip. The hospitals have been told to prepare for 100 000 casualties during the first twenty-hour hours of hostilities. We have something up our sleeve that the Germans don't know about. London and Paris will be roaring furnaces within a week. Our Air Force is twice the advertised size. G.H.Q. has removed to Bristol. We have bought Rumania's oil output for two years. Half the German tanks are cardboard. And so on and so forth.

March 22 *Wednesday*

After the theatre Bertie van Thal and Jock coaxed me to sup out of my usual orbit. They took me to the Moulin d'Or, next to Kettner's. Excellent. But what a trap for a critic! I had just been to see a screen flash-back of Sarah Bernhardt. "There", said I, in my loudish voice, "was a personality. You would have recognised Sarah at the bottom of a coal-mine. Modern actresses have no personality. I suppose I have seen Carol Goodner and Constance Cummings twenty times at least. But if they were to walk into this restaurant now I wouldn't be able to tell t'other from which!" Whereupon two ladies sitting at a table not two yards away, and whose beauty and charm I had already remarked, sat up like offended rattlesnakes. "Those", whispered

Jock and Bertie simultaneously, "are Carol Goodner and Constance Cummings!"

April 17 Monday

Of a six-foot-four figure whom we saw striding along Regent Street this afternoon Jock said, "Dante without the poetry; Irving without the mystery; Mephistopheles without the fun." It was Sir John Reith.

July 25 Tuesday

Nouveaux Contes Scabreux, No. 7. This is a tale of a rosy-cheeked schoolboy who turns his head to the master flogging him and winningly remarks, "Excuse me, sir, but this is pleasing me more than it is hurting you!"

WAR

September 6 Wednesday

I used to agree with Hazlitt's "Egotism is an infirmity that perpetually grows upon a man, till at last he cannot bear to think of anything but himself, or even to suppose that others do." In war-time this does not hold. I realise that I have become a person of no distinction, and it is this which I find disconcerting. *Per contra*, all sorts of people one had regarded as amiable noodles now turn out to be of immense importance. They burst upon the club in uniform and hold forth where they used to listen. I feel like Kipling's Eustace Cleever, "decorator and colour-man in words", who found himself abashed in the company of young men of action.

September 7 Thursday

Anatole France, in one of his novels, refers to a satirical drawing made by Gustave Doré during the Crimean War. This shows a monk writing in his cell while all around him is carnage. The monastery is on the verge of collapse, and in the doorway of the monk's precariously poised cell a hand-to-hand fight is going on. In the midst of all this the monk, whose name I suspect to be Brother Edward, still keeps his nose in his manuscript and continues to write. France has the comment: "Voilà ce que c'est que de vivre dans les bouquins! Voilà le pouvoir des paperasses!" What I want to know is what else the monk should have done. I propose to glue my nose to *Ego* as long as I and it have sticking power.

September 23 *Saturday*

Leo came to lunch. He told me that originally *The Importance of Being Earnest* was written in four acts, and was cut down by George Alexander to three. The original third act contained a scene in which Algernon Moncrieff was arrested for debt. When told that he would be taken to Pentonville Algernon said, "Never. If Society thought that I was familiar with so remote a suburb it would decline to know me." Leo said, "I know all about this because from 1906 to 1909 I was the official German translator of Wilde's plays. In this capacity I got to know Baron von Teschenberg, who had a copy of the four-act version. He became a great friend of mine, and swindled me out of five hundred pounds."

October 10 *Tuesday*

Brother Edward sends me this from York:

"There are those who can move their ears, one or both, as they please; there are those that can move all their hair towards their forehead, and back again, and never move their heads. There are those that can counterfeit the voices of birds and of other men, cunningly: and there are some who can break wind backward continuously, that you would think they sung".—St Augustine, *De Civitate Dei.*

October 11 *Wednesday*

The depressing thing about *Music at Night* which bored me stiff at Malvern last year and which I had to endure again to-night, is to find Priestley falling into the small-town error of imagining that all smart and successful people are, *au fond* and if they would be honest with themselves, miserable. Take the case of the gossip-writer in this play. I know many gossip-writers, all of whom find writing gossip an admirable way of fulfilling their empty selves. Now Jack cannot see himself as a gossip, unless, of course, it is one of the esoteric variety chattering about Time and Eternity. Therefore nobody can be a gossip and be sincere about it, whence it follows that the *courriériste* in this play must be wearing a mask. Then take the courtesan. It is inconceivable to Jack that a courtesan best expresses herself by being a courtesan. To him an unfortunate is a woman who has been abused. "C'est si facile de nier ce que l'on ne comprend pas!" said Balzac. "If I disapprove of a thing it doesn't exist!" booms Priestley. "My Snoops Linchester and all the rest of the world's Snoopses are good little girls lisping songs of innocence until they meet some nasty millionaire who takes advantage of them." (It never occurs to honest

Jack that the Snoops Linchesters spend their entire time, whether appearing to listen to music or anything else, in calculating how much advantage they can reap from being taken advantage of!) Wherefore Snoops turns out to be only Marguerite Gautier all over again— "J'ai rêvé campagne, pureté; je me suis souvenue de mon enfance— on a toujours eu une enfance, quoi que l'on soit devenue"—and must, when she opens her heart to us, babble of green fields and girlhood's buttercups and daisies. As Olivier de Jalin, in Dumas's *Le Demimonde*, so nearly said: "Il faut arriver de Bradford pour avoir cette idée-là."

October 12 *Thursday*

Stanley Rubinstein reports complete success with all creditors. Horses turned out to grass, car turned in, chauffeur sacked, income taken over, cheque-book exchanged for one marked "Private Account", into which a pittance will be paid every Monday morning. I feel like a remittance man who has *not* been packed off to Australia.

October 13 *Friday*

"It was in this year that my uncle began to break in upon the regularity of a clean shirt" (*Tristram Shandy*). To-day for the first time in history I put on yesterday's shirt.

October 30 *Monday*

Seventeen days of sitting up till four and five in the morning working at my anthology for the Forces, *Speak for England*. Clemence Dane gave me the title; it is the phrase shouted in the House the other day when Arthur Greenwood got up to speak on the declaration of war. After wasting a lot of time and going through agonies of indecision I drew up a set of rules which I then rigidly adhered to:

1. War to be background only.
2. Connecting thread of anthology to be Rupert Brooke's "the thoughts by England given".
3. Anthology must hang together.
4. Must be intelligible to average soldier.
5. Nothing to bore or depress.
6. The note to be R. B.'s sonnet transposed into the key of "If he, *i.e.*, another, should die . . ."

I found snags everywhere. Modern poetry too grim. Sassoon's

horrors put him out of the question. I tried hard to have that moving poem of Wilfred Owen with its exquisite concluding line, "And each slow dusk a drawing-down of blinds." But then there was that first line, "What passing-bells for these who die as cattle?" Hardly encouraging to open the anthology at a poem called *Anthem for Doomed Youth*! Tom Driberg thought the sailors might like Hopkins's *Wreck of the Deutschland*. Just don't see how the average A.B. is going to cope with a rigging full of nuns, or the gushing of a "lush-kept plush-capped sloe mouthed to flesh-burst". The prose selections were just as difficult. I had decided upon Thackeray's magnificent passage in the ninth chapter of *Esmond* beginning "Why does the stately Muse of History", but had to reject it in view of General Staff's susceptibility in the matter of a C.-in-C. who would steal "a portion out of a starving sentinel's three-farthings". However, I got the anthology done at last, and delivered to the hour.

December 1 *Friday*

To the Embassy last night to see a modern-dress version of *Julius Caesar*. I hate this preciosity, the argument for which presumably runs something like this. The Elizabethans saw these plays acted in the costume of *their* day. Why shouldn't we, the audiences of 1939, see them acted in the costume of *our* day, the idea being that the modern audience is a feeble-witted thing which will be put off if the clothes are other than those which it is accustomed to see in the street? All right, let's agree! But since what is sauce for the eye is sauce for the ear also, then this poor, feeble-witted, modern audience must be equally put off when the language used in a play is not that which it is accustomed to hear in the street. This being so, why not rewrite the plays to suit the modern ear? Why all this old-fashioned stuff about the "Bay'd, brave hart," hunters "signed in thy spoil and crimson'd in thy lethe," dishes carved for gods, dumb mouths opening ruby lips, and so on? To-day a dictator is bumped off or not, as the case may be. Reading Damon Runyon's story *The Brain Goes Home* in bed last night, I came across a passage which only wants some alteration in the names to be a perfect transcription of Shakespeare's Act III, Sc.1. Reading Daffy Jack as Brutus, the Brain Caesar, Homer Swing Metellus Cimber, Big Nig Mark Antony, and the teller of the story as Lepidus, here is the passage:

> Now what happens early one morning but a guy by the name of Brutus hauls off and sticks a shiv in Caesar's left side. It seems that this is done at the request of a certain party by the name of Metellus Cimber, who owes Caesar plenty of dough in a gambling transaction, and who becomes very indignant when Caesar presses him somewhat for payment. It seems that Brutus, who is considered a very good shiv artist, aims at Caesar's heart, but misses it by a

couple of inches, leaving Caesar with a very bad cut in his side which calls for some stitching.

Mark Antony, the crap-shooter, and I are standing at the corner of Fifty-second Street and Seventh Avenue along about 2 a.m., speaking of not much, when Caesar comes stumbling out of Fifty-second Street, and falls in Mark Antony's arms, practically ruining a brand-new topcoat, which Mark Antony pays sixty bucks for a few days back, with the blood that is coming out of the cut. Naturally, Mark Antony is indignant about this, but we can see that it is no time to be speaking to Caesar about such matters. We can see that Caesar is carved up quite some, and is in a bad way.

Of course we are not greatly surprised at seeing Caesar in this condition, because for years he is practically no price around this town, what with this guy and that being anxious to do something or other to him, but we are never expecting to see him carved up like a turkey. . . .

Shall work this into something for the *S.T.*, ending with a reference to those "ever-loving" wives Portia and Calpurnia.

Christmas Eve

Dense fog. Looking through the week's papers, come across a letter to *The Times* in which A. J. Munnings complains that Braque sees oranges square. Why not? I am not worried when Modigliani paints a woman sitting on a high chair with her chin in her hand and her elbow resting on the floor. The reason I'm not worried is that Eric Newton has taught me not to look for sense in pictures, but to listen to them as though they were music. In painting I can just about manage this; indeed, the picture I like best in my little collection is a de Pisis in which a man looking like Edwin Evans is walking into a free library with a tree growing out of his hat. I don't even pretend that this is the Tree of Knowledge!

Where I begin to jib is in music. *Pace* Ernest Newman, I fear I shall never be able to stop listening—I listen with pleasure to Scriabin and Poulenc and Milhaud—and substitute reading, the matter to be read being the composer's musical thought. I jib still more when I am told that a poem can dispense with rhyme, metre, and even meaning so long as it discovers "evocative rhythms" and "image sequences". It isn't that I don't like some modern poetry. I like a little of it enormously. Straight, I do! I find much of Edith Sitwell imaginative and stimulating —in short, fun. But when in music I hear the atonal stuff I say like Antony to the Roman messenger, "Grates me: the sum." When I read Dylan Thomas's *January* 1939, beginning,

> Because the pleasure-bird whistles
>   after the hot wires,

> Shall the blind horse sing sweeter?
> Convenient bird and beast are lodged
>   to suffer
> The supper and knives of a mood,

I think of Coleridge's "To please me, a poem must be either music or sense; if it is neither, I confess I cannot interest myself in it." Compare John Betjeman's *Upper Lambourne*, which sings like Tennyson:

> Feathery ash in leathery Lambourne
>   Waves above the sarsen stone
> And Edwardian plantations
>   So coniferously moan
> As to make the swelling downland,
>   Far surrounding, seem their own.

That I should like *some* modern stuff in all the arts—to me Epstein's moderns are as sympathetic as Eric Gill's ancients are revolting—is of extreme importance. If I did not I should have to consider giving up my job on the *S.T.* The position of the dramatic critic who takes himself seriously is extremely delicate. His job is to encourage to the best of his ability whatever is new and genuine, and to refuse to be hoodwinked by the new and bogus. He must hold the door wide open, and shut it tight. He is at once explorer and watchdog. About one thing I am absolutely determined. This is not to be afraid of saying No to pretentious rubbish because fifty years ago Clement Scott made a fool of himself over Ibsen.

Christmas Day

Fog-bound and unable to get to Monty's party, the second time I have defaulted in ten years. Fortunately, Leo Pavia is marooned here with me, and has been for two days. Have never known anybody with more catarrh or wit, and I spend the day listening to his snuffles, gurgles and *bons mots*. It is incredible that so much malice should have a background of so much childishness. He comes into the room saying, "There's a young woman at the Telephone Exchange who insists that it's six-fifty-nine exactly. I tried to argue with her, but she wouldn't listen." I then found out that he had rung TIM for the first time in his life and didn't know she was mechanical.

1940

March 11 *Monday*

Leo is still in good form and temper. Began to-day by asking whether one should correct mispronunciations in others. I said, "Only when they are our social equals." To which Leo at his most Johnsonian: "To correct the lower orders is useless and therefore unkind. To instruct our own class is impertinent. To put right the people who hold themselves to be our social superiors is more than a duty: it is a pleasure."

April 8 Monday

Nouveaux Contes Scabreux, No. 10. Based on a conversation I had years ago at a suburban dinner-party. My neighbour, who appeared to be wearing Gertrude Jekyll's gardening boots and looked like one of the Old Ladies of Llangollen, said, "Tell me, Mr Agate. What is a sadist?" I said, "Imagine that somebody climbs a tower and from the top of it pours molten lead into the navel of an infant pegged out on the ground below. That would be an act of sadism, and the perpetrator would be a sadist." The old lady said, "He would have to be a good shot!"

April 10 Wednesday

In the little play at the Gate Theatre called *The Jersey Lily* Mrs Langtry is made to allude to an epoch in which the dressers of star-actresses were invariably their mothers: "You can't think what a bad dresser my mother would make." The Prince of Wales, to whom this is said, answers, "Mine would be rather good."

April 11 Thursday

Jock and I lunched at 90 Piccadilly. No other guests. Hugh Walpole at his pinkest and most cherubic. He and I jabbered incessantly; Jock, with more sense, devoted himself to the food and drink, with an occasional "That's right" and sometimes "That's wrong." Afterwards we dropped our cigar-ash into a wooden bowl painted by Gauguin, and admired Hugh's latest acquisition—the scarab ring which Wilde never stopped twirling throughout the trial. He has bought, by the way, the smaller of Monty's two Matisses. I told him that, out of excess of delicacy, when going through the final proofs of *Ego* 3, I suppressed my parody of his Lakeland style. He was indignant at my thinking he might be hurt, and made me promise to insert the pastiche in my entry for to-day. Here it is:

'Twas early morn. The dew was still on the grass, and the grass was still underneath the dew. Presently the sun would get hotter and there would be no more dew. But the grass would remain. When the dew had gone the grass would be dry, and Susan Saddleback would be able to sit down. She decided to wait. Below her was the lake of Derwentwater. Behind her were the fells, to the right the jaws of Borrowdale, to the left the pikes of Langdale. Above her, both right and left, was the sky. At her feet were larkspurs, raising their heads to salute first the songsters and songstresses of the waking day, and second the spurs of the lakeland hills which held her as rapt as they had done a week come Tuesday. Susan was nothing if not self-analytical. Why, she asked herself, whenever she glimpsed Great Gable did she always think of Clark?

April 12 *Friday*

Mrs Patrick Campbell is dead. Of her Paula Tanqueray that unimpressionable critic William Archer wrote after that first night of May 27th, 1893: "Never was there a more uncompromisingly artistic piece of acting. It was incarnate reality, the haggard truth." Neither Shaw nor Max was gammoned by the play itself. Yet both used the then-significant word 'glamour' in connection with the unknown young woman chosen to play Paula. There followed a round of great parts in which the changes were rung on Pinero, Ibsen, and Sudermann— she was the best by a hundred miles of all the Magdas I have seen. Her Juliet and Ophelia had been but so-so, but now in 1898 came her ever-memorable Mélisande to the Pelléas of Sarah Bernhardt. I remember one afternoon soon after the turn of the century when I stole from my office-stool to see Mrs Campbell. The play was Echegaray's *Mariana*, and all I recollect of it now is a long scene in which Mrs P. sat quite still and told of an incident in Mariana's childhood. She was being snatched up out of her cot, and her mother's lover was crying, "Be quick! be quick!" She was lovely in those days, and filled the mind with a haunting sense of baffled importunacy, and sympathy for all creatures engaged in strange and romantic quests. Her voice was like Casals' 'cello, and her silences had the emotional significance of Maeterlinck's shadowy speech. This was an actress who, for twenty years, had the world at her feet. She kicked it away, and the ball rolled out of her reach.

"I am not like the things I do," says a character in Allan Monkhouse's *Mary Broome*. I attribute this great player's failure to stay the course to the fact that she came to resemble the things she said. To them she sacrificed her material, her art, and, finally, herself. Gloriously witty things which burned her mouth as money burns my pocket. Despicably cruel things, as when, at a party, she went up to a clever child standing beside a distinguished actress well on in her sixties and said, "My dear, how young you look, next to everybody!" It is a rule of golf that nothing a player can do can deprive him of the half he has already gained. Twenty sorry years could not cancel out the earlier and glorious twenty. One can only say that our young people can never have known this artist at anything like her best. In my life I have seen six great actresses, and six only. These are Bernhardt, Réjane, Mrs Kendal, Ellen Terry, Duse, and Mrs Patrick Campbell.

May 19 Sunday

And now for my goddess Malibran! Bunn says of her [in *The Stage; Both Before and Behind the Curtain*]:

> The energy of her character eventually destroyed this astonishing woman; and the only wonder to me is that the melancholy and premature event which we shall have by-and-by to record did not take place sooner. The powerful and conflicting elements mingled in her composition were gifts indeed, but of a very fatal nature— the mind was far too great for the body, and it did not require any wonderful gift of prophecy to foresee that in their contention the triumph would be but short, however brilliant and decisive. Themistocles, in accounting for his own watchfulness, used to say that the trophies of Miltiades would not let him sleep. The idea that the fame of any living artist could approach hers was enough to eat her heart away, if nothing else had ever preyed upon it.

Espiègle enfant ce soir, sainte artiste demain is Musset's phrase for burning the candle at both ends. Here was Malibran's way, according to Bunn:

> During her late professional visit to London, I was leaving the theatre one evening, and going into Malibran's room I found her, after the performance of *La Sonnambula*, dressing for an evening concert. I remonstrated with her, pointed out the inroads she was making on her constitution, and urged her to send an excuse. She promised to do so; and in a belief she would keep that promise I bade her goodnight, and drove home to Brompton. I was reading in bed about half an hour after the midnight chime, when the bell of the outer gate was rung violently, and on its being answered, I heard a voice say, "Tell Mr. Bunn not to get up—I am only come for a little fresh air in his garden." I dressed and found in one of the walks Madame Malibran, Monsieur de Bériot, and Monsieur Thalberg, from whom I learnt that, despite all my injunctions, she had been to TWO concerts, gone home afterwards to undress, and dress, and had taken a fancy to this slight country trip at such an extraordinary hour. I had supper laid under a huge walnut-tree which overshadowed the entire southern aspect of the house; and beneath its umbrage some viands, especially aided by a favourite beverage of hers—home-brewed beer—and (don't start, readers!) ONIONS. She pulled them fresh from their beds, and, thus humbly entertained, she seemed to be as happy as possible. She warbled,

as late as three into the morning, some of her most enchanting strains, and wound up by saying, "Now I have had my supper I will go and steal my breakfast"; and running into the hen-house emptied every nest, and started off to town.

I have already described in *Ego* this singer's astonishing performance in Balfe's *Maid of Artois*. At the end of the opera she had a prolonged shake on B flat in alt, and Bunn quotes the critic of the *Morning Post*:

It was, in sooth, a wondrous burst, and it was cruel to demand it a second time. The curtain however drew up, and she again went through what would on the score appear an almost incredible task. A storm of cheering summoned her after the act-drop fell, and Templeton led her forward, when the waving of hats, handkerchiefs, etc., could not be exceeded even at La Scala.

To explain the incredible encore Bunn has this:

I had occasion, during its last rehearsal but one, to express myself in strong terms at her leaving the stage for more than an hour and a half, to go and gain £25 at a morning concert. Neither the concerted pieces of music, nor the situations of the drama in which she was involved, could possibly be proceeded with, and the great stake we were then contending for was likely to be placed in jeopardy by an unworthy grasp at a few pounds, to the prejudice of a theatre paying her nightly five times as much. She knew she had done wrong, and she atoned for it by her genius, while her pride would not have permitted her to do so. She had borne along the two first acts on the first night of performance in such a flood of triumph that she was bent, by some almost superhuman effort, to continue its glory to the final fall of the curtain. I went into her dressing-room previous to the commencement of the third act, to ask how she felt, and she replied, "Very tired, but" (and here her eye of fire suddenly lighted up) "you angry devil, if you will contrive to get me a pint of porter in the desert you shall have an encore to your finale." Had I been dealing with any other performer I should perhaps have hesitated in complying with a request that might have been dangerous in its application at the moment; but to check *her* powers was to annihilate them. I therefore arranged that, behind the pile of drifted sand on which she falls in a state of exhaustion towards the close of the desert scene, a small aperture should be made in the stage; and it is a fact that, from underneath the stage through that aperture, a pewter pint of porter was conveyed to the parched lips of this rare child of song, which so revived her, after the terrible exertion the scene led to, that she electrified the audience, and had strength to repeat the charm, with the finale to the *Maid of Artois*. The novelty of the circumstance so tickled her fancy, and the draught itself was so extremely refreshing, that it was arranged, during the subsequent run of the opera, for the negro slave at the head of the governor's procession to have in the gourd suspended from his neck the same quantity of the same beverage, to be applied to her lips on his first beholding the apparently dying Isoline.

May 24 *Friday*

Lunched with Francis Sullivan at the Coq d'Or. Came across this in Sydney Smith:

> There is not a better man than Lord John Russell; but his worst failure is that he is utterly ignorant of all moral fear; there is nothing he would not undertake. I believe he would perform the operation for the stone—build St Peter's—or assume (with or without ten minutes' notice) the command of the Channel Fleet: and no one would discover by his manner that the patient had died—the Church tumbled down—and the Channel Fleet been knocked to atoms.

June 2 *Sunday*

Having no money is teaching me what Timon of Athens learned— that the only result of paying for other people is their rage when it stops.

June 3 *Monday*

Long pow-wow with Stanley Rubinstein, who says that he is bound to tell me that I can get out of all my financial difficulties, including income tax, by going bankrupt. But that he is a hundred per cent against such a course. To which I reply that I am two hundred per cent against it unless I am badgered into it! I agree with Stanley that any- thing of the sort would be unpatriotic and disgraceful. But the badgering may leave me no other way out. The difficulty, as usual, is the income- tax people, who cannot be brought to understand that I am unable to reap my articles unless I first sow them. Here, for example, is a story gleaned this week from the Café Royal. It was told me by a naval officer in charge of one of the ships during the Dunkirk episode. An English Army officer who was all in, finding no place to sit down, let alone lie, finally espied a life-boat containing flags and covered with a tarpaulin. Creeping under the tarpaulin, he fell into a deep and blissful sleep, from which he did not awake till some hours later. Lifting the tarpaulin and peeping over the edge of the boat, he found that he was back at Dunkirk. He had done the round trip!

That little yarn *makes* the article in which it is going to appear. Now say my supper-bill for the week comes to £3. And say I get £25 for the article. Deducting £3 for expenses and £8 6s. 8d. for my one-third share, which is what Rubinstein allows me, the transaction leaves my creditors with a net profit of £13 13s. 4d. On the other hand, sitting on my behind at Bognor produces just exactly nothing at all, except a net loss of 4d. on the cup of cocoa which my creditors will presumably not deny me. The sentiment may be Skimpolean, but the logic is the logic of fact.

The trouble is that I understand arithmetic and that the Revenue authorities don't. Stanley says that they would prefer my smoking a bad cigar, writing a bad article, and losing my job, to a good cigar, and a good article ensuring the continuance of that job. And that when, putting it in language that a child could understand, I say what about the bad cigar making me sick, and the bad article making my editor sick of me, they merely shrug their shoulders. It's the old puritanical passion for preaching all over again; so long as the Revenue can indulge in its habit of scolding naughty boys it doesn't mind whether it gets the money or not. In a way I understand. No man who had the imagination to conceive a debt (Balzac) and no man whose horizon was not blotted out by a smokable cigar (Agate) would be a tax-collector.

But I warn the Revenue and my creditors generally that I am nearing the end of my patience. It is a long worm that has no turning, and the turn this worm will take if not left reasonably alone is Carey Street. If my creditors do not want me to earn money for them let them shut me up altogether; if they want me to go on earning some thousands a year for them let them shut up. Since January 1st, 1939, they have had eightpence out of every shilling the worm has made. At nine-pence it gets restive, and at ten-pence it turns.

June 10 Monday

Every schoolboy knows what the weather was like on the night before Caesar's murder. Other than schoolboys asked themselves what to-day's weather portended—a dense, Ancient Mariner-like, white mist with a small copper sun. I have never seen anything like it even in November, and it lasted all through this day on which Mussolini declared war on France. Is the Pathetic Fallacy less fallacious than we think?

A Week Later

France has surrendered, and this country is back in 1805, 1667, 1588, 1066, or 55 B.C. If at this point I am expected to say something about the inviolacy of the British hearth and the sanctity of the British home, the Union Jack in a word, I am afraid I shall disappoint. But as a dramatic critic I still retain my sense of good and bad style in drama. It is worse than fustian, it is untrue, to say that the future of the country

is on the knees of the gods. It isn't. It is in our own hands. I do not
believe in the Powers of Darkness except as a play. What said Shakespeare's Bastard? "Come the three corners of the world in arms. . . ."
Well, they have come, and it is not we who are going to rue.

I would break off here but for the fact that I should be ending on a
note I have sedulously avoided. Harking back to my proper key, it
occurs to me that I have not recorded any of my dreams. Here is one
I had last night. I am looking into the *Dictionary of National Biography*
in the year 3000, and I find this:

> AGATE, James (late 19th–middle 20th century), diarist and brother
> of the great wit. Is believed to have written criticisms of the theatre,
> which still functioned in England at that time, though no trace of these
> remains. In 2792 the Diaries, of which *Ego* 4 is generally regarded as
> the best, were translated into German by Dr Ebing von Afterkrafft,
> with Introduction and Notes by Professor Beinzieher; the twenty-
> four volumes contain the passages suppressed during the author's
> lifetime, and full transcripts of the 180 *Contes Scabreux* and *Nou-
> veaux Contes Scabreux*. As a prose-writer Agate is vigorous, though
> here and there obscure. In the year 2907, and in the hope of throw-
> ing further light on English morals and manners in the 20th cen-
> tury, the diarist's grave at Southend was opened. Nothing was found
> except writs.

EGO 5

July 1940–August 1942

July 28 *Sunday*

"You realise", said Jack Bergel, "what bringing this out now means?"
This was *Ego* 4. "It means that you regard your Diary as more important
than the war." I said, "Well, isn't it? The war is vital, not important."

I take it that to Schönberg atonalism, to Hindemith serialism, and
to both the inter-relationship of chromaticism, mathematics, and
acoustics are more important than whether the British can destroy
Hamburg before the Nazis destroy Hull. If at this point somebody
tells me that a Nazi victory would put an end to music both tonal and
atonal I just say, "Bosh!" Look at this matter from another angle.
Because I am suddenly stricken with cancer, must cancer become my
whole world? Again I say, "Bosh!" Cancer has become vital to me,
but not important; except in so far as I am a coward it does not fill
my mind. It was advisable recently that I should have the coping of
my house attended to; on the day when I found a large lump of stone
lying on my door-step I realised that "advisable" had become "im-
perative". But I have still no interest in coping-stones; though they
cut my head open, my mind remains closed to them. In other words,
coping-stones are vital, not important. Should I, finding myself looking
down the barrel of a Nazi rifle, hold that piece of ironmongery to be
more real than *Ego*? Yes, and I should be wrong, and to know how
wrong I have only to ask which will be more real after the shot is
fired, seeing that if I still have a name in the world it will be as a writer
of diaries and not as a facer of firing-squads.

I spent ten minutes yesterday afternoon gazing in the window of
Hawes and Curtis's shop in Jermyn Street, admiring some new gloves
of a shade half-way between primrose and daffodil with a wonderful
dusty bloom on them, and regretting that I couldn't buy half a dozen
pairs, or even one pair. But I was compensated by the recollection of
Claude Vignon and his famous *gants jaunes*. And I realised with an

almost physical intensity of realisation that Balzac's world is one which Hitler cannot touch. I was profoundly impressed at the end of the last war by the alacrity with which writers of all sorts dropped a subject which had become tedious, how quickly war books and war plays and war films went out of fashion. I believe that, whichever way this war ends, the moment it is over it will be the last thing anybody will want to read about. Do I seriously mean that the re-opening of the Proms next week is of greater interest than, say, what Stalin is or is not going to do? The answer is yes. Not now. Perhaps not while this Diary is writing. But in twenty years certainly. In a hundred years, when my big toe began to ache and when it stopped aching will be of more interest to anybody coming fresh to this Diary than the Peace Terms. It will be news; they will be merely history.

August 10 *Saturday*

The urge behind this diary is something more than egotism. It is the desire to take up certain leases. N. C.'s [Neville Cardus] prose will look after itself, but there remain Brother Edward's letters, unculled Montague, the quiddity of Gemmell [a remarkable character in the world of horse-dealing], the charm of humble friends. If this diary lives, then something of these lives.

August 24 *Saturday*

Café Royal. Some Bloomsbury ass braying about platonic love, I told him of a letter which appeared in *The Saturday Review* some time in the 'nineties. The writer had overheard this conversation in a Paris café and taken it down:

> FIRST COCOTTE. Mon ami me dit qu'il n'a pour moi que de l'amour platonique. Que'est-ce que c'est que ça?
> SECOND COCOTTE. Je ne sais pas au juste, mais pour moi ça a l'air d'être quelque sale cochonnerie.

I once heard Edgar Jepson wind up a dinner-table discussion on the subject by saying in his dry, precise voice, "I know nothing about platonic love except that it is not to be found in the works of Plato." And I remember Leo saying about two Platonists, "They are always in a state of miserable enthusiasm about each other."

September 1 *Sunday*

I turn on the wireless and I hear: "It was a great moment when Stanley met Livingstone. But can it have been as momentous as when Bud Flanagan met Chesney Allen?"

September 2 *Monday*

Leo Pavia presented me with a hat-brush with the date 1845 dyed into the bristles. This was given to his grandmother by Rossini.

September 7 *Saturday*

Lunch at Lord's with Alfred Chenhalls, and had long discussion on how we are going to get Henry Wood the O.M.

The biggest air attack launched on London to date started at 5.30 this afternoon and has been going on ever since, the time of writing being 2 a.m. From the roof of the Café Royal got a fine view of the blaze, the Tower Bridge being cut out like fretwork. In one corner of the foreground a large flag fluttered, making the whole thing look like one of those old posters of *A Royal Divorce*, Napoleon's cavalry against a background of red ruin.

September 17 *Tuesday*

E. C. Bentley, the inventor of the Clerihew, reviewing *Ego* 4, hints that it is about people who don't matter. I woke up this morning murmuring:

Mr Bentley
Said evidently
Whoever thinks Balzac, Beethoven, Benson, Bernhardt, Daudet, Duse, Flaubert, Ibsen, Maupassant, Meyerbeer, Montague, Wagner, Walkley, Wilde, and Zola among the dead, and, among the quick, Beaverbrook, Beerbohm, Cochran, Coward, Gielgud, Hambourg, Horowitz, Isherwood, Laughton, MacCarthy, Moiseiwitsch, Newman, Rachmaninoff, Sayers, Shaw, Sibelius, Stein, Tempest, Thorndike, Walpole, Wood, Zuloaga, and lots more matter
Is as mad as a hatter.

September 28 *Saturday*

Letter from Alfred Douglas, beginning "Devouring time that blunts the lion's paws has slightly modified my feelings of dislike towards you."

September 30 *Monday*

Bertie van Thal's friend, John Byron the actor, having found me rooms at Oxford, I am now installed where I have always regretted not being educated.

October 4 *Friday*

Oxford is not the hub of modern culture I expected to find it. Seeing two ladies vainly exhorting a dog to get into a motor-car, I prodded it with my stick, repeating Cyrano's command to Christian: "Monte donc, animal!" The elder lady gave me a severe look and said,"I think that was most uncalled for."

October 11 *Friday*

Read Bernard Darwin's reminiscences called *Life is Sweet, Brother*. Very well done. Signs that the famous urbanity is part of the Cambridge manner, something cultivated like a golf course cut out of a forest. But there is plenty of jungle left, witness the liking for tigers like John Mytton, benevolent leopards like Osbaldeston, and the jackals of murder. Here B. D.'s taste is irreproachable. A "harmless little fellow like Crippen" is hardly worth considering. Palmer's his man, not Pritchard. And always he asks the right questions. Who was the person with the odd walk seen coming down St Paul's Road, Camden Town, at a quarter to five in the morning after Phyllis Dimmock had been killed? Who was the man that Helen Lambie saw coming out of Miss Gilchrist's flat? Who wrote the note to Rose Harsent at Peasenhall, with those characteristic capital P's in the middle of a word, which brought the poor girl downstairs to her death in the middle of the night and a thunderstorm? Who telephoned the message to William Herbert Wallace which sent him on that fool's errand to the non-existent Menlove Gardens East, from which he returned to find his wife murdered? Was it William Herbert himself? And why did he choose Qualtrough for a name? In my view the Wallace case is the best of all modern crimes; chess figures in it, and the case for and against is as well balanced as a match between great masters.

Personally I have always taken the best of the vintage crimes of a hundred and more years ago to be the murder of William Weare by John Thurtell, aided and abetted by those two unsavoury scoundrels Hunt and Probert. Darwin likes Thurtell because he belonged to the world of prize fighters and billiard sharps and touts. "The women in the case, sleepless and terrified upstairs, hearing something heavy being dragged across the garden, are full of the right quality, and have a touch of De Quincey and Ratcliff Highway." Bernard approves of Thurtell because he knew Belcher; I approve of him because he was always prating of his friend Edmund Kean, of whom he gave an excellent imitation. For the rest he was born to evil, a crook and a blackguard whose only job of work was to act as second to the bruisers of the day. He figures under the name of Tom Turtle in Hazlitt's account of the fight between the Gas-man and Bill Neate. Hazlitt sits next to him on the coach going down to the fight. "My friend the trainer was confined in the topics to fighting dogs and men, to bears and badgers; beyond this he was quite chap-fallen." Borrow, who put Thurtell into *Lavengro*, described his features as "a blending of the bluff and the sharp". His kind are still to be seen wherever greyhounds are raced, though they no longer rise to the dignity of murder. Bernard is good on Thurtell, though he doesn't seem to know that Robert Surtees witnessed the execution of Thurtell's accomplice Probert, hanged in the following year for horse-stealing in company with two others convicted of the same crime, and a burglar. The account found among Surtees's papers concludes: "The drop suddenly fell, and a thrill ran through the crowd as those four white-covered heads assumed the same sideway attitude as they were launched into eternity."

October 15 *Tuesday*

To G. W. Stonier
of the "New Statesman"
on failing to review "Ego 4"

Some people write for *Comic Cuts*
And some for journals tonier;
Some journalists the 'phone affect,
Others are even phonier;
Some seed must fall on stony ground,
But need that ground be Stonier?

October 22 *Tuesday*

My brother Edward died on Friday last during an operation. He did not know the true nature of his disease, deep-seated and unsuspected, did not fear the operation, and had no mental suffering. Even if he had, he possessed the stoicism to meet it. He was buried in the family grave at the Unitarian Church at Monton Green, Manchester, and as the coffin was being lowered a near-by siren wailed. I thought of Macbeth's "Nothing can touch him further". Nothing could touch Edward at any time. He made for himself a way of living and was not to be turned from it. Hardened to seeing his gifts unrecognised, he would do nothing to secure their recognition, or to turn them to commercial advantage. He was invited to collaborate in a film about Cyrano de Bergerac but declined "out of respect to (*a*) the original Cyrano, (*b*) Rostand, and (*c*) myself". He would not hear of compromise. "Que je pactise? Jamais, jamais!" He would spend months translating the works of Klopstock or Platen, not knowing or caring whether they would find a publisher. He was dissuaded with difficulty from translating the fourth part of Heine's *Reisebilder*. When the question of market was raised he exuded vitriol. "There ought to be one," he would say with finality. He pursued the unreadable just because it was unreadable. He sought out the librarian of a well-known library and demanded to be shown the store-room to which were relegated uncalled-for books; these he insisted on arranging and cataloguing, "as they must obviously be the best". In some ways he never grew up, and to the end of his life remained ignorant of the things with which the average child is familiar. He was a formidable wit with a dual mind, half Thersites and half Mr Dick, and could change from one to the other in the course of a single sentence.

October 25 Friday

Spoke at the Union. The motion was the establishment of a Chair of Drama at Oxford, proposed by Leslie Banks and opposed by A. G. Macdonell. One of the undergraduates made the excellent point that you can't mix dead languages and living drama, and that if Oxford dons were allowed to contact the living drama they would kill it. I summed up the debate with a distinct bias against the whole business of National Theatres. Talking about idealists and the harm they do I suggested that the proper way to deal with the C. P. Scotts is to behead them in the morning, give them an Abbey funeral in the afternoon, and canonise them in the evening. So with the proposed Chair of Drama. Establish it in the morning, chop it up for firewood in the afternoon, and in the evening make a bonfire of it on the steps of the Martyrs' Memorial. "What about the black-out?" piped some vulgar little boy. The motion was carried handsomely, 231 votes to 89.

November 19 Tuesday

Letter from Alfred Douglas:

> 1 *St Ann's Court*
> *Nizells Avenue*
> *Hove* 2, *Sussex*
> *Nov.* 18, 1940

DEAR JAMES

The Importance of Being Earnest was originally planned to be an eighteenth-century play (costumes of the *School for Scandal* period). Oscar told me the idea of the play two or three times before he wrote it. I suggested that it would be much better to make it modern, and he said "I believe you are perfectly right," and he adopted my suggestion. It was originally in four acts, and I think it is quite likely that the Baron Teschenberg, whose German translation you mention, got hold of a typed copy of the original draft of the play. When Oscar was sold up at Tite Street immediately after his arrest. all sorts of letters and documents disappeared. Brokers and masses of other people wandered about the house and no doubt some of them pinched anything they could lay hands on. Probably some one took this draft of the play, and later on, after Oscar's death, this Baron Teschenberg may easily have bought it from a second-hand dealer. The play was cut down to three acts chiefly, I believe, because George Alexander suggested that it wanted some cutting. Oscar, of course, consulted me about this and I agreed, but until you brought up the question I had almost forgotten all about it. I do vaguely remember something about "Mr Gribsby" of the firm "Gribsby and Parker." No doubt they figured in the original draft. I distinctly remember that "Lady Brancaster" was the original name of Lady Bracknell. Oscar invariably took for his characters the names of places where he and I had stayed together, *e.g.* Worthing, Goring, and Basildon. My mother's country house, at which he stayed two or three times, was near Bracknell; Bracknell was the railway station. Brancaster was a place in Norfolk at which I stayed with a tutor who was coaching me in the vac. while I was at Oxford. So he took the name, but afterwards changed it to Bracknell. All this is first-class stuff, and I am heaping coals of fire on your head by giving it to you considering the shabby way you have always treated me in the matter of reviewing and noticing any of my publications. However there you are!

Yours ever,
ALFRED DOUGLAS

December 15 Sunday

Archie Macdonell motored me to Bray, where Barry Neame was giving a luncheon-party to launch Maurice Healy's new book *Stay Me with Flagons*. This is a wine book, and you know the kind of thing: "Claret is an intellectual wine." "I confess I find the Rhône wines lacking in a sense of humour." "Pontet Canet is the least temperamental of Clarets, always conscious of its duty to please and refresh." All this strikes me as nonsense but amusing.

We began with oysters and champagne, after which lobster mould, partridge, creamed mushrooms, toasted cheese, a white wine and *six* vintage clarets in magnums. I had on one side of me Charlie Cochran, in great form despite years, infirmity and stagnation in the theatre world, and on the other the daughter of Charles Morgan's French translator. I thought of asking her the French for "perdurable hypostasis", but refrained.

In the evening I went to a musical party given by Nevil Coghill. About twenty dons and graduates. We began with a Sonata for two violins by Handel. Then a young woman, I think a Pole, played some Bach, Rameau, and Mozart quite well, after which came an earnest young man who treated us to Byrd on the virginals, which he prefaced

by saying in a tone of contempt, "I can't think why you want to listen
to this instead of some jolly, romantic stuff on the modern piano."
I couldn't think why we did! Sandwiches and mulled claret. And
then, just when I thought we were all going to talk, the pianist announced
Beethoven's Sonata, Op.110, after which, believe it or not, there was a
duet for two recorders, actually recorder and violin, the sort of thing
we shall hear a lot of if Clifford Bax ever writes a play about Mary,
Queen of Scots. Last, Brahms's E minor 'cello Sonata, *magnificently*
played by a young Russian girl. Coghill, whose party it was, is a man
of great charm, a combination of Owen Nares, Young Brooke in
Tom Brown's Schooldays and, as he says himself, the Apollo Belvedere.

1941

January 13 *Monday*

Talked to the Playhouse company about *Hedda Gabler*. Have
arranged to insert a leaflet in the programme of *Housemaster* to-night
and every other night this week. A very imposing affair, four pages
long, with the heading in bright red. "TAKE THIS HOME!"

January 14 *Tuesday*

Only two copies of the leaflet were found on the floor after the
performance last night, showing that the audience had obeyed my
injunction. Query: Is the vulgar thing that works better than the
exquisite thing that doesn't? This is a matter for the highbrows: I
made up my mind about it years ago.

January 15 *Wednesday*

Julian d'Albie has roped me in to help with the production, in which
he plays Judge Brack. My first shot at anything of the kind, and I
find it very exciting. Full of problems, since the cast must be got *out
of the company as it is* without any intrusion of guest-artists. Which
means that since most of them are playing against their personalities,
they have got to *act*. After some hours I got rid of much of d'Albie's
charm, which is too genial, and got him to replace it by the cold suavity
of your man of the world. Contrived, too, to persuade handsome
John Byron's Eilert Lövborg not to look at his first entry as though he
had just made a century in the Varsity Match. Mrs Elvsted, generally
flaxen, is to be played by a dark-browed girl who looks like a gipsy.
As she acts the part most sensitively I am not going to have it ruined
by a wig which would turn her into a platinum-blonde Jewess. So

Mrs Elvsted remains dark which, since Hedda has Titian-red tresses, makes nonsense of the latter's remark about Thea's "irritating hair". But it's the lesser of two evils.

January 17 *Friday*

Greatly shocked by the death of Archie Macdonell. In London I had not known him very well, but here at Oxford we have been thrown together quite a lot. He paid me many little attentions, but then he went out of his way to be kind to everybody. There was a paradoxical dandyism about this huge, virile Scot, and at the railway station in the mornings he would stride along the platform with his red carnation smiling and his glasses frowning. His mere presence banished dullness.

January 18 *Saturday*

Went to town yesterday to see Donald Wolfit's tercentenary performance of Ford's *'Tis Pity She's a Whore*. Wolfit has everything a great actor should have except classic features. As Othello, for example, he looks like a golliwog. Jock declares he is the best Shylock he has seen, and I say the same about his Falstaff, judging by the *Merry Wives* embodiment which he plays in a lovely shade of Matisse pink, or like Miss Mitford's description of her father in his vermilion eighties. Yesterday he had made himself up to look like a sentimental French postcard, in spite of which he was very fine, and in the death scene immensely moving.

January 19 *Sunday*

Stayed the night at Fairfax Road. Completely quiet. Took Pavia to lunch. When I told him that Jock and I held Liszt's B minor Sonata to be noisy rubbish, he said, "You're wrong, James. Some of it is quiet rubbish!" And he reminded me that when Lizst played it to Brahms the latter fell asleep, for which Liszt never forgave him.

Got back in time for the dress-rehearsal of to-morrow's play, much of which was a shambles. Consoled myself with the lovely dresses Tony Holland has designed and made for Hedda. The first is a white silk morning wrapper, the kind of thing Sarah would have worn as Théodora. The second is a snaky thing in greenish gold. The third is a black satin which, with Pamela Brown's Titian-red hair, is pure Yellow Book. The first dress, the white one, is the most ravishing thing I have ever seen on any stage. They tell me that I must not judge Pam by her performance to-night, that she needs an audience, when she takes fire in all sorts of unexpected ways. I have arranged that she uses her reception at her first entry to stand stock-still and survey the Tesman lay-out with icy disfavour. Am having the last scene between Hedda and Brack played almost in a whisper (*a*) because of the presence of Tesman and Mrs Elvsted who are not supposed to overhear, and (*b*) because if the players have done their job they can afford to sit still and let the audience act the scene for them. And now all I can do is to sit still and wait for to-morrow.

February 2 *Sunday*

Here, in the *Observer*, is Ivor Brown on *Hedda Gabler*:

> At Oxford there has not, I believe, been a new play for a year or so, and the business, as I saw, is grand. Also the quality of the acting. This is a first-rate company, which ought not to be spending all its time on the "repertory" treadmill. Its *Hedda Gabler* was an adventure, if not a novelty, and it was justly given the public's eager support. Were I a dramatist I should be very happy to have my leading feminine part 'created' by Miss Pamela Brown, whose Hedda was much spoken of—and rightly so.
>
> She gave that lady rather less than the usual weight and sense of grandeur. When Mrs Pat was Hedda she seemed to be the daughter not only of General Gabler but of the entire Norwegian War Office: Miss Brown's Hedda might only be the daughter of a half-pay major. But, taking the great rôle a little lightly, she gave it an admirable sense of humour, which the heavier Heddas usually miss. She held the stage triumphantly, in speech or silence, with a beautifully firm picture of all Hedda's pretentious self-martyrdom and third-rate aesthetic posturings, as well as the devouring jealousy and fever of possession.

Both Jock and Ivor stress the lightness of this Hedda. It was intentional. One day at rehearsal I asked Pam to give me a little more. She said "But I'm only twenty-two, I shan't be able to give what you want till I'm thirty-two, and I'm not going to force it," I said "Very well. We'll build the whole performance up to twenty-two and no more." And so it was.

February 14 *Friday*

A carpet divided Gilbert and Sullivan; Jock and I have split over a typewriter. After eighteen weeks of release from the damned thing— all the time I was at Oxford—he finds he cannot return to the old drudgery. I should have foreseen this. He was with me fourteen years, five months, and some odd days.*

---

* A classic example of J. A.'s use of 'the higher truth' (see *Preface*). Not a word about his attempt to reduce Jock's salary or that the typewriter was the original one, fourteen years old, which J. A. refused to replace. *Ed.*

May 24 Saturday

The *Hood* sunk by the *Bismarck*. Thirteen hundred men killed in a land battle is an incident; a loss at sea of the same dimensions is a tragedy. The ship acts as proscenium.

May 25 Sunday

"The pursuit [of the *Bismarck*] still continues." Yes, but will the couple of torpedoes we have put into her slow her up enough to let us catch her? Everybody doubts it.

May 26 Monday

News from Crete bad. Actually considered as book-keeping, it would be better to keep Crete and let the *Bismarck* go. But sentiment is all the other way. Have spoken to several sailors to-day all of whom say, with complete conviction, "The boys will get her."

Pursuit still on. Hope getting fainter.

May 27 Tuesday

The first intimation I had was looking out of my window at about twelve-thirty and seeing a sailor come down the road, waving his arms and stopping everybody. "We've got the ——!" he said. Listened to the one o'clock news and knew it was all right from the excitement in the announcer's voice.

May 28 Wednesday

America is in the war as near as makes no matter. Roosevelt is the greatest jockey the human race has known.

May 31 Saturday

Sat up late last night writing a long letter to Hugh Walpole, reported by *The Times* as having had a bad heart attack. I have ragged Hugh for years, unmercifully and in print about being slipshod as a writer, and the letter was an attempt to square accounts as between my affection for him as a friend and the plaguey business of disliking his handling of words.

June 1 *Sunday*

Hugh did not live to get my letter. I heard the news over the wireless as I was waiting to begin a broadcast. We had some first rate rows. In the summer of 1938 I wrote to Hugh offering him space in *Ego* 4 to explain why he had forbidden Macmillan's to send his new novel to the *Daily Express*. The letter ended "Come, you old badger, let me draw you". Hugh replied in due course and there was a long rally, both of us coming up to the net to smash. But when it became necessary to shorten that book, this correspondence had to go. I give Hugh's return of service here:

> *Perran Bay Hotel*
> *Perranporth*
> *Cornwall*
> *July* 24, '38

My Dear Jimmie,

I dont' want you to review my books and for two reasons:

1. I don't want you to review them because you don't read them. What you do is to open my new book, find a piece of English that isn't *your* English, pick it out, pillory it under your fat caricature in your paper, make a mock or two, and so leave it.

Now, you are a first-class journalist and I always read you with joy, but I can never reconcile your serious, devoted attitude to the theatre and your flippant, casual patronage of current literature.

I *doubt* if you've ever read a *whole* book by any one right through in your life! Have you? If so, what?

Now, you may be right in your attitude to current literature, but, as *you* know, a book *is* a book to the author of it. One has been a year or more living with it, caring for it, cursing it. Why should one deliver it over to some one who will certainly mock it without reading it? All the same it *would* be so delivered over were it not for the second reason.

2. I have a great regard for our friendship. It has had some ups and downs, but by now I value it for its entertainment value and because I like you. Now, I know that a contemptuous view by you who have *not* read my book will only make me, for a time at least, think you a patronising, job-shirking bastard. Of course, you are *not* that, but I, in company with others whom you have mockingly patronised, would for the moment think so. As you are not that I don't want to think you are.

After all this you will think me super-sensitive and cowardly perhaps. I'm *not* cowardly, but I am sensitive where you are concerned—

> and am
> Your affectionate friend,
> Hugh Walpole

Magnanimity came naturally to Hugh. Discussing Maugham's *Cakes and Ale*, he said to me, "I shan't forgive Willie easily. The beggar had drunk my claret!"

The reason I found Hugh unreadable is his *inexactness*. "A flock of angels cut the brilliant air like a wave breaking through mist." What would Macaulay have said if Montgomery had perpetrated this simile? Take that last article Hugh wrote:

> I will confess that I would sacrifice my life, my books, my possessions, everything except my friends if in exchange I might have written *Alice in Wonderland*, Boswell's *Johnson*, *Wuthering Heights*, the best of Hazlitt's Essays, or Hans Andersen's Fairy Tales, and gone down to history as the author of any one of them. The big banging masterpieces are so beyond me that I can't begin to think of myself as author of them, but Dodgson, Boswell, Hans Andersen, even Dickens, seem within chatting distance.

If this means anything it is that Boswell's *Johnson* and *Pickwick* are not "big banging masterpieces". "My mind floats in a kind of summer mist", wrote Hugh in *Roman Fountain*. Exactly! Amanda Ros described Delina Delaney as "sister to cloudy confusion". The moment Hugh took up the pen he became brother to that muddled young woman.

Balzac writes somewhere of "L'honnête artiste, cette infâme médiocrité, ce coeur d'or, cette loyale vie, ce stupide dessinateur, ce brave garçon". Heart of gold, soul of loyalty, tried and trusted friend—Hugh was all these, but the rest of Balzac's judgment would not be too severe. His tragedy was that his fine qualities have nothing to do with being a great novelist. With Desmond and all the other critics I may be mistaken about Hugh's final place in English letters. I *know* that he would not have bated a jot of his generosity, of his simple goodness, to gratify his lifelong ambition. He leaves a gap. His steady blue eyes, his willing smile, his resonant voice, his high scorn, his skill in banter, his sense of fun—all these things had become part of the fabric of literary London.

June 17 *Tuesday*

Leo Pavia has now installed himself in Jock's place. Henceforth I look to find my typing witty, inventive, and in inessentials, wildly inaccurate.

June 18 *Wednesday*

"Yes", I said. "But suppose I start to read Proust *now*, how much of my life shall I have to give up to him?" The Proustian said, "All of it". And for this, frankly, I am not prepared. "The English bishops have been vivacious almost to wonder," writes Fuller, commenting on their lordships' tenacity of life. I want a word for insistence on many-sidedness.

> So many hours must I tend my flock;
> So many hours must I take my rest;
> So many hours must I contemplate;
> So many hours must I sport myself;

How shall a man know all about books, bridge, painting, boxing, music, cricket, golf, horses, the theatre? How shall he be an authority on Proust and Culbertson, Jonathan Wild and Jimmie Wilde, William Morris and Old Tom Morris, Beethoven and Bradman? Were I a *rentier* with nothing to do in life, how still could I hope to know all about surrealism and atonalism, chess-openings and the best order in which to tackle the Lake hills? How make myself master of Proust and the Hackney Stud Book as well?

September 12 *Friday*

Greatness in acting requires a combination of things not all of which are under the artist's control. Enough height and not too much; beauty, or if not beauty, then the power to suggest it; brains and the ability to conceal them; physical health and the nervous system of an ox; indomitable spirit and natural grit; the flair for the right opportunity; luck or the knack of turning bad luck to account; a ruthless capacity to trample on all competing talents; *a complete lack of interest in the drama except in so far as it provides the actor with striking parts.* In addition to all this the great player, male or female, must possess that indefinable something which makes the ordinary man abase himself without knowing why. When, after her performance of Pelléas in Maeterlinck's play at the Theatre Royal, Manchester, Sarah Bernhardt walked through the winter garden of the Midland Hotel supported by two Florentine lackeys, hard-headed cotton manufacturers who had never heard of her stood up and removed their bowler hats, and common stockbrokers, abashed and open-mouthed, left their stories in the air.

October 8 *Wednesday*

For some unexplained reason I feel well to-day, but really well, as I used to feel in the summer holidays when I was a boy. I feel that I could go out and fight a battle, without worrying over much whether I should come back. I have always understood and sympathised with Spintho's remark in *Androcles and the Lion*, which I quote from memory: "I mean to die in the arena like a martyr and go to heaven. But not to-day. Not until my nerves are better."

December 31 Wednesday

When I handed over my affairs to Stanley Rubinstein I assessed my liabilities at £2 200. Here is a letter from S. R. showing how wide of the actual mark I was:

> 5 & 6 *Raymond Buildings*
> *Gray's Inn*
> *London W.C.*1
> 30*th December* 1941.

DEAR JIMMIE,

When I took over your affairs at the outbreak of war you were in debt to 52 private creditors, 2 moneylenders, the Bank, your horse account, and the Revenue for arrears of income tax and surtax—roughly £5 000.

The road has been rough and hard—but (mixing the metaphors) I perceive calmer waters ahead, and I have great pleasure (and pride) in telling you that I have paid off all your private creditors, both the money lenders, the Bank, and surtax up to date. All you owe now is the balance of your horse account (they're eating your head off), and arrears of income tax. In other words I have reduced your indebtedness from £5 000 to just over £1 500—and you've lived!

> Yours,
> STANLEY

P.S. A Happy, Peaceful and Prosperous New Year.

P.P.S. Would you like to take over the management of *my* affairs and try and be as clever!

1942

New Year Resolutions

1. To refrain from saying witty, unkind things, unless they are really witty and irreparably damaging.
2. To tolerate fools more gladly, provided this does not encourage them to take up more of my time.
3. To be more patient with Leo. To bear with that all-pervading aroma of stale Vapex, those scented yet acrid plugs, twists, and flakes, that October-to-March sniffling and snuffling, the sneezing and coughing with which he draws attention to himself whenever I am telephoning, the eternal jeremiads, and the physical clumsiness which, one day last week, caused the

following incident. Too blind to see whether the fire was alight
or not, he lifted a live coal in his fingers, found it was hot, and
let it roll under the piano ten feet away where it burned a hole
in my carpet the size of a five-shilling piece. And then the typing!
At this very moment Lady Macbeth looks up at me from my
desk and intones:

"O, never shall son that moral sea!"

Today, January 2nd, 1942, I resolve henceforth to tolerate all this,
and to set against it the feast of malice, the flow of wit, and the fine
temper of the musician who, when he has driven me half frantic, will
go to the piano and play Beethoven more Beethovenishly than any
living virtuoso, sing in a cracked voice the *tuttis* to the concertos, and
improvise his own cadenzas.

January 11 Sunday

The Jews are often blamed for that ostentation which is merely the
expression of their lavish hospitality. This is unfair. Some of the
hospitality is shrewd, but a great deal of it is pure generosity. Edgar
Cohen, the father of Madeleine, who for thirty years kept open house
in St John's Wood, when remonstrated with for not knowing half his
guests, would say, "I shall worry if I know them! If they come to see
me, good. If they come for a meal, also good. Much I shall care what
they come for."

Louis Sterling, who every Sunday evening before the last war used
to entertain from thirty to fifty uninvited guests, said much the same
thing to me today. "If they come to see me, they are my friends;
if they come for the food, perhaps they need it."

January 22 Thursday

Telegram:

THANK YOU INDEED FOR YOUR MAGNIFICENT AND GENEROUS REVIEW
OF MY WORK STOP MAY I CONTINUE TO DESERVE IT OF YOU AND THE
PUBLIC STOP GARRICK IS MY YARD-STICK HE HAD VERSATILITY AND A
ROUND FACE TOO STOP WARMEST REGARDS—DONALD WOLFIT.

Here is a player who, in the last four years, two of these being war
years, has played the Fox in Ben Jonson's *Volpone*, Giovanni in Ford's
'Tis Pity She's a Whore, and appeared under his own management as
Othello, Bottom, Shylock, Richard III, and Hamlet. Probably the
list could be extended, but it's enough. It is owing to Wolfit that for
four weeks in succession, *en pleine guerre*, there have been four revivals

of plays by Shakespeare played to full or nearly full houses. But
this is no reason why the London playgoer should lay flattering unction
to his soul in the matter of improved taste. D. W.'s manager telephoned me this morning to say that at each and every performance
Czechs, Poles, Norwegians, Belgians, and French had accounted for
50 per cent of the audience and sometimes 75 per cent. "The rest have
been Jews; had we relied on the Christians we should have played to
empty benches." All the same I don't like Wolfitt's Hamlet. Indeed, I
disapproved so greatly of what I saw yesterday that I sat down round
about midnight and again wrote my notice by hand, which I do only
when I am excited. Finished at 2 A.M. and shall print the thing as it
stands. Highly pleased with the conceit that D. W.'s round face
"bespeaks as much melancholy as a small boy at the pantomime
extasié'd by Monsewer Eddie Gray." There are lots of fine things in
Wolfit's performance, and I have given him credit for them. But it
isn't Hamlet.

January 26 *Monday*

From an unknown correspondent who has dug the following out
of the *European Magazine* for 1787, and suggests that it is the perfect
Damon Runyon story:

EVERET *v.* WILLIAMS
Suit instituted by Everet for an account of partnership profits

The bill stated that the Plaintiff was skilled in dealing in several
commodities such as plate rings watches &c., that the Defendant
applied to him to become a partner: that they entered into partnership, and it was agreed that they should equally provide all sorts
of necessaries such as horses saddles bridles, and equally bear all
expenses on the roads and at inns taverns ale-houses markets and
fairs: that the Plaintiff and the Defendant proceeded jointly in the
said business with good success on Hounslow Heath, where they
dealt with a gentleman for a gold watch; and afterwards the
Defendant told the Plaintiff that Finchley in the County of
Middlesex was a good and convenient place to deal in, and
commodities were very plenty at Finchley, and it would be almost
all clear profit to them; that they went accordingly, and dealt
with several gentlemen for divers watches rings swords canes hats
cloaks horses bridles saddles and other things; that about a
month afterwards the Defendant informed the Plaintiff that there
was a gentleman at Blackheath who had a good horse saddle
bridle watch sword cane and other things to dispose of, which he
believed might be had for little or no money; that they accordingly
went, and met with the said gentleman, and after some small
discourse they dealt for the said horse &c.: that the Plaintiff and
the Defendant continued their joint dealings together until

Michaelmas and dealt together at several places, via: Bagshot, Salisbury, Hampstead, and elsewhere to the amount of £2 000 and upwards.

The rest of the bill was in the ordinary form for a partnership account.

The bill was dismissed with costs to be paid by the Counsel who signed it. The Solicitors acting for the Plaintiff were fined £50 each. The Plaintiff and Defendant were hanged.

January 27 Tuesday

Disappointed with Edward G. Robinson in *The Sea Wolf*, a psychological film about a rascally captain with a split mind, whereas I had been looking forward to two hundred lashes in Technicolor.

February 4 Wednesday

Indoors again. Worth while being laid up to have the chance of really reading Haydon's *Autobiography*, hitherto only glanced at. I can't make up my mind how far H. was an artist at heart. There is Hazlitt's:

> I did not think he had failed so much from want of capacity, as from attempting to bully the public into a premature or overstrained admiration of him, instead of gaining ground upon them by improving on himself; and he now felt the ill effects of the reaction of this injudicious proceeding. He had no real love of his art, and therefore did not apply or give his whole mind sedulously to it; and was more bent on bespeaking notoriety beforehand by puffs and announcements of his works, than on giving them that degree of perfection which would ensure lasing reputation.

As against this we must set Haydon's prayers, the sum of which is less "Let me be a great painter", than "Let Art be great in my time, and let me be her chief minister".

Has the irony of Haydon's end been sufficiently noticed? I do not mean that he found it necessary both to cut his throat *and* blow out his brains. Consider that the final act was brought about by the failure of his two vast canvases—the *Banishment of Aristides* and *Nero playing his Lyre while Rome is burning*. To exhibit these he had hired a room in the Egyptian Hall. But alas, another room had been taken in the same hall by, of all people, General Tom Thumb! The public flocked to see the modern oddity and left the heroes of antiquity severely alone, and in this manner was giantism vanquished by a dwarf. I like to think that Haydon threw up the sponge in a moment of pique, that he was spared the anguish of realising that he was not, had never been and could never be, a great painter. Of the second string to his bow—his genius as a diarist—he was unconscious. It is by his *Auto-biography* that he lives. Woe to other Diarists who have no master-piece in another art to fall back upon!

February 7 Saturday

Dickens Fellowship Luncheon. Mr Wemmick did some conjuring tricks, Miss Skiffins sang "in a trifling lady-like amateur manner that compromised none of us", and just before I got up to speak, the Aged, complete with ear-plugs, batteries, and sounding-boards, established himself in the vacant angle of the T-table just under my nose.

Told them how Dickens was obsessed by Shakespeare, and that Macbeth was his King Charles's head. Steerforth, shaking off his depression, says, "Why, being gone, I am a man again. And now for dinner, if I have not, Macbeth-like, broken up the feast with most admired disorder, Daisy." The shade of the young Canterbury butcher whom David defeated after throwing away the late Miss Larkin's faded flower rises in his memory "like the apparition of an armed head in *Macbeth*". Miss Tox's "most domesticated and confidential garments hung like Macbeth's banners on the outward wall". At the wedding of Florence Dombey and Walter Gay "The Amens of the dusty clerk appear, like Macbeth's, to stick in his throat a little". And how Hall Caine suggested that *Edwin Drood* is Shakespeare's tragedy all over again with the substitution of Jasper for Macbeth, Drood for Duncan, Neville Landless for Malcolm, and Rosa Budd for the crown of Scotland.

Ended by reading them an extract from John Coleman's account of the Farewell Dinner to Macready organised by Dickens.

March 30 Monday

At the end of my lunch with Ernest Helme the other day I asked him to let me have a résumé of what he had said. He promised, and here it is:

> *Catalani.* Catalani was the most famous soprano of her day, was the possessor of a voice of phenomenal range, and was engaged for a musical festival at Winchester for the *Messiah*; being very much a *prima donna assoluta*, she selected the arias of the other soloists and had them transposed to suit her voice. *Comfort ye* as well as *Why do the Nations* were so treated. But this was not all; Monsieur Valabrègue, her husband, proceeded to demand the fees of the remaining soloists, and on the festival committee remonstrating, is said to have rejoined "Et pourquoi pas? C'est ma femme, et les autres ne sont que des poupées."

Madge Kendal. I well recollect the agitation aroused by the fact that, as Lady Gay Spanker, Mrs Kendal lifted her green riding habit up to within a few inches of the top of her riding boots, which she gently tapped with her riding whip. Never was there a more astute bit of theatrical business. The réclame was enormous; first in London amongst the Victorian matrons, and next in the provinces, where houses were sold out. The Canons' wives were rocked with curiosity at this hint of impropriety on the part of one always held to be the legitimate successor to the dear Queen's beloved Helen Faucit. The manoeuvre was the sole topic of conversation in the Close of each cathedral city visited by her company, and the County was divided as to whether its blushing daughters should be taken to the theatre on the evenings when *London Assurance* was to be played.

April 4 Saturday

Baffled more than ever by that odd creature, Leo Pavia, who drinks the drains of other people's tea-cups, puts the butt-ends of my cigars into his pipe, and at the Café Royal the other day, seeing that a total stranger at the next table proposed to leave a leg of chicken, stuck his fork into it, and, transferring it to his plate, snarled, "I disapprove of waste". I have been looking recently at his "Journal", a quarter-of-a-million-word haggis informed by a spite, rancour, and venom unequalled in my reading. As the reader guesses, the best of it is unprintable and unquotable, besides furnishing the Courts with enough libel actions for twenty years. I have advised him that in the unlikely event of his book being published, he should call it by some such name as *Contortions and Grimaces*. Here are a few extracts described by Leo as "harmless":

INTAGLIO

Deux Bangeuses. Sophie Menter played with such force that she hardly left a hammer intact. I remember an amusing caricature in the *World* depicting the pianist performing with her usual ferocious expression, hair falling down, boots burst asunder, and keys and piano strings flying in all directions including the faces of the audience in flight.

Equally vigorous was Teresa Carreño, who was also a pugilist, and nearly murdered her three husbands. She made such a noise that no one could stay in the same room, and guests were invited on to another floor. Her recitals at St James's Hall were unsuccessful at first, because people became stone-deaf. Afterwards hardly anybody appeared at all, a great crowd gathering in Regent Street, people having discovered that one could hear the Señora quite as well from there without having to pay for admission. Finally, the matter was adjusted, and when the Señora gave a recital in St James's Hall, the audience was accommodated in the Bechstein Hall.

New Material about Goya. Kathi Klosettuch, a blue-stocking in the best Hôtel de Rambouillet tradition, tells me of an interesting meeting at a refugee concert with an old Spanish painter of some repute, whose father knew Goya intimately. "A most delightful old man, this Spaniard. His name is Don Sierra de Garbanzos y Tortadilla, and he claims to be the stepson of Pablo Cantankeranos. He told me that Goya in his old age conceived a passion for English jam, and would often drop large flakes of this sticky compound on to his pantaloons. Don Sierra's father noticed how fond the children of Madrid were of the old painter, and how they would clamour to sit on his knees. But there was always so much jam on them, and indeed, on the front and back of his coat as well, that the little dears found it impossible to detach themselves, and thus Goya could often be seen walking round the Sol des Guergas with adhesive infants sticking to every part of his body. This story interested me hugely, as I can find no mention of it in any of the Official Biographies, neither in Tortas de Hombres, nor Schreinacher, nor the new book on Goya by François Poteloptoptopemos." I congratulated the Fraulein on the dexterity with which she pronounced this last. She said, "But it's on everybody's tongue."

Sexual Aberrations. Are you interested in Sexual Aberrations? Of course you are, if you are an ordinary, normal, clean-minded Briton. Well, I have just finished reading a German book on the subject; it is called *Die nervosen Storungen des geschlechtlichen Adernsystems*. It is by Dr Hans Pfitzermann, and was published in Berlin in 1936. Among the interesting cases are those of the young Czech poetess who would run for hours after old men with no teeth, Klara N——, the Munich mannequin who was excited by chewing match-boxes, the Hungarian Baroness three times arrested for attacking young men in the street with a horse-whip dipped in vitriol, and the forty-year-old chef, Karl Schutz of Lübeck, who was so much obsessed by tennis balls that he served them as *oeufs à la cocotte*. And, of course, the astounding case of Johanna Leschauer, a nurse in Leipzig, who murdered and ate seven of her lovers within six months. She confessed that the wild ecstasies which the devouring of these caused her were as nothing compared to the thought of eating her own dead body. "It is difficult to see," adds Dr Pfitzermann, "how she hoped to accomplish this." Most interesting of all, perhaps, is the case of the lion-fetishist. Dr Magnus Brausesalz, the eminent brain-specialist, was in the habit of giving lectures at which visitors with some problem to solve were received. The Doctor said on one of these occasions, "I have an interesting case in my waiting-room." Whereupon he called the patient, and a bespectacled little man appeared and was introduced as Dr X., Professor of Egyptology at the University of Klopstock. The Professor said, "Gentlemen, I am a Zoophilist. I love lions. From my earliest youth I have been attracted by lions. When I go to a Zoological Gardens and watch the lions I . . . but perhaps I need not particularise." At this point Dr Brausesalz, who was not famous for his sense of humour, interrupted: "I should point out, *meine Herren*, that this predilection of the Professor has up to the present been singularly devoid of reciprocity."

April 27 Monday

Marie Tempest about again after her illness, and holding court at the Ivy. When the time comes my old friend will *act* the twenty-third chapter of *Villette*. I remember a commemoration luncheon some ten or twelve years ago after the public had refused to flock to see her in *Mr Pim Passes By*. It was a brilliant performance, but alas, the public passed it by! The point is simply that the familiar is the enemy both of the worse and the better. An actor or actress who makes a real success in a part, and provided that part be not of the grand order, makes that part his or hers for life. No player can monopolise Hamlet: but whoever first plays, say, Aubrey Tanqueray, bags him for good. George Alexander may or may not have been a good actor, but while he lived his was the first and last Mr Tanqueray. The partakers of the funeral baked meats that day were three: Marie Tempest, Graham Browne, and myself. She wept, he wept, and I wept, until the *Caneton à la Mauvaise Presse* was a wet and soggy business. At last one of us spoke, and he said, "My dear Mary, if you were three times better than Irene Vanbrugh you wouldn't be half so good!" Whereupon Mary mopped an eye which had never been really wet, smiled bravely with the other, and said that, after all, everybody *at the beginning of their careers* must expect reverses. She was sixty-five then. The luncheon ended in extreme gaiety.

June 5 Friday

From a review of *Here's Richness!** in a publication called *Shell Magazine*:

> If provocativeness in a writer is a sign of talent, then Mr James Agate is as gifted as he gives the impression of thinking himself to be, for I know of no modern essayist, critic, and journalist who is capable of affording so much annoyance to so many by the expression of so few really significant thoughts.

That's Shell, that was!

June 6 Saturday

John Gielgud was anxious, even insistent, that I should not write in the *S.T.* about last night's performance, on the ground that he is tired, the cast has had casualties, and the production is about to go into dry-dock prior to London. I promised, telling him that *I* was tired, but with a

---

* An anthology of and by James Agate, with a foreword by Osbert Sitwell (Harrap, 1942).

mental reservation about *Ego*. And so behaved exactly like the Witches "That keep the word of promise to our ear, And break it to our hope!" John will never be happy vocally with Macbeth; his voice is neither deep enough nor resonant enough. But what sheer acting ability can do, he does. His is the only Macbeth I have ever seen who has kept it up all the way through; the last act, where most of them fall down, is superb. In the lounge before lunch Gwen sought to show by metaphysical X, Y, and Z that Lady Macbeth is a frail little thing, all nervous energy and no physique. Lady M. can't contemplate a murder without taking something to steady her nerves. ("That which hath made them drunk hath made me bold.") She can't carry one through and has to invent an excuse. ("Had he not resembled my father as he slept, I had done't.") She is given to fainting and sleep-walking, and cracks up in the end. All very persuasive, and I don't believe a word of it. I don't and won't see Lady M. as a kind of Rosa Dartle. If I can't have Mrs Siddons give me Mrs Vincent Crummles. The vast Pavilion was crowded. Many were service men, some of whom had to leave before the end. It was still bright day, and each time a soldier crept out, the golden sunlight peeped through the blanket of the dark.

July 3 *Friday*

To the Proms with Gwen Chenhalls. Superb performance of the *Symphonie Fantastique*, grandly conducted by Basil Cameron. But why didn't Berlioz end the symphony with the "Marche au Supplice"? Sheer composer's vanity, of course, and some nonsense about finishing the story. Also because, like Wagner, he had no sense of the point at which, in the hearer, saturation is reached. The "Marche" is one of the most final things in music, in the sense of bringing a work to an end; there is no more going beyond it than you can go beyond the buffers at Euston Station. The "Ronde du Sabbat", immensely fine though it is, must always be an anticlimax, since not even genius can end a work twice. But no. Berlioz was the victim of his own *idée fixe*, and because he could twist and turn his theme still further, we must stay to listen. In my view he should have added a bit to this pretended last movement and turned it into a symphonic poem on the same theme.

July 10 *Friday*

Here is what I am saying on Sunday about the revival of Macbeth:

> Shakespeare in this play set Mr Gielgud, the actor, a problem which he proceeded to solve as nearly as it admitted of solution; Mr Gielgud, the producer, wilfully, and with his eyes open, set himself another problem which he did not solve—the actress to lead with him. Walkley divided actresses into mouseys-pouseys

and roguey-pogueys: I will never rank Lady Macbeth among the teenie-weenies.

The first poser was the old difficulty of reconciling Ross's description of Macbeth as "Bellona's bridegroom" with the hag-ridden neurotic. Mr Gielgud failed here, as every Macbeth worth seeing must fail, Nature not having seen fit to endow cart-horses with the nervous system of thoroughbreds, or successful generals with a genius for the introspective. Heaven protect us from the Macbeth who strides on to the stage like Kitchener at Omdurman, and for the rest of the evening barks the poet's lines as though they were words of command in an Aldershot review. Mr Gielgud did his audience at the Piccadilly the courtesy of pretence; he gave Macbeth at his first entry a swashing and martial outside, though low in tone, gaunt and sombre like an El Greco. Having discharged the formal reply to his sovereign, and with the gloriously delivered "Stars, hide your fires," Mr Gielgud dropped the warrior and bent up each corporal and intellectual agent to the terrible feat of interpreting the most poetic of all murderers. He spoke the verse beautifully throughout, and was, I thought, particularly fine in the Dagger soliloquy, and the "Seeling night" and "To-morrow" speeches. Of the last, one would repeat what Mr Maurice Baring wrote about another player: "One felt that for the perfect utterance of beautiful words this was the Pillars of Hercules of mortal achievement."

But to speak Macbeth beautifully is not to act him fully; the actor still fails who is content with being *profond et rêveur* in the Lemaître manner. Mr Gielgud was not thus content. His collapse immediately after the murder was a masterpiece of nerves well matched by the truly magnificent virtuosity of the Banquet Scene, where the actor went all out. Contrary to most Macbeths, with whom going all out means petering out the rest of the way, Mr Gielgud went on to finer achievement in the immensely difficult Apparition Scene, and overtopped this by holding together those final fragments where, if anybody is in danger of going to pieces, it is Shakespeare. All of this shows the command by the actor of immense reserves of nervous force, to which one must add imaginative control. Too often the short-long speech about the "yesting waves" is a mere gabble; Mr Gielgud united the winds very much as three nights previously we had heard Sibelius untie them in the Prelude to *The Tempest*. If not the whole of Macbeth, then "a piece of him", as Horatio would say.

I think it is Goethe who maintains that the play ought to have been called *Lady Macbeth*. Which, of course, settles the Lady's size. If that is not enough, there is our old friend the *optique du théâtre* which in this case I should prefer to call *l'optique du sens commun*. There is no law of Nature which ordains that in real life murderesses shall not be little women and bad wives, and it can be plausibly argued that the soul of a Goneril is fittingly encased in the body of a Miss Mowcher. On the stage such a Goneril would not look right, any more than a strapping Cordelia or a plain Juliet would look right. *And that is all there is to it.* Miss Ffrangcon-Davies is a delightful actress in comedy whom we last

saw as Gwendolen in Wilde's farce. But could she have swelled
to the overpowering architecture of Gwendolen's Mamma? I
think not. And if not Lady Bracknell, then a hundred times not
Lady Macbeth. She does not fill the eye. The question is not one
of mere inches; Rachel had very few more than Miss Davies. But
the deep tones in which the French actress delivered Phèdre's
apostrophe to the sun

> Soleil! je te viens voir pour la dernière fois—

are part of theatrical history; they are the tonës which Lady Macbeth
must use for her

>   O, never
> Shall sun that morrow see!

Miss Davies's light mezzo-contralto simply hasn't got these tones;
with her the observation is merely barometric. Scorn is the deepest
note in this actress's register; scorn accompanied by an expression
of faint disgust. She can neither speak daggers nor look them. I am
compelled to say of this Lady Macbeth that which, changing the
pronouns, Lewes said of Macready's Thane: "She was irritable
where she should have been passionate, querulous where she should
have been terrible." In place of the master mind, the nagging spouse;
so that one questioned whether the likes of 'er would have succeeded
in putting it over the likes of 'im. More Shakespeareanly, "Nought's
had, all's spent" sums up a clever, well-thought-out, and always
courageous tackling by a gifted actress who is not a tragédienne
of a part which makes the maximum call on tragic implementation.

Mr Nicholas Hannen bestows upon Duncan the Maeterlinckian
quality of sweetness in old age. Mr Leon Quartermaine endows
Banquo with a beautiful honesty, and Mr Francis Lister gives
Macduff his full pathos. Mr George Woodbridge's Porter is
allowed to indulge in caperings which hint that this play is the
next to be taken in the balletomane's ravishing stride. If this is so,
I suggest that whoever is interested should borrow Messrs Ayrton
and Minton's scenery and Mr Walton's music, and get it over.

The plain truth of the matter is that John ought not to have offered
Ffrangcon-Davies the part, and, alternatively that she should have had
the strength of mind to refuse it.

July 14 *Tuesday*

From James Bridie:

At 3 *Camstradden Drive East,*
Bearsden,
Dumbartonshire,
July 13, 1942

DEAR JAMES AGATE,

In your abstract and brief chronicle of Gielgud's Macbeth I think that you record a piece of History that will mislead Posterity. You may be right and I would not go so far as to say that you are wrong, especially as everybody seems to agree with you, but you have missed an essential point about Gwen Davies's Lady Macbeth. There is nothing whatever in the text that makes Lady M. a giantess with the face of a horse. It is one of these foolish tumours that grow on the stage, that tradition. I shouldn't be surprised if Fielding was trying to kill it in *Tom Thumb the Great.* On the contrary, the Woman is a correct Pictish heroine. How Shakespeare invented her with what must have been a very superficial knowledge of Picts I do not know. The fact remains that his creation fits a picture very familiar to anyone who has lived in the Highlands or read their stories and legends.

Gwen is a Pict and everything she said and did and felt was, as far as I can judge, absolutely authentic and very frightening indeed. These little blackavised things, who never have a grey hair in their heads when they are eighty and smile with their mouths only and could charm the sea-water heart out of a jellyfish, have, among other things, a burning fire of loyalty in their bodies that burns up all common decency and ruth. Prince Charlie, who was a dead loss and a wet smack, was never given up by the Highlanders because they knew that their wives would poison them most politely at the first sign of funny business—and would not let them know by a flicker of an eyelid that they had suspected anything. They are very subtle and full to the neck of the most peculiar emotions. They manoeuvre and cheat these emotions, too, in the extraordinary way. Have a look at Pegeen Mike and the Widow Quin. Neither of them is Lady Macbeth, but you can't understand Lady Macbeth without knowing them.

"And your point, Mr Russell?" My point is that Gwen is the first actress I have ever seen or read of to give us a real Highland Lady Macbeth, subtle, hysterical and bloody and restrained, and it is a pity that she has had no credit for it. All this may be in the eye of the beholder, but I don't think so. I thought I'd tell you.

With the kindest regards,

Sincerely yours,
JAMES BRIDIE

My reply:

10 *Fairfax Road*
*N.W.*6
July 20, 1942

DEAR BRIDIE,

Your letter has given me extraordinary pleasure without
carrying the least conviction. It is, like everything of yours, well
and subtly argued. But it is based on the absurd supposition that
Shakespeare cared two pins about ethnology. The string-pulling
Lady Macbeth may in real life have looked like Graham Moffat's
Bunty, but I don't believe Shakespeare saw her as anything of the
kind. I remember standing with George Bishop on the deck of a
steamer going down the Mediterranean. Presently we sighted the
featureless strip of land which is Tangier. George said, "Not my
notion of Africa!" Gwen's Lady Macbeth is not my notion of the
character, and I feel in my bones that it was not Shakespeare's.
Even if right racially it is wrong dramatically. As a dramatist
you must know that Shakespeare is not reconstructing a Highland
crime for the benefit of a Highland coroner, but writing a play
about Scotland for the delectation of a London audience. It is
quite possible that the real Lady M. never betrayed anything by
the flicker of an eyelid. But what, pray, has that do do with her
stage counterpart? The stage Lady Macbeth asking the spirits to
unsex her, thicken her blood, take her milk for gall, and all the
rest of it, must look as though she meant it. I don't say Gwen
didn't mean it. I could see her trying to mean it. But she didn't
convince me that Lady M. was meaning it; she just hadn't the
voice and look to mean it with. "In each of her eyes sat a devil."
Charlotte Brontë could never have said this of Gwen.

I don't demand that Lady M. should be a "giantess with the
face of a horse." But I insist that she fill the mind, and it helps if
the actress can begin by filling the eye. Charlotte Brontë's Vashti
was "but a frail creature." Yet we read: "As the action rose and
the stir deepened how wildly they (the evil forces) shook her with
their passions of the pit! They wrote HELL on her straight, haughty
brow. They tuned her voice to the note of torment. They writhed
her regal face to a demoniac mask. Hate and Murder and Madness
incarnate she stood." This, all but the madness, is what Lady
Macbeth should be. I found none of it in Gwen's performance.
Please don't deduce from this that I think poorly of a very clever
player. Hazlitt writes: "Of Miss Campbell's Lady Macbeth we are
almost afraid to speak, because we cannot speak favourably of it;
yet a failure in this part is by no means decisive against the general
merits of an actress." This goes for Gwen too.

But enough about Lady M. I thought I should have got into
more trouble with you over her better half. Macbeth must always
give both actor and critic a lot of trouble. He is a soldier whose
springs of action have been weakened by excess of imagination.
He is rotten as a pear is rotten.

> Then comes my fit again: I had else been perfect,
> Whole as the marble, founded as the rock . . .

applies not only to his fears but to his attacks of poetry, after which he returns to his action-plot just as your recovered epileptic will go about his ordinary business. In all my experience I have only seen two Macbeths who combined the warrior with the poet. Benson did it by throwing together his Henry V and Richard II. Whether he knew what he was up to I don't know; he was the best Macbeth I ever saw. Next was old William Mollison, who alternated dourness with a habit of going off into trances; it was as though some spiritualist medium had taken control. I have it from his son William, the producer, that this was exactly what his father intended. Your ideal Macbeth is a man of action breaking down into the poet almost as science tells us that matter breaks down. Now Gielgud is never a soldier. He is a poet first and last, who from time to time remembers that he must build himself up into a soldier. An exquisite performance, not quite right. And never can be. Again a matter of physical limitations. I think Quartermaine's Banquo is the best I have ever seen.

From your old friend

JAMES AGATE

July 15 *Wednesday*

An extract from Jock's notice in *Time and Tide* of *The Man who came to Dinner*. I heard rumours of this at the time, but did not see the article.

Sheridan Whiteside is a roaring, tearing monster of a petted and pampered dramatic critic. He is a hurly-burly of a man, too witty to be wise, kind by fits and starts but unkind continuously, and as designing as any boy of five caught near a pantry door. His friends dread him, and his enemies make allowances for him. Early in life he has discovered that he possesses charm, and he uses this mysterious power to elaborately illicit purpose, cowing secretaries, dispelling duns, and warding off all decent obligations. He manages it shrewdly. He uses it to temper his harshness, condescension, prevarications, or sheer insults. He turns it, at will, into wheedling, cajolery, and a gift for making his satellites do things against their own desire and, of course, to his own advantage. He has a peculiar talent for making those he has wronged feel mean about not forgiving him. He has a genius for eating his cake and still having it. He adores tripping up anybody and everybody. He is malicious, yet somehow too big to be quite petty. He is easy to malign, but never sufficiently maligned. He is an odd and impossible, yet perfectly human and quite irresistible compound of Skimpole and Quilp and Mr Micawber. He somehow obtains everything in life—nay, life itself—at a considerable discount, and he somehow makes all those feel base and common who dare to grudge him the lordly privilege. He is too small in one sense to be called truly great in any sense. He is exactly what Ellen Terry meant when she called D'Annunzio a "great little fellow". His writings amuse half the world, and set the other half by the ears. He is a vulgar exquisite, an exquisite vulgarian. He is a living, breathing, writing, talking paradox; a pest and a menace, a pest and a delight. He is, in short, as like as life to Mr Alexander Woollcott or to his English counterpart on the *Sunday Times*.

EGO 6

August 1942–December 1943

August 21 *Friday*

Fatras. A correspondent avers that in a novel by Ouida he has discovered this passage: "Entering her palatial music-room filled with all kinds of instruments, Eloise sat down at a spinet incrusted with lapis lazuli and silver, and flooded the room with the rich, voluptuous strains of Wagner's *Tristan and Isolde.*"

September 3 *Thursday*

"The President of the Immortals, in Æschylean phrase, had ended his sport with Tess." "Come, children, let us shut up the box and the puppets, for our play is played out." Let who will prate of Hardy's and Thackeray's famous endings. My vote goes to the more modern "He went to live at Wolverhampton and died of cirrhosis of the liver."

September 4 *Friday*

Let women write on subjects they know about. I do not want to read some Wimbledon spinster's views on the amours of a Spanish bull-fighter any more than I want to hear from a Swedish miss about the love-life of an Arsenal centre-forward. The play to-night was all about British saboteurs in France, at the end of which a glamorous authoress came forward. Afterwards to the Café Royal, where at the next table sat two young American airmen arrived in England the same day. One of them leaned over to me and said, "Say, buddy, d'ya think we could take a coupla women to our hotel?" I asked what hotel they were staying at, and he mentioned one of the most respectable hostelries in London. I told him they could not possibly do such

159

a thing. "Aw," says airman No. 2, "don't get us wrong. We don't mean a coupla women each!" Perhaps some young woman would like to write a war play about American airmen?

September 8 Tuesday

A sergeant air-gunner writes: "I don't suppose you have spent eighteen months in a desert. Or sat in a gun-turret for four hundred and fifty hours, eight hours at a stretch. Or been shot down and wounded. If you had, perhaps you would take a more kindly view of the enclosed poem." I have replied: "No, I shouldn't. Your poem, badly rhymed and worse scanned, did its job when it took your mind off the desert and the gun-turret. Having done this, it became waste paper."

September 18 Friday

"I told you so" is impermissible only when a catastrophe is calamitous, not, I hold—using "catastrophe" in its dramatic sense—when it is triumphant. Readers of *Ego* 5 may remember how I came to be interested in Pamela Brown. "But she's amazing!" said everybody after the first act of *Claudia* last night, and again at the fall of the curtain. But I wasn't amazed, being in the position of the chemist who, having poured sulphuric acid on to zinc, isn't surprised to see hydrogen released. I had already seen the flame of Pamela's talent. In the autumn of 1940, at the Oxford Playhouse, I noted a performance of extreme distinction by a young and unknown actress. Her attack, intelligence, and quality generally convinced me that she could play Hedda Gabler. Now the saving grace of a repertory company is that it will listen; your commercial manager has ears only for finance. I proposed the play, Eric Dance gallantly acceded, and six weeks later the new Hedda was launched and received great praise from the principal London critics. But did any London manager inquire further? I heard of none. I tried to get the piece transferred to town for a matinée. The company was eager. Dance offered to sacrifice the evening's receipts and I pointed out that, any modern set serving, there would be no expenses except the front of the house and a man to pull the curtain up and down. The managers refused to listen. They went on with the old game of wringing their hands and deploring the lack of new talent. The newcomer has the *petite frimousse éveillée* which was Sarcey's way of describing Réjane's departure from conventional good looks. She has great gift of facial expression, and when she feels emotion can show it, and the kind of emotion. When she must express grief she does not, as more trumpeted discoveries have done, bury her head in a cupboard. Her acting possesses both pace and variety. It is good enough to stand up to a heroine who is a tiresome combination of the innocent in Besant and Rice's *Golden Butterfly*, Ibsen's Nora, and Bret Harte's M'liss, to which is added a strong infusion of mother-complex. *Now*, perhaps, some manager will give us a play that can stand up to Pamela. Why not a matinée of *Hedda*? I should not dream of suggesting a run for this masterpiece unless one could entice the public with a cast including Deanna Durbin as General Gabler's daughter, Harpo Marx as Tesman, Bing Crosby as Lövborg, and W. C. Fields as Judge Brack!

September 29 Tuesday

Leo amused us with a story about Hans von Bülow, who once travelled to Birmingham to rehearse the Emperor Concerto with a well-known orchestra. Bülow, always like a Prussian general, said "Begin!" Whereupon the orchestra gave out the first chord of E flat. "Now the tutti," commanded the pianist. "But, Herr von Bülow," remonstrated the conductor, "you haven't played your solo before the tutti yet." "Bah," said von Bülow, "I do not come to hear how *I* play; I come to hear how *you* play!"

November 3 Tuesday

The last three days taken up in reading *Sodome et Gomorrhe*. This is the only book of Proust's into which I have not dipped at one time or another, and when I found a beautiful copy (Knopf) at the Chenhalls's I determined to make a frontal attack. I know now that I shall never be a Proustian, though perfectly remembering how Walkley declared the first two books had given him "more pleasure than anything in modern French". I recognise the genius of Proust and marvel at his craftsmanship; a blind man reading him in Braille would be dazzled. Yet he does not hold me as Balzac holds me. The snobbery? Rather like those dinner-parties at Eaton Gate, when Monty Shearman would suddenly recover his social sense and say to Maurice Ingram, "Yes, yes, Maurice, but tell me about your Ambassador's wife afterwards. James isn't interested," and turn to me and ask if I had seen any exciting cricket at Lord's recently. (More and more I miss Monty's never-failing sympathy and counsel.) The hypocrisy about Albertine? I just cannot be bothered to read "him" for "her" six times a page. When I knew Albert he was, I suppose, about fifty, and had acquired a certain saturnine distinction. He told me, a year or so after Proust's death, that he had some four hundred letters from him "which, when it rains, will keep me". But it never rained. "Monsieur Albert est mort," I was told the next time I went to Paris, "d'une pneumonie féroce."

November 20 *Friday*

Jock showed me a delightful review of *Ego 5* in the *Manchester Guardian*. After comparing me with Nero and Pepys, the review concludes:

> It is a poor heart that cannot find diversion from the gloom of the time in the aesthetic amours and vendettas which he continues to pursue with all the swagger of Cyrano, something of the irony of Swift, and that sure feeling for certain sorts of perfection that is his prime claim upon an audience.

At last a reviewer who sees what I'm after! Get home to find in the *Daily Telegraph*: "There is a lot about dull people." What the inexact fellow means is: "He writes uninterestingly about lively and exciting people." But he doesn't say this and so I pink him, very much as I did his predecessor two years ago:

> The *Telegraph*
> (Don't make me laugh)
> Holds that Baring, Beecham, Beerbohm, Belloc, Bridie, Cocteau,
> Coward, Henson, Hicks, Lutyens, Margot, Maugham, Priestley,
> Shaw, Wells, my beloved Rebecca, and some six hundred illustrious
> and witty dead whose names I cull,
> Are dull.

December 7 *Monday*

I really don't care very much whether there is life on Mars or why Hannibal turned back at Cannae. There's nothing logical about the things which puzzle one person and not another. Or even oneself. For example, I care nothing at all whether Wagner's father was or was not a Jew, while desiring immensely to know the answer to the Shake-speare-Bacon riddle. Rossini's idleness intrigues not me: no, nor Congreve's silence neither. But I am practically on fire, as Damon Runyon would say, to know why Rimbaud abjured poetry. I am not in the least anxious to continue *Edwin Drood*, whereas I hanker after more of the *Weir of Hermiston*. I want to know the identity, not of the Man in the Iron Mask but of the Third Murderer in *Macbeth*. I would not cross the road to know whether Mary Queen of Scots connived at the killing of Darnley, but would go all the way to Liverpool to learn who killed Mrs Wallace. To the permanent fascination of the *Marie Celeste* mystery another has been added during the last few days— meaning that I have been dipping into Cyril Foley's *Autumn Foliage*. The mystery is that of Alletson, the Notts cricketer, who in the Notts *v.* Sussex match at Hove, in 1911, during the thirty minutes of cricket which Foley was privileged to see, scored 139 runs. He finished up by making 115 out of 120 in seven overs, hitting Killick for 22 in one over, and 34 (4, 6, 6, 4, 4, 4, 6) in another, there being two no-balls, and scoring 34 off two overs from Leach, or 90 in four overs. The mystery is not how Alletson came to do this but why he never tried to repeat it. Foley writes:

> After these fireworks his appearance at Lord's against Middlesex was eagerly anticipated. An enormous crowd assembled to see him. He certainly made a fair score, including a gigantic drive over the clock, but was otherwise disappointing. From then onwards he retired into his shell and absolutely refused to hit. Later in the season I went to see him at the Oval and happened to sit in the Notts dressing-room next to A. O. Jones, the Notts skipper. "Jonah" was in despair. He said to me, "The man can't be normal. I've told him that I will play him in every match right through the season, even if he makes recurrent cyphers, as long as he will hit, but he just won't do it. You'll see for yourself presently." And I did. In came Alletson with a huge crowd on tiptoe with excitement, and made the most scratchy 11 runs possible. Never once did he attempt to hit the ball. As he was not a bowler he had to be dropped from the side.

What is the psychology of the cricketer, who, knowing that he can hit and knowing also that he will be dropped from the side if he doesn't, refuses to make the attempt? Why should that two-handed engine which was Alletson stand ready to smite once, and smite no more?

December 13 *Sunday*

Andrade did me a witty turn yesterday at the Savage Club. An elderly and obvious bore, a visitor, coming up and saying, "Mr Agate, I generally agree with the things you write in the *Sunday Times*, but today . . . ," Andrade cut him short: "Excuse me, Professor, this is not Mr James Agate, the critic. This is his cousin, Mr William Agate, a stocking manufacturer from Dorking." Whereupon the old gentleman withdrew after profuse apologies. The philosophy of boredom has been insufficiently explored. In my case it is quite simple, and can be put into one sentence: I don't want to talk to anybody unless I can get something in return. I am not like Leo, who will talk to the fronts of empty houses if he can't get people to talk to; in fact, he has been seen in the street doing it. Put Leo in a bar among complete strangers and in ten minutes he is entirely happy. But that is because he is eternally young, and talking to impress is one of the qualities of youth. Whereas I am old and curmudgeonly: I want to be paid for my talking. Most of all I hate conversation about the theatre. When anybody says to me, "What did you think of Gielgud's Macbeth?" my mind goes back to those four days of hard and painful thinking compressed into a column. Am I now to go through the further labour of condensing that column to a sentence which shall express what I think exactly? And this for the benefit of some silly fellow who only wants to misquote it to somebody else.

December 14 *Monday*

Gerald Moore says that if he had his time to come over again he would ask the gods for one gift—that of being unable to play a single note on any instrument. With this asset he feels that he could have climbed to great heights in the world of recording, broadcasting, conducting and musical criticism. He told me how the other day one of the Big Noises at H.M.V. insisted on a passage being played differently. "Show me!" said Gerald, getting up from the piano-stool, whereupon Big Noise perforce collapsed.

1943

January 15 *Friday*

Took the chair at the meeting called by Leslie Henson at the Saville Theatre on behalf of the Opening of Theatres on Sundays. Had Lewis Casson on my right and Will Hay on my left. It was all most amusing and muddle-headed, and I felt like the calm spot in the centre of a vortex in a whirlpool of red herrings. Nobody put forward the essential thing to be debated—that if the general weal demands Sunday opening the profession should acquiesce and arrange its conscience and its business affairs accordingly. In my view actors and actresses who cannot do this should abandon the profession in favour of those who can, and see if they have any better luck as printers, nurses, and everybody else who has to work on Sunday night. I kept this to myself, however, and gave no inkling of which way my sympathies lay.

Some time after midnight a well-known actress rang up. She and her husband were coming round to the Villa Volpone. I tried all sorts of things—including my Sarah record—to keep them off the vexed question. But it was no use, and what, after all, can an elderly critic do when a beautiful woman throws herself at his feet like Mrs Kendal at the feet of Mr Kendal in *The Ironmaster*? They had ordered a taxi for two o'clock, and at half-past I suggested that the driver might like a drink. They acquiesced, after which the lady resumed her impassioned appeal to be allowed to spend Sunday evening darning her husband's socks with her husband looking on. Bed around four.

February 17 *Wednesday*

A passage in *The Merchant of Venice* tonight (Frederick Valk at the New Theatre) struck me as a perfect picture of Leo:

> But hear thee, Gratiano:
> Thou art too wild, too rude, and bold of voice;—
> Parts that become thee happily enough,
> And in such eyes as ours appear not faults;
> But where thou art not known, why there they show
> Something too liberal. Pray thee, take pain
> To allay with some cold drops of modesty
> Thy skipping spirit; lest, through thy wild behaviour,
> I be misconstrued in the place I go to,
> And lose my hopes.

"Skipping spirit" is exactly Leo. Many a time and oft I have taken the old thing to some pie-faced dinner party, promising myself that if he behaves properly at dinner he will be invited to play in the drawing-room afterwards. I generally arrange to sit within frowning distance of the old boy, after which I experience increasing agony. During the earlier stages of the meal he will sit like a model for Humpty Dumpty's Impenetrability, but I know that presently the dam will burst and something will be said which will blow the hostess out of the room. I remember one occasion on which the talk came round to Cora Pearl, and I told the guests how when she played in *La Belle Hélène* her abominable French set the audience on a roar. Somebody saying I was mistaken and that Cora had never appeared on the French stage, Leo could hold himself in no longer. He said, "Of course James is right. She appeared at the Bouffes-Parisiens in 1867, and my dear aunt, who was a great friend of hers, sang in the chorus." At this revelation of low life some of the guests sniffed audibly. But Leo went on: "Some people have said that my aunt was a whore. I deny this. She was not a whore; she had lovers, which is a very different thing. Sometimes one lover, sometimes two. I dislike over-statement. My aunt was never a whore!"

February 25 *Thursday*

Dined with Sir Pelham Warner at the Conservative Club. A man of great charm and with enough modesty to go round a whole room. During dinner I contrived that the talk should all be about cricket. Among other things, P. W. said that he once asked Ranji who in his opinion was the world's greatest batsman. Ranji replied, "On a hard, fiery wicket, W. G., easily. But on all wickets, Charlo." (This was Ranji's name for C. B. Fry.) Warner talked a lot about Fry. How he saw him make his record long-jump, how the measurements were taken over and over again, and how the crowd shouted at the announcement of a world record. He remembered the famous match between Oxford and Blackheath. How Fry could run like a stag, and how if he failed to tackle his man it didn't matter because he could run after him, catch him up, and tackle him again. How in the match against Blackheath Fry outran and out-manoeuvred the opposite backs and scored three tries, grounding the ball each time in the dead centre of the goal posts. How after the match the crowd, cheering, followed him all the way back to Wadham. A lot more talk about the great cricketers of the past. In return for which I told him the story of how I bowled out W. G. Grace first ball. I was seven at the time, and the family was staying, I think, at either Blackpool or Llandudno. I was playing cricket on the sands, and presently a huge man with an immense black beard offered to bowl to me. He did not seem much good at bowling on the soft pitch with a tennis ball, and I hit him all over the place. Being a well-brought-up little boy, I presently asked whether the gentleman would not like an innings, for which purpose, I handed him my tiny bat. I bowled, the ball hit on a flat pebble, and instead of bouncing slithered between the two walking-sticks which were the wickets, the Great Man having played about two feet over it! (He would have ricked his back if he had done anything else.) I remember my father, who was sitting on the promenade pretending to watch, but actually reading the *Manchester Guardian*, laughing a great deal and telling me that I had bowled the world's greatest batsman. Which, let me confess, seemed to me a perfectly natural thing to do. After dinner, we adjourned to the smoking-room, where I thought it only fair to exchange P. W.'s shop for mine, as he is very keen on the theatre. Wherefore I trotted out some of my best anecdotes, and the evening ended all square.

May 30 *Sunday*

Here is something from Ernest's column in the *S.T.*:

> Score-reading is absolutely indispensable, in more ways than one, to anyone to whom listening to music in the concert-room is something more than a sort of ear-bath, anyone who really wants to know what, so to speak, the composer is talking about. The disparagers of score-reading seem to imagine that the pure essence of a work is embodied in the sound of it, with the corollary that when we have heard the sounds we have necessarily heard the work. I propose to try and show that this is pure delusion, that we can hear a given piece of music a hundred times and yet, if we do not know it also from the sight of the notes the composer has put on paper, get no further than the outer rim of his thought.

Which has inspired me to the following one-act drama:

ERNEST AND HIS COOK

Play in One Act

SCENE: *Ernest's dining-room. Evidence of cerebration everywhere. Over the mantelpiece a portrait of "Béla Bartok's Musical Make-up" by Twerpp. On the piano, whose keyboard has been removed, is the score of Jacob Britain's Concertante for bagpipes, foghorn, siren, road-drill, and Wurlitzer, with a marker to tell Ernest where he left off reading. It is lunch-time.*

ERNEST. An excellent pudding, my love.
MRS N. I'm glad you like the flavour.
ERNEST. Flavour? What has flavour to do with it?
MRS N. (*mildly*) Then what is it you like about it, dear?
ERNEST (*testily*) Flavour is mere mouth-wash.
[*Correcting himself*] I should have said tongue-bath. What interests me is the thinking behind the pudding. Pray ask cook to write out her recipes for me in future. I hate getting no further than the outer rim of her culinary thought!

CURTAIN

June 9 Wednesday

I was asked to-night why I refuse to have truck with intellectuals after business hours. But of course I won't. 1. I am not an intellectual. Two minutes' talk with Aldous Huxley, William Glock, or any of the *New Statesman* crowd would expose me utterly. 2. I am too tired after my day's work to man the intellectual palisade. 3. When my work is finished I want to eat, drink, smoke, and relax. 4. I don't know very much, but what I do know I know better than anybody, and I don't want to argue about it. I know what I think about an actor or an actress, and am not interested in what anybody else thinks. My mind is not a bed to be made and re-made.

July 8 Thursday

Letter from Pamela Brown, who has left the cast of *Claudia* through illness kept at arm's length for months:

> Wingfield Hospital
> Headington
> Oxford
> 3rd July, 1943

DEAR MR AGATE,
I write to you because I always write to you when I am taking any kind of step, not that this is exactly a "step" but I felt I'd like to write all the same. I have gone on playing Claudia until I

really ceased to be able to walk, let alone run up and down stairs
and pretend I was nineteen. I should be doing it still, I expect, but
God sent me a temperature of 101½ for no reason at all and the
matter was out of my hands. Sir Arthur Hurst, who is a wise and
wonderful man, got me in here, where they have everything there
is to cure legs that refuse to work. I won't bore you with details,
but I am to have gold injections to cure the bug, and every sort
of device to stop the legs from stiffening up. It may be a longish
job—a matter of months rather than weeks, but I am not coming
out until I am better.

So remember, if all the plays you have to see suddenly seem
boring—and the theatre despair—that Sunday morning is made a
better thing for me because I can read your *Sunday Times* article.
Or am I too bold? Yes I am.

Love from

PAMELA

In reply to which I wrote:

Flat 1
Queen Alexandra Mansions
*Grape St., W.C.*2
July 8*th*, 1943

MY DEAR HEDDA (no, *not* Claudia),

Do you remember Mr Nicodemus Dumps? He comes in *Sketches
by Boz*, the story called *The Bloomsbury Christening*. Dumps is the
godfather of Master Frederick Charles William Kitterbell, and
here is part of the speech he makes at the "sit down supper"
after the ceremony: "I hope and trust, ladies and gentlemen, that
the infant whose christening we have this evening met to celebrate
may not be removed from the arms of his parents by premature
decay: that his young and now *apparently* healthy form may not
be wasted by lingering disease. You, I am sure, will concur with
me in wishing that he may live to be a comfort and a blessing to
his parents. But should he not be what we could wish—should he
forget in after-times the duty which he owes to them—should they
unhappily experience that distracting truth, 'how sharper than a
serpent's tooth it is to have a thankless child. . . .' " In other words,
I do not think that you can look forward to a time when your state
of health will permit you to be whirled about the stage in the manner
of Juanita and the Ganjou Brothers.

Dear Pam, let's face it, you may never return to the stage.
Having squared up to this tragedy—for that it would be—let's
look around and see if we can espy any comfort. I think we can.
I'm not going to tell you that victories are not always won on
battlefields. You are an artist, and any consolation to be found
for you must be such as befits an artist. Very well, then, I am not
discouraged.

I foresaw all this at Oxford. I said to myself, "Here is a great
little player who may, or who may not, have the health to grow
into a great big one." I then bethought me of my favourite passage
in all literature. It occurs at the end of Théophile Gautier's

Mademoiselle de Maupin: "Combien sont morts qui, moins heureux que vous, n'ont pas même donné un seul baiser à leur chimère!" I determined that you should have your heart's desire and greatly play a great part. This you did. Nothing can take from you the knowledge that, judged by the highest standards, you were as grand a Hedda Gabler as an actress of your age could hope to be. I am not lying to please you. I stake my critical reputation, such as it is, on the beauty and understanding of your performance. You followed this up by glamourising tosh—a great triumph, since the mark of the second-rate actress is that she is no good in anything except the masterpieces. If you return to the stage, be sure that if I am alive I shall be there to welcome you. If you do not return, may I be a perpetual guest in the theatre of your mind? Attend first nights with me in spirit. Let me write you from time to time what I really think of that wan blossom, Miss X, and that splendacious orchid, Miss Y.

Now cheer up. The summer's flower is to the summer sweet, though to itself it only live and die. But it wasn't summer—it was February, if I remember aright. And your Hedda lived triumphantly.

Ever your sympathetic

JAMES AGATE

July 28 *Wednesday*

A. V. Alexander, at lunch at the Club to-day, lectured me on where I had gone wrong in my criticism of Esther McCracken's *Living Room* and insisted on its superiority over Shaw's *Widowers' Houses*. I listened with a brilliant assumption of patience. When he had finished I said, "Would the First Lord like to hear my views on naval strategy?" Am bound to say he took it very well.

August 31 *Tuesday*

Entertain at the Ivy George Lyttelton, a nice, large affable creature in the early sixties. We talk about *Ego*, and I tell him how nothing— which includes nerves, fatigue, worries, and what is supposed to be my work—has been allowed to interrupt it. I tell him something of the manner of its writing, how it is part written by hand, part dictated; typed, corrected, re-typed and re-corrected; how I sit up till four in the morning over it; how, since the war, one copy has been "evacuated" to my brother at York, and another deposited at the typist's. How some of the pages are re-written five or six times. How every alteration down to semicolons (but not commas) is sent to Brother Harry. How, every three months, there is a small revision, and every six months, a grand one. How the sheddings are so great that what ultimately appears is less than half of what I originally wrote. At this point Lyttelton asks why I don't write a supplementary volume containing all the things I have so obviously avoided. I say: "Meaning conduct, religion, sex, and all that?" He says "Yes. You could deposit it with the British Museum with instructions that it shan't be printed for a hundred years." I say: "My dear fellow, have you seen Edward D. Johnson's *Don Adriana's Letter?*" He says he hasn't. I go on: "This shows how in the course of the Letter's twenty-five lines Bacon inserts the words 'See the Design', and then in a faultlessly symmetrical pattern insinuates no fewer than seventeen statements as to who wrote *Love's Labour's Lost.* I have been as liberal as Bacon with my pointers." We then go on to discuss religion, the colour bar, and A. E. Housman, and lunch ends with G. L. inviting me to go down to Eton and talk to his boys.

When I get home I take up David Masson's study of De Quincey and read once more the pathetic story of his love for the little Oxford Street drab. Am struck by a passage of immediate, personal concernancy. "He had not told the *whole* truth about his London vagrancy, he said, because that was impossible, but he had told nothing but the truth." Later I glance at the *Illustrated London News* and read how somebody has discovered two new planets, the nearer of which is associated with the double star 61 Cygni, 75 million million miles away! And I reflect that if G. L. were present I could give him my views on all the things we talked about. Briefly these are: That sometime, somewhere, somehow two people who have wished to be united in this world shall be united in the next independent of age, station, colour or any other bar. As I wrote in *Responsibility*, the most bizarre conceptions assail me in the matter of what I should consider a satisfactory Heaven. I want a Heaven in which Jack shall have Jill, and Darby, Joan; in which poets shall find their Evelyn Hopes and their Shropshire lads; a Heaven in which Narcissus will not tire of his body's perfection, and Leda shall dally with her Swan, and Sappho burn no longer. I conceive an ingenious metaphysical limbo where one has one's desires though they may run contrary to the other person's, where all love is requited though the requiter may know nothing about it. Here Madame Potiphar shall enjoy her Joseph without the knowledge of that simpleton, Lady Booby ensnare her footman without diminution of his virtue, Lady Wishfort have her fill of unwilling gallants, and the rich socialite smooth out the crinkles in some bored jazz-drummer's hair. Myself? I want to meet again my first grand passion, with whom, more than fifty years ago in a Derbyshire lane, I exchanged fewer than a dozen words. To go back to where we started. I hold that if those two specks, De Quincey and Little Ann of Oxford Street, are not reunited, then, despite its 75 million million of miles the Scheme of Things shrinks to a Joke in Singularly Poor Taste.

December 12 *Sunday*

My carefully prepared speech last night at the Water Rats Cabaret and Ball called for some quick revision. I arrived at the Queensberry Club to find it crowded from floor to ceiling with American and Australian troops, which meant that references to Dan Leno and Arthur Roberts, and even Harry Tate and George Robey, would be lost. However, I got through somehow, and the fact that nobody knew what I was talking about gave, I understand, a tone to the proceedings. Mark played, the First Lord spoke, and all very jolly. I noticed that the speakers looked to a box on the left and began their speeches with "Your Highness." Asking who the Highness might be, I was told it was the Crown Prince of Arabia. Therefore I, too, began "Your Highness." At the end of the speech the M.C. said that the Prince had graciously consented to say a few words. Whereupon, the band struck up what appeared to be the Arabian National Anthem, we all stood, and down the stairs came a magnificent specimen of Oriental humanity attended by a woolly Ethiopian who was obviously His Highness's secretary. Splendiferously turban'd and caftan'd, the Prince took the centre of the stage with enormous dignity. And then, at a signal from the M.C., the band struck up a popular dance tune, and the pair fell into a buck and wing dance. This concluded, Bud Flanagan presented each of them with a pound note, and two of Soho's duskier denizens passed out of history. Taking my cue from Damon Runyon, I personally do not think this Crown Prince is any more Arabian than Mr Fred Emney.

EGO 7

1944

January 17 *Monday*

The management of Studio One had a notion amounting to genius when it prefaced the revival of *Un Carnet de Bal* with something called *Dreams Come True*. This picture showed Frances Day first as a soubrette singing Hungarian folk-songs in a Viennese café, and then warbling the same ditties from the tops of hay-carts, weeding a herbaceous border, to the little pigs in the farmyard, to the swans of some stately river. Whereupon the parents of the Boy realised that the Girl, though she might be an actress at night, must, in view of such warbling, be possessed of daytime purity. At which the cultured French audience, assembled to see Duvivier's masterpiece once again, broke into low but audible derision. It was interesting to note now much one remembered of *Un Carnet de Bal*. Yes, there it all was, just as it had been in the mind's eye any time these ten years or whatever length of time has passed since its making. That dream-waltz in those dream-clothes, taking place in a ballroom of unimaginable splendour, beneath incredible chandeliers, amidst what Balzac called "le luxe insolent et écrasant"—one remembers asking oneself how in circumstances of unheard-of grandeur Christine could possibly have picked up those lovers whose point is not shadiness of character but mediocrity of station. One of them becomes a hairdresser, another runs a night-club, the third is a grocer, the fourth an abortionist—not one of them has elegance. It is not until the end that one realises that the grandeur of the ball existed only in Christine's sixteen-year-old imagination. There she is twenty years later dancing once more in the scrubby, flag festooned dance-hall of the little country town, surrounded by girls in frocks of flowered gingham and cretonne, courted by hobble-dehoys in ill-fitting dress suits. Time has not laid a finger on this film's magnificent acting; the picture would be worth going to see if only for the priest of that great actor, Harry Baur. Then there is the Provençal of Raimu, the ignoble shyster of Louis Jouvet, the inimitable clowning of Fernandel, the exquisite playing of Françoise Rosay, and the brilliant self-effacement of Marie Bell, who never allows Christine to be more than a necessary peg. One could write a whole essay on the minor characters in this film. Characters like the old housekeeper in the first episode, or the blackmailing little rat, or the abortionist's wife. And with what delicacy is the whole thing rounded off! "One's first ball," says Christine to her adopted son, "is as important as one's first cigarette." And then, as the curtains close, you hear her say to herself, "Just as important. And no more." It seems to me that with this film the art of picture-directing came to an end. I have never seen anything since which has been within measurable distance of it, or if I have it has been a French film.

February 10 *Thursday*

Bertie van Thal is getting more and more like Tenniel's Dormouse. Showed me his War Diary, pretending that it is modelled on *Ego*. Here is the enchanting beginning:

> *May* 1, 1941. The season has opened brilliantly with the death of old Lady Tweedle. . . .

February 11 *Friday*

Bobby Andrews tells me a new story about Mrs Pat. Terribly bored by an elderly scientist drooling away about ants—"They are wonderful little creatures; they have their own police force and their own army"— she leaned forward and said, with an expression of the utmost interest and in a voice like damson-coloured velvet, "No navy, I suppose?"

February 21 *Monday*

Deciding to give myself a rest—the first for many months—I come down to Brighton on Saturday afternoon and find the Pavilion Hotel maintaining its reputation for hospitality. Am taken by Charles Smith to the Brighton Theatrical Club, where we do a lot of drinking and talking. Spend Sunday morning cutting 10 000 words out of *Ego* 6 and reading Hazlitt. Excellent lunch, after which I am persuaded to interview a boy of twenty, Don Sinden, who has been playing in Charles's repertory company. He is the son of a chemist, and according to Charles has some notion of acting. Will I say whether, in my opinion, he should go on the stage or stick to cabinet-making, to which he has already served his apprenticeship? Murmuring "Stick to your fretwork, young man!" I prepare to go to sleep. But Charles won't have it, and presently I find myself taking stock of the boy. Enough height, an attractive head, something of the look of young Ainley, a good resonant voice, vowels not common, manner modest yet firm. Straightway and without fuss he gives me a taste of his quality—Wolsey's Farewell— and after a bit I am playing Cromwell! We then go through Bucking- ham's last scene, and I find myself suggesting that even the "mirror of all courtesy" can't be supposed to *enjoy* going to the block, that the whole of the "All good people" speech should be spoken in the light of this, and that "Lead on, o'God's name!" is not a pious com- mand but shows Buckingham at the end of his tether. Afterwards the young man does a scene from *On Approval* quite badly, and I tell him to stick to Shakespeare, beginning at the bottom of the ladder. Which advice may ruin his career; the giving of it certainly wrecks my after- noon. Washing my hands of him—I will *not* have another protégé— I am settling down for a snooze when Charles comes to tell me that we are starting at once for a camp eleven miles from anywhere to see his production of Coward's *Private Lives*. A perishingly cold night, the last half of the journey accomplished under an arch of searchlights. Fair performance, after which we bring the company back for supper, and all very jolly and boring, as George Mathew said of Bach's Christ- mas Oratorio.

March 16 *Thursday*

Letter from Harley Street suggesting that I must be ill:

> Take your criticism that Francis Thompson's immortal lyric *The Hound of Heaven* is only a "stained-glass window" in comparison with Wordsworth's *Ode on the Intimations of Immortality*. I yield to no one in my admiration of Wordsworth, but both Thompson and Shelley's best lyrics I think outshine those of the Lakeland poet. I have never been truly able to decide between Percy Bysshe and Francis, and as I am a descendant of the former, and the only person (besides an occasional nurse) who sat beside the deathbed of the latter, I think I may fairly claim to have thought a lot about them both.
>
> > *Queen Alexandra Mansions W.C.*2
> > *March* 16, 1944

DEAR SIR

You may be a descendant of Lord Nelson and have held Lord Kitchener's hand as he went down in the *Hampshire* and yet know very little of navigation. Besides, you quote me less than perfectly. What I said was that Francis Thompson's poetry bears to the poetry of Wordsworth the same relation that a stained-glass window bears to a field of buttercups and daisies. On reflection I think I was wrong in my comparison of art and Nature. The correct parallel is between Thompson's artifice and Wordsworth's art. Can't you see how in every line and every word Thompson is straining for effect? Whereas in Wordsworth the lines seem to come of themselves. Don't you realise that

> Adown Titanic glooms of chasmèd fears

is not poetry but a perfect description of alcoholic depression and incipient D.T.'s? Can't you see that Thompson's stuff is much too poetic to be poetry? Compare the overworked, over-decorated

> Across the margent of the world I fled,
>   And troubled the gold gateways of the stars,
>   Smiting for shelter on their clanged bars
>   Fretted to dulcet jars
> And silvern chatter the pale ports o' the moon

with the sober splendour of

>   Waters on a starry night
>   Are beautiful and fair
> The sunshine is a glorious birth
> But yet I know, where'er I go,
> That there hath past away a glory from the earth.

I am quite content to rest my view of the matter on Rebecca West, who said to me at the Buckingham Palace tea-party yesterday afternoon: "My dear James, of course your're right. Compared with Wordsworth, Thompson's stuff is pure wedding-cake. The difference between God and Gunter's!"

> Yours faithfully,
> JAMES AGATE

March 30 *Thursday*

> *Ibstone House*
> *Ibstone*
> *Nr. High Wycombe, Bucks*
> *March* 27*th*, 1944

DEAR JAMES,

I have been working hard ever since that Palace party, which I greatly enjoyed. Did it strike you that at last the family which entertained us had, by dint of certain noble efforts, made themselves as civil, as well bred, and as English as your parents and mine? I admired the great-grandmother, the grandfather, and the father, with all my heart, but I would not have conceded them *that*. But what a one-sided entertainment—we can only hope that we repaid them, according to the dream-like quality of the afternoon (rather like Drury Lane pantomime seen in childhood, I thought)—

175

De mon service de vierge
De ton bonjour d'écolier.

I think Francis Thompson a horrible poet, an artificial flower-maker by temperament, and a *boozed* writer—I don't care where the wine goes so long as it doesn't get into the style—and just look at that passage after "Ah, must—Designer infinite. . . ." The man says he is a piece of charred wood, then makes the assertion that his "freshness spent its wavering shower i' the dust" (what *does* this mean?). Then his heart is a fount, and his mind a tree, not apparently charred at all, but thoroughly and unpleasantly wet—and the next minute he is a fruit with a rind and a pulp. He should have made up his mind what he was. And then the ascription of disgusting motives to God passes the frontiers of blasphemy. God would not say to any of us, "Alack, thou knowest not how little worthy of any love thou art!" He is the one person conceivable who never could think that—and in that surely lies His Godhead. "Whom wilt thou find to love ignoble thee save Me, save only Me?" This is the authentic voice of the worm's wife in Nathaniel Gubbins' column. A *low* poem, pawing about the English language, and vulgarising religion. It's odd that Francis Thompson didn't think of another verse where God threatened him with a breach-of-promise case.

My best wishes to you.

Yours ever,
REBECCA WEST

April 26 *Wednesday*

A letter:

Ledbury
Garratts Lane
Banstead
April 23*rd,* 1944

DEAR MR AGATE,

To-day's mistake in French makes the third in recent months.

1. "Mille" meaning thousand does not take an 's.' The translation of "ten thousand copies" is "dix mille exemplaires."

2. "Le son du cornemuse" should have been "de la cornemuse;" this word is feminine.

3. "Vous dîtes" means "you said", not "you say". "You say" is "vous dites".

Sorry I've forgotten the dates.

Yours pedantically,
J. H. NEWBOLD

My reply:

Queen Alexandra Mansions, W.C 2
26th April, 1944

DEAR SIR,

My secretary is sand-blind, semi-deaf, demi-paralysed, seventy, uncertain of his step, and deprived for long periods of the senses of smell and taste. He is not, alas, dumb! I cannot do more than take my Zola down from the shelf, and give him the passage to copy. Only yesterday I find him making me write in a film article: "It looked as though Mr Maugham was going to state the case for *patriotism*—except that there is no case." Actually I had dictated "pacifism", and only by a miracle of luck happened on the error. I do not plead remissness in the matters of the extra 's' and the unnecessary accent.

Remains "cornemuse". Odd though it may seem to you, I could not remember the French word for bagpipes and I do not possess an English–French dictionary. So I ring up the library at one of my papers, and the following three cornered conversation ensues, my secretary, one Leo Pavia, grunting from his chair:

J. A. What is the French for bagpipes?
LIB. Cornemuse.
J. A. Masculine or feminine?
LIB. Masculine.
J. A. Are you sure? Look again.
LIB. It's masculine. There's an 'm' after the word. It says "cornemuse, m."
SEC. (*interrupting*). It doesn't sound right to me.
J. A. Nor to me. But perhaps it's one of those odd French things like calling a cabin-boy "mousse," which looks feminine but is masculine.
SEC. Cabin-boys don't play the bagpipes.
J. A. That's a non-sequitur. Why must you drag in red herrings?
SEC. The captain wouldn't allow it. Unless, of course, it was a fishing-boat with a Scotch captain, and even then . . .
(*With a scream like the madden'd beach dragged down by the wave J. A. rings off and sets down the offending "du."*)

Yet I submit that reasonable care was taken. But care will not do everything. Caroline Lejeune of the *Observer* tells me that she has had to cease referring to the film *Un Carnet de Bal* because the printer insists on printing *Un Carnet du Bal*.
Since 1921 I have written, including my forty books, seven million words, or very nearly double Balzac's output. And you expect me to see with my own eyes that every 'i' is dotted, and every French accent correct? My dear sir, your letter is a grotesque and gratuitous impertinence. All the same, I am obliged to you

for it. By the way, did you see that a first edition of *The Cloister and the Hearth* fetched £280 at Sotheby's yesterday, doubtless because it contained the sentence: "She threw her face over her apron"? Now perhaps you can understand why your letter to me is like a rag to a red bull.

Yours sincerely,
JAMES AGATE

June 4 *Sunday*

Why is *The Winter's Tale* unpopular? Some people have alleged the gap between the third and fourth acts to be the reason for their aversion. On the theory, perhaps, that devouring Time blunts more things than lions' paws—to wit, theatrical interest. Have given to-day's *S.T.* readers a slice of Quiller-Couch, to whom for many years I meant to write but never did. I should like him to have known that of all the critics of Shakespeare he has pleased me most. About this play "Q" wrote:

> Shakespeare, master of resources though he was, could hit on no device to avoid having to present, in an action of some three hours, the children Marina and Perdita first as babes exposed, helpless as innocent, to the surge of the sea and the beasts of the forest, anon as maidens grown up to reunite parental hearts long astray, redeem inveterate wrongs, cancel old woes, heal the past with holy hope.

But "Q" possessed in addition to his sympathy great store of sanity and shrewdness, and could on occasion get down to the gist of the matter as forthrightly as Hazlitt or as bluntly as Johnson. By the way, if I were asked for my favourite stroke of Shakespearean criticism it would be one of Samuel's notes to *The Merchant of Venice*. Lorenzo asks who comes with Portia, and Stephano replies, "None but the holy hermit and her maid." Whereupon Johnson growls, "I do not perceive the use of this hermit, of whom nothing is seen or heard afterwards." "Q" dismissed the bear—I mean the one in *The Winter's Tale*—with the remark: "The bear is a naughty superfluity." Reverting to why people dislike this play, I don't think it necessary to look for reasons. I don't believe an audience is worried by unexpected Third Murderers, hermits of whom no more is heard, frisking Time, improbable bears, and sea-coasts as far removed from their proper place as a modern beauty's eyebrows. But if I had to find a reason I should say it is because Hermione talks too much, and in an idiom that is too difficult. One of the reasons *Hamlet* is a popular play is because it is comparatively easy to take in. In the version normally performed I can think of only one passage which gives the average playgoer any trouble. This is Gertrude's

> This is the very coinage of your brain:
> This bodiless creation ecstasy
> Is very cunning in.

I doubt whether the average person realises that what the Queen is saying in the last two lines is no more than: "People who are mad are very good at imagining things, and believing them to be real." But Hermione's talk is nothing but the most difficult jargon. For example:

> Cram's with praise, and make's
> As fat as tame things: one good deed dying tongueless
> Slaughters a thousand waiting upon that.
> Our praises are our wages: you may ride's
> With some soft kiss a thousand furlongs ere
> With spur we heat an acre.

Yes, I know all about "When daffodils begin to peer". Which does not prevent Autolycus from being a sad dog who tires me in very much less than a mile-a.

June 7 Wednesday

Took the chair for Robert Sherwood debating about the theatre at the Churchill Club, in Inigo Jones's exquisite Ashburnham House in Little Dean's Yard, Westminster. John Mason Brown, dramatic critic and gallant naval officer, was to have been the other speaker, but could not come. Raymond Mortimer deputised, and in place of the fat, elderly, pompous highbrow I had expected he turned out to be thin, youngish, amusing, modest, and in every way charming. The room was crowded, the audience consisting largely of Americans, from officers of high rank to privates, overflowing into the next room and half-way down the stairs. I began by saying some nice things about Sherwood, after which, in order to get the show going, I accused Mortimer of being a highbrow and of believing (1) that if the lower classes had bathrooms they would use them; (2) that the uglier music sounds the more beautiful it is; (3) that the dustman would be a more efficient dustman if he could be persuaded to read Proust; and (4) that if German youth could be taught to recite "Mary had a little lamb" it would drop the *Herrenvolk* nonsense for ever. Having got the audience into a highly receptive mood, I sat down, lit a cigar, and prepared to listen and enjoy myself. But it was not to be. After six minutes Sherwood said he had no more to say about the theatre, and Mortimer said that as he seldom or never went to the play he had no views on the subject. Obviously I couldn't allow any meeting of which I am chairman to flop in this disgraceful fashion, so I set to work, let off a lot of impromptu fireworks, and finally got them both talking again.

And what nonsense did they talk! Mortimer said that the only nineteenth-century playwrights who remained alive were Ibsen, Strindberg, and Tchehov. Sherwood said that in his opinion all art ought to be didactic and propagandist, and that the only hope for the theatre was that the new generation would bring a new mind to it. Whereupon I set about both and told them to put their thinking in order. I told them that they were confusing the art of drama with the business of entertainment. I told Mortimer that on the first of these two planes he was right about Ibsen, Strindberg, and Tchehov, but that all three were as dead as mutton on the plane of playhouse draws unless there was some other bait such as the presence of a Mr G. or a Vivien Leigh. Then I told Sherwood that he was right about the new mind provided that he too was talking in terms of abstract drama, but that as far as filling the theatres was concerned the British public wouldn't stand for new minds. That it would with difficulty accept new *material*, and then only on condition that the new playwright wove the old sentimental twaddle around it. In the end the evening turned into a raging success.

June 9 *Friday*

Dined last night with Lady Cunard at the Dorchester—one of those ultra-smart parties where somebody says, "You know Booboo and Snooky, of course", and you spend the evening wondering who these fellow-guests are. I recognised Kenneth Clark, but have no idea of the identity of the colonel who was also a connoisseur of pictures, the lady who had been a Russian princess, and the striking beauty from the Chilean Embassy. It was both instructive and amusing to hear from the horse's mouth, as it were, what the upper classes talk about when they think they are among themselves. I minded my *p*'s all right, but dropped a few *q*'s. One was when X's name cropped up, and I said he was a snob and an ass who had made a mess of every ministerial post he had occupied and was loathed by the people he hadn't met even more than by the people he had. Whereupon it turned out that the politician in question was the friend of every bosom round the table! Good food, two bottles of native wine contributed by the Chilean lady, some excellent brandy, and a vile cigar. I had a frantic desire to descend into the restaurant and buy one, but decided that this might be thought odd in Mayfair. Left early, and got to the Café Royal in time for the whiskey-and-soda and smoke I was dying for.

June 26 *Monday*

Trouvailles
He had the most voluptuous lips in Nottinghamshire.
LESLIE ROBERTS, *Feathers in the Bed*

June 28 *Wednesday*

A slight breeze with the B.B.C. in connection with my broadcast
in the Forces programme about the revival of Korda's *Lady Hamilton.*
B.B.C. "Do you mind prefacing your talk with the statement that
whereas you hold a high opinion of Nelson's seamanship you have a
low one of his morals?" J. A. "Yes, I mind very much." B.B.C. "But
don't you realise, Mr Agate, that you are talking not only to the soldiers
but also to their mothers and wives, who don't think that their sons
and husbands should be told that women like Emma Hamilton exist?
Or that a woman such as you have drawn could ever be the mistress of a
great national hero." J. A. "I don't care a damn what the mothers and
wives of soldiers think." B.B.C. "Perhaps not, but we have to."
J. A. "Then I shan't give the talk at all." Rings off. What was in my
mind was something Stevenson wrote about Sir Richard Grenville of
the *Revenge*, and how he declined to surrender to the Spaniards and
ordered the ship to be scuttled. "Some one said to me the other day
that they considered this story to be of a pestilent example. I am not
inclined to imagine we shall be ever put into any practical difficulty from a
superfluity of Grenvilles." And I am not inclined to imagine that this
country will ever be put into any practical difficulty from a superfluity of Nelsons with mistresses like Emma Hamilton. But I just
haven't time to read Stevenson's essays to B.B.C. officials concerned
for the morals of the British fighting man. Presently Norman Collins
intervenes, and I consent to say that while the film presents an idealised
view of Emma, there is also a realistic view which I propose to put
forward whether the moralists approve or not.

July 11 *Tuesday*

Justice is Coming—it ought to have been called *The Four Who Were
Hanged*—the news-reel issued by the Soviet Film Agency which I saw
to-night at the little Tatler Theatre, is entirely sickening and should be
exhibited all over the country. The first scoundrel to be examined is
Captain Wilhelm Langfeld, of the German Intelligence. To me he
doesn't look the officer-type; he is obviously uneducated and has none
of the gloss which these swine use to cover up their brutality. He admits
putting one hundred civilians to death. The next is Retzlaw Reinhardt,
of the Gestapo. This precious fellow has a mouth like a shark, no
chin, and a forehead straight out of Lombroso; he admits to ordering
the citizens of Kharkov into the van in which they were to be
asphyxiated. The third is Lieutenant Hans Ritz, of the S.S. He is a
blond, rather sheepish-looking young man who might be a shop
assistant or something equally harmless; we learn that he is a sadist
of exquisite depravity who slaughtered women and children with
his own hand. The fourth is one Michael Bulanov, who is a decent-

looking fellow and might be mistaken for any Russian concert-pianist;
he drove the murder-van. Well, of course they have got to hang, and
they do hang. But their hanging leaves one with a sense of frustration.
After all, they were only carrying out orders, and the highest in rank
among them was only a captain. What we want to get at is the colonels
and the generals and the people above colonels and generals. It never
does to neglect Unser Shakespeare. Well, let us see what Unser
Shakespeare has to say on the subject of people like Hitler and Himmler,
Goering and Goebbels. The trouble is that they have only four lives
between them, and one remembers Othello's

> I would have him nine years a-killing.

And

> Had all his hairs been lives, my great revenge
> Had stomach for them all.

And again

> O, that the slave had forty thousand lives
> One is too poor, too weak for my revenge.

So I take another play of Shakespeare, and turn to the lines in which
Macduff promises Macbeth his life:

> Then yield thee, coward,
> And live to be the show and gaze o' the time:
> We'll have thee, as our rarer monsters are,
> Painted upon a pole, and underwrit,
> "Here may you see the tyrant."

My own way with the quartet would be to turn them into a travelling
circus and send them round the once-occupied countries, each immured
in a bullet-proof glass cage. These cages would have to be nicely warmed,
because each of the quartet would be naked, with his uniform and
decorations fastened to the glass at the back. Over the whole show
would be emblazoned: "Here may you see the *Herrenvolk!*" The
captives would be given plenty to eat and drink, but they would be
compelled to listen, day in and day out, unceasingly, endlessly, to the
torrents of their own eloquence reproduced by exceedingly loud
speakers and diversified only by selections from *Mein Kampf* and the
more idiotic bits of Nietzsche. The circus to be entirely managed,
run, and policed by Jews. Here an even brighter idea strikes me. This
is to send the circus, not to the once-occupied countries, but to Germany! It would be appropriate if it were to start from that beer-cellar
in Munich.

July 14 *Friday*

Letter to Pamela Brown:

MY DEAR PAMELA,

What's this about your wanting to play Marguerite Gautier? Garrick's widow is supposed to have said to Edmund Kean: "Sir, you are a very fine actor, but you cannot play Abel Drugger." Madam, you are a very clever actress, but you can no more play Marguerite than Sarah Bernhardt could have played Miss Prism! Marguerite is the *courtisane sentimentale*, and there is not an ounce of sentimentality in your make-up; suggestion of a knife-edge brain with a core of sentiment hidden away is something very different.

I beg you not to be another of the great ersatzists in the part, one more of those brilliant performers who have substituted something else and labelled the substitution Marguerite. Take warning by Duse, who turned Dumas' heroine into what Lemaître described as "une grisette extrêmement distinguée et un peu préraphaélite, une grisette de Botticelli." Never for one moment he went on, could you imagine this Marguerite "riant faux dans les soupers, allumant les hommes, s'appliquant à leur manger beaucoup d'argent." Duse just couldn't suggest this. She played the first and second acts, says the French critic, deliciously, but just as she would have played Juliet or Francesca da Rimini. During the last three acts she found it convenient to forget all about that little matter of Marguerite's profession. "Ce n'est plus que l'aventure très touchante de deux amants très malheureux, séparés on ne sait bien par quoi." And when old Duval put in an appearance all that the spectators saw was "une pensionnaire grondée par un vieux monsieur très imposant."

But then they have all come to grief, each in her different way. When Sarah gave Armand that camellia it was with the shyness of one unaccustomed to sincerity; whereas Cécile Sorel went through the motions of a statesman laying a wreath at the foot of a cenotaph. I won't bore you about Jane Hading-Gautier, who, as a wit of the period said, interpreted the part in terms of Sarahbesques; about Nethersole-Gautier, Rubinstein-Gautier, Pitoëff-Gautier, Tallulah-Gautier, and even Garbo-Gautier. Do you imagine that your voice has the tones in which to half-sigh, half-murmur, "On nous abandonne, et les longues soirées succèdent aux longs jours"? Can't you realise that as a relentless little realist of to-day you can have nothing in common with a demi-mondaine of a hundred years ago not only reclining upon plush but speaking it? Can't you see that you will make nonsense of "On a toujours eu une enfance, quoi que l'on soit devenue," just because you will look like a child with your past still to come? Hear my alternative suggestion. This is that you should tackle Meilhac and Halévy's *Froufrou*, a play with some, at least, of Dumas' sentimental quality, and a great deal more wit. You may not be able to wear a crinoline, but you can have a bustle, and in the first act you wear a riding-habit! The story is all about a feather-brain who runs away from her too serious husband and dies of mingled T.B. and repentance. The part was first played by Aimée Desclée and later by Sarah and by Modjeska. Don't you know, dear Pamela, that you have the power of appearing extremely young? Consider the impression you have to make on your audience at your first appearance. It is Valréas, your would-be lover, talking: "Froufrou? Une porte qui s'ouvre, et, tout le long de l'escalier, un bruit de jupe qui glisse et descend comme un tourbillon . . . Froufrou . . . Vous entrez, tournez, cherchez, furetez, rangez, dérangez, bavardez, boudez, riez, parlez, chantez, pianotez, sautez, dansez, et vous vous en allez, Froufrou, toujours Froufrou . . ." I know no actress on the stage to whom I would sooner say, "Squirrelisez!"

I agree that the play dates, but I maintain that it dates much less than the Dumas play. The world of to-day contains no more Marguerites, but there are still plenty of Froufrous. Our best film actresses are always pretending to be a Froufrou of one kind or another. Turn my proposal down, my dear Pam, and Claudette Colbert will hear from me by the next mail!

Your devoted

JAMES AGATE

July 20 *Thursday*

Letter from Pamela Brown:

36 *Soho Square, W*.1.
July 18*th*, 1944

DEAR MR AGATE,

A most spirited management, the Cambridge Arts Theatre Trust, are anxious to present *La Dame aux Camélias* (with me in it), to be directed by Norman Marshall. He has always wanted to produce it, as I have to play in it: so we seem all set for good adventure.

But you are against it.

I think the memories of actresses who have played Marguerite Gautier have a little fogged Dumas' original conception of the character. May I quote him a little, a very little? "Elle avait vingt ans." Well, you say, I have "the power of appearing extremely young". All right, But you also say, "You would look like a child with your past still to come." This delights me because it's an almost exact description of Marguerite. "On voyait qu'elle était encore à la virginité du vice." . . . "On reconnaissait dans cette fille la vierge qu'un rien avait faite courtisane, et la courtisane dont un rien eût fait la vierge la plus amoureuse et la plus pure."

There she is: her seductive charm lay in her virgin appearance, however lewd her speech "riant faux dans les soupers". Sentimentality? I think I know why you say "There is not one ounce of sentimentality in your nature." It is because there wasn't any in my Ophelia; and that there should have been, I quite agree. I was a rotten Ophelia.

Anthony Holland, the designer, and I planned a production of *La Dame* five years ago at Oxford, but the war intervened. During odd bits of leave from the R.A.F. he has worked out a simplified setting, practicable for 1944. So let me have a shot at it anyhow. I think *Froufrou* sounds a delicious idea, and I have this morning procured a copy from the London Library (now again open) and look forward to doing it—Claudette Colbert permitting.

Love from
PAM

I have replied:

Queen Alexandra Mansions, W.C.2.
July 19th, 1944

DEAR PAM,

What a lovely letter! I shall give it a treasured place in *Ego* 7; for which I have ordered from Tunbridge-Sedgwick a beautiful photograph of your wide-awake little mug. This is the phrase Sarcey used for Réjane. "Petite frimousse éveillée" sounds better.

You make a very good case for your child Marguerite, and I have no doubt that was Dumas' intention. But I doubt whether he brought it off in the play. Take the speech in the second act:

"Nous paraissons heureuses, et l'on nous envie. En effet, nous avons des amants qui se ruinent, non pas pour nous, comme ils le disent, mais pour leur vanité. Nous sommes les premières dans leur amour-propre, les dernières dans leur estime. Nous avons des amis, des amis comme Prudence, dont l'amitié va jusqu'à la servitude, jamais jusqu'au désintéressement. Peu leur importe ce que nous faisons, pourvu qu'on les voie dans nos loges, ou qu'elles se carrent dans nos voitures. Ainsi, tout autour de nous, ruine, honte et mensonge."

These are not the thoughts of the girl of twenty who is still finding life full of fun, but of the woman of thirty who finds that the fun of that particular way of life begins to pall. Then again that speech in the third act:

"Ainsi, quoi qu'elle fasse, la créature tombée ne se relèvera jamais! Dieu lui pardonnera peut-être, mais le monde sera inflexible!"

I just cannot feel that any young woman thinks of herself as a "créature tombée". But then again I may be wrong, and you may be right in thinking that I am a little betrayed by the Marguerites I have seen, all of whom have been fully grown women. (I wonder how old Doche was then she created the part?) Shall we put it this way—that I shall be extremely interested to see your Marguerite.

And then what will happen? You will have done the spade-work, after which that astute little Jewess, the Bergner, will come and clean up.

No, your Ophelia was not rotten. It was a fine performance of the wrong thing. The poor wretch, you remember, turned everything, affliction, passion, hell itself, "to favour and to prettiness". Pray, what did you turn it to?

By the way, I think our not meeting is charming. I still see you enthroned on that rickety chair on the stage of that Oxford theatre, very tiny, and endeavouring to conceal shyness by an imperiousness that would have put to shame Cleopatra, Queen Elizabeth and the Empress Catherine of Russia! The aloofness repeats the Shaw–Campbell, Shaw–Terry pattern. Anyhow, doubt that the stars are fire, doubt that the sun doth move, and so on. But never doubt that you are much in the thoughts of

Your old admirer

James Agate

July 21 Friday

There is this to be said for Ravaillac, Charlotte Corday, and Wilkes Booth—at least they were not bunglers. Which is more than can be said for Graf von Stauffenberg, who merely scotch'd the Hitlerian snake instead of killing it. The worst of failure in this kind is that it spoils the market for more competent performers.

August 11 Friday

Wrote to George Lyttelton, quoting a nice thing out of D. B. Wyndham Lewis's article in this week's Tatler: "We greatly esteem the modern school-master type, which is very often such a cultivated, easy, genial man of the world that we'd entrust anything to it, except maybe a child's future."

August 20 Sunday

The Express has given me five hundred words in which to tell its readers what I think about Henry Wood, who died yesterday. Well, I think simply that Wood was a great man. I can remember greater conductors. But I know of none who had a greater love of music for its own sake, and not as the means through which his own virtuosity could be recognised. Just as many years earlier Hallé had determined to make Manchester musical, so Wood determined to make music a part of the intellectual life of London. There can be no doubt that he succeeded; to-day London without the Proms would not be London.

He was a great innovator, and to him, chiefly, the public was indebted for its first acquaintance with the works of Tschaikowsky, Strauss, Sibelius, and Vaughan Williams. Whatever shortcomings may be alleged, even if his powers were a part of talent rather than genius, it must always be remembered that while his predecessors were all of foreign extraction—Jullien was French, Costa and Mancinelli were Italian, Manns, Hallé, and Richter German—Henry Wood was the first great English conductor. And it is no small part of his fame that he did more than any other man to improve the status of the orchestral player in this country. Here is what I am saying in the *Express* to-morrow:

When Henry Wood first raised his baton he found this country a highly unmusical nation. There was a lot of Italian squalling in the neighbourhood of Covent Garden during the months of May and June, and a lot of pretence by the tiaras and starched shirts that they understood what it was about. But the general notion of music was the Overture to *William Tell*, followed by Somebody's Lancers or Quadrilles. Except, of course, once a year when everybody traipsed out to the Crystal Palace to hear five thousand sopranos and contraltos, tenors and basses, bleat that they, like sheep, had gone astray.

Wood did for this country's potential music-lovers what Lilian Baylis did for its potential drama-lovers. He popularised music, but not in the sense in which that word is generally used. A "popular" edition of the works of some great dramatist or novelist generally means cheap paper, ramshackle binding, execrable print, abominable illustrations. Wood's notion of popularising music was to give the best performances of the best stuff in the best way at prices within the reach of the man in the street. Talking of streets, did anybody ever go on foot to Covent Garden? No. Did broughams drawn by spanking bays, or, in later years, the more expensive miracles of the motor-engineer, collide in Langham Place? No. Henry Wood conceived his job not as bringing music to the best people, but as bringing the best music to the people.

How good a conductor was he? Shall we say that he was an all-rounder? Yes. And a great all-rounder? Yes. Was Henry a great man? Yes. Hazlitt has laid it down—in an essay on the Indian Jugglers, if you please—that there are four tests for greatness. Has a man great power? Has that power produced great effects? Has a man shown greatness in a way that cannot be hid or gainsaid? Has he filled up a certain idea in the public mind? Wood came through all four tests with flying colours. To the average man he became identified with—nay he *was*—London's music. The average man trusted Henry. He knew that if Henry thought a work worth performing it was worth his, the average man's, listening. He preserved the best in the old music and was a courageous innovator. And behind it all he gave you the conviction that he knew his job. Even more important, he impressed you as putting the composer first, the orchestral and solo players second, and himself last.

Wood was not a man of excessive culture, though he could hold his own in a profession where virtuosity is often a polite name for half-wittedness. His voice was high and squeaky. His English was not impeccable, and nobody wanted it to be. His remark to the fiddlers, "Wot d'you think you're a-doing of, sawring away regardless"? has become legend. They called him "Timber," and rightly. The timber was of oak. He died in the fulness of time and achievement. His work was done. He knew himself beloved. He is a part of musical England for ever.

August 23 *Wednesday*

The liberation of Paris was announced in the one o'clock News. In the words of the announcer: "Fifty thousand of the armed forces of the interior and several hundred thousands of unarmed patriots. . . ." Not unarmed, I think, but armed haphazardly!

There is a transcendentality of delirium—the reader must know the phrase by now—about B.B.C. matters which baffles me completely. I have known them fade out in the middle of the Hallelujah Chorus, the last page of *Tristan*, and the last ten bars of the Hammerklavier Sonata. And always in favour of popular muck. What I have never known them do is to fade out muck in any circumstances whatever. To-night I listened in to a special programme in honour of France. Incidentally, there was a long speech supposed to convey the views of the Man in the Street. This was uttered in an announcer's voice and contained the words "garish" and "pristine". But let that pass. The point is that to-night, of all nights, the B.B.C. chose to fade out in the middle of the *Marseillaise*! After which a female voice said, "You are now going to listen to *Cap and Bells*, a late-night revue with . . . etc., etc." Gibbering like Othello, I rang up the B.B.C., and, getting hold of the Biggest Noise in Charge, said: "This is James Agate speaking. Do you know that you have faded out in the middle of the *Marseillaise*? Goats and monkeys! May the Corporation rot, perish, and be damned!" And rang off. Either the principle of elasticity is admitted by the B.B.C., or it isn't. If it isn't then it is surely a matter of timing and rehearsal. Why didn't they time and rehearse properly? If there are Other Factors I Know Nothing About, then the B.B.C. must appoint a Director of Unknown Factors whose job it is to foresee and prevent *gaffes* like to-night's. Salary £5000 a year. Any *gaffe* to entail instant dismissal. Otherwise I expect to hear any evening now: "At 11 A.M. to-day the General in Command of the Axis Forces on the Rhine asked for an armistice, which the Allies granted on the following terms . . ." (*Female voice interrupts.*) "Listeners will now hear *Pop Goes the Weasel*, a late-night revue featuring Miss Naomi Thickhedde and the Uvula Boys. . . ."

August 24 *Thursday*

In a letter from a major serving abroad:

> How right you are about the impossibility of educating the lower
> classes. The lower class educated is the lower class spoilt. Let them
> remain what they should be—rough and tough, raw and dumb.
> Give them more football grounds, boxing-rings, and dog-tracks;
> more Metropolitans and Bedfords; more Florrie Fordes and Bud
> Flanagans; more gin palaces and fish and chips and winkles;
> let them have great roaring whores with feather boas. Man should
> be a lusty beast, not a niminy-piminy. I have more than three
> hundred men under me. They come from North and South,
> East and West, labourers, farmers, drivers, butchers, factory
> hands, and bricklayers. They drink, they swear, they whore—if
> they get a chance. But there's the devil's glory in them. Day and
> night, in North Africa and Italy, they have driven heavy lorries
> over mountain roads in snow or rain, across the plains in the heat
> and the dust. They are always undefeated, undefeatable. What do
> they want to go back to after the war? A new world? Not if they
> can help it. To the old world, glorified and magnified. Stronger
> and cheaper pints of beer, bigger wins on Saturday afternoons,
> better clothes, the same food but cheaper and more plentiful,
> the same houses but lighter and healthier. They want to work hard
> and play hard—but at their own sort of work and their own sort
> of play. They are men—there are no men like them. I hear and
> know little of the plans devised by our Elder Statesmen for an
> England after the war. But I fear we are condemning a race of
> demi-gods to a perpetual Surbiton.

"Great roaring whores with feather boas" is superb. And I hope
original. This letter stands for something that most highbrows and
certainly the *New Statesman* gang refuse to understand. The one constant thing in my political economy is my belief in the non-educability
of the non-educated. I agree with the gallant major that to educate
the working classes is not only infeasible but undesirable. I am, and
always have been, entirely consistent about this. I find in *Ego* 3, in an
entry made almost exactly eight years ago to the day, the following:

> Coming back in the car, George and I talked about the Black-
> pudlians, and agreed that the outstanding feature of the working
> classes is their self-containment. They don't want the things the
> rich want—travel, clothes, jewels, expensive food and wines,
> grand opera, and hand-painted pictures. They prefer Blackpool to
> Biarritz, cloth caps to Ascot toppers, beer to champagne. Their
> notion of music and pictures is Gracie Fields, and their idea of a
> racehorse is something not to own, but to bet on.

I will only add to this that it is no use trying to foist on the lower
classes better minds or better manners, for the simple reason that they

don't want better minds or better manners. Intellectuals have never understood this, and never will. The education of the masses is all my eye and Kingsley Martin!

August 26 *Saturday*

Part of a letter from Los Angeles:

> Those who saw Irving at his best know that to-day none stands in such lonely splendour. Greatest when he had assistance from the greatest; recall *Macbeth*, Act i, scene 5. Ellen Terry seated in huge high-backed chair by fire in massive hearth, loose-robed in peacock blue, shimmering silver ornaments in fair hair—every inch a queen of the stage—reading a letter, each syllable dropping clear as water from an icicle. Fiercely she seizes Opportunity, no milk of human kindness in her, clutches at her breasts under the blue robe, furiously appeals to hell for aid, grasps at the murdering dagger, cries "Hold, hold." . . . Suddenly enter from behind the arras . . . Macbeth, "Great Glamis!" Has he heard her? No, no. Recall how Irving paused to stare in wonder, as she, exulting, embraces him and murmurs, "Great Glamis! worthy Cawdor!" (What an entrance, nothing in all the entrances in all the plays excels it.) Then in four lines she tells him her intent. . . . They were always very careful about entrances. Recall Act i, scene 7, Irving ending his soliloquy, almost in tears, voice trembling, sorry for himself. . . . Terry rushes in from doorway lower R. . . . He turns on her terrified. "How now," a scream of dismay, has some one overheard? No. It's only you. "What news?" he gasps, struggling to smile, and again she sweeps him into the flooding tide of her iniquity. In that brief scene (they took it slowly) every phase of human emotion came from their voices, gestures. He self-centred, reluctant to risk. She, annoyed, bitter, sarcastic, contemptuous. He sulky, turns back on her. She works herself up into a fury, dashes hands against the battlements. He gives way. Her "we fail"—the splendid scorn in her cry. She draws him aside, lowers voice, outlines the design. Irving shouts admiration, wonder, his eyes dilated, whole body quivering with homage for such a wife. "Bring forth men children only." At that curtain I remember Gladstone in a box, hand behind ear, intent with admiration, rising to applaud with the whole house, old Drury Lane (actually the Lyceum), gloriously rejoicing.
>
> As I knew his sons, Harry and Laurence—we were boys together—occasionally, I saw something of rehearsals. Irving was careful for other entrances. Act v, scene 3. Macbeth feels safe from Birnam Wood and man not born of woman. Suddenly enters a Messenger with bad news. Irving leaps at him, catches him by the throat, nigh chokes the fellow. "The devil damn thee black." How he spat it out, shaking his sliver out. That was rehearsed a dozen times, and the man had to drink three pots of beer to recover.

Again, without his wife Macbeth is self-centred, Act v, scene 3, "I have lived long enough. . . ." Irving utterly dejected, voice bitterly miserable. For her still hoping. "Canst thou not minister. . . ." Eager pleading like a child shut out, exquisitely the words fell. Furious at refusal he turns away, as one would shout, "You and all your stuff be damned." The last blow, her death. Irving is utterly alone, naked in spirit, facing his enemies. "Creeps in this petty pace from day to day." He is walking at his own funeral. Each word uttered like a stroke of the Passing Bell.

Great actor, he took great care for stage setting; simplicity and strength in his surroundings were manifest. Many memories of him return as I write. Shylock to Terry's Portia. The Jew money-lender of the period, stalking the stage with clutching feet like the claws of a bird of prey, shoulders flapping like ill-omened wings. He seemed physically a vulture. Marvellous make-up, indescribable gesture.

August 28 *Monday*

Jock called. Reminded me that at the last broadcast of *Everyman* they faded out the Voice of God, saying, "You will now hear Sandy Macpherson on the organ. From the Granada Cinema, Tooting Bec." Or some such place. We agreed that the first condition of high office at Broadcasting House is to have eaten of the insane root that takes the reason prisoner.

September 3 *Sunday*

Waiting for my bus the other evening, I heard a woman who had just come away from *Cosi fan Tutte* at the Prince's say to her friend, "Oh, I *liked* it, dear. The costumes were heaven! But couldn't they have got some *other* music for it?" ! ! ! !

A friend tells me that in one of the intervals of *Peer Gynt* he over-heard this in the foyer:

HIGHBROW (*holding forth to a circle of admirers*). Of course it's sheer vandalism to hear foreign masterpieces in a translation. One should hear them *only* in the original.

COMMON LITTLE MAN (*butting in*). But I 'ave 'eard this in the original.

HIGHBROW. You have? How very thrilling! Tell me, what did it sound like? Marvellous, of course.

COMMON LITTLE MAN. Dunno about marvellous. To me it sounded like the News in Norwegian!

191

September 12 *Tuesday*

Some people think when I write "highbrow" I mean "intellectual". I don't. Perhaps Johnny Morton's best story will help:

> A soldier said to an old lady, "So when we got to Wipers——" "*Ypres*," said the old lady. The soldier resumed: "So when we got to Wipers——" "*Ypres*," said the old lady. The soldier heaved a sigh, and began again: "So when we got to Wipers——" "*Ypres*," said the old lady. "Cor," said the soldier, "you ain't 'arf got 'iccups."

A highbrow, in my connotation, is an intellectual with hiccups.

September 13 *Wednesday*

Flabbergasted to find that G. M. Trevelyan's *English Social History* has the following Publisher's Note: "An American edition of this work was published in 1942, but owing to paper shortage over here in war-time it has only become possible to publish it in Great Britain in 1944." The book, which is a miracle of erudition, contains, roughly, a quarter of a million words. I have found out from authoritative sources that during the years 1942 and 1943—that is to say, in a time of total war—2967 works of fiction were published in this country. Taking it that sixty-seven of these were not the usual pin-headed drivel of the kind I wade through week after week, this means that paper was found for some 250 000 000 words of utter punk! But, of course, in the case of Trevelyan's work, paper couldn't be found for some 250 000 words of something akin to genius. Let the social historian of five hundred years hence try to explain *that* away! Mind you, I don't want a censorship of books. I hold that publishers should be free to print what they want. But I also hold, and hold strongly, that when this country produces a masterpiece the publishers should get together and say, "We are going to produce this book by hook or by crook, willy-nilly, and whatever the state of the paper situation. We'll pool it. Or we'll toss up which of us is to have it, and the rest of us will each contribute a bit of paper for it." I know publishers meet because I have addressed a meeting of publishers! Am suggesting in the *Express* that next time a book of first-class importance appears on the horizon the publishers shall call a meeting and address themselves!

September 15 *Friday*

As I sat attentive at Olivier's *Richard III* to-night I seemed to see an extraordinary succession of images—Charles II plotting mischief, any old actor's Robert Macaire and Alfred Jingle, any good actor's

Iago and even Iachimo, and above all a great deal of Irving's
Mephistopheles. People still talk of the way in which the Old Man
would say about Martha, "I don't know what's to become of her—*I*
won't have her!" Yes, there was a great deal of Irving in to-night's
performance, in the bite and devilry of it, the sardonic impudence, the
superb emphases, the sheer malignity and horror of it. If I have a
criticism it is that Olivier is a little inclined to step out of the picture.
Richard is immensely tickled at the virtuosity with which he proposes
to take the world-stage, and in his hero's opening soliloquy Shakespeare
is at great pains to convey this relish. But Olivier makes that speech
rather more than something overheard. This Richard means us to
overhear; we are positively tipped the wink.

> Now are our brows bound with victorious wreaths;
> Our bruised arms hung up for monuments;
> Our stern alarums changed to merry meetings,
> Our dreadful marches to delightful measures.
> Grim-visaged war hath smooth'd his wrinkled front, I don't think:

Olivier may not say those last three words; his eyebrows certainly
signal them.

This Richard coheres from start to finish, and there is a complete
presentation of the character as the actor sees it and his physical means
permit. Yet one has to close one's ears to certain disadvantages.
Take that moment when Stanley says "Richmond is on the seas,'
and Richard has his tremendous "There let him sink, and be the seas
on him!" Like Irving, Olivier has not the voice for this. And it was
here that old Martha came to mind, that I seemed to hear Irving
chuckle "There let her sink, and be the seas on her!" It is a moot point
whether Richard's "There is no creature loves me" should or should
not crook a finger at pathos. Olivier says "No" firmly. This Richard
is bent on carrying the joke through. And on the note of

> March on, join bravely, let us to't pell-mell;
> If not to heaven, then hand in hand to hell

he brings the drama to a jaunty, Jingle-esque conclusion. To sum up,
I don't think that this is Shakespeare's Richard. It could not be said
of Laurence Olivier's Renaissance villain at the end that "The bloody
dog is dead". (The boar was Gloucester's device, and "dog" is Shakespeare's equivalent.) But this Richmond wouldn't be able to say "dog".
What he would say over Olivier's corpse is: "We have scotch'd the
snake *and* kill'd it!" But even if this Richard is not Shakespeare's it
is very definitely Olivier's. In one respect only do I fault John Burrell's
production; it is too glittering and too band-boxy. Everybody, like
Pinero's French governess, is over-gowned and over-hatted. Let it
be recorded that, according to the programme, Ralph Richardson
appears as "Earl of Richmond, afterwards King Edward VII" ! !

September 17 *Sunday*

Our Ernest [Newman] is at it again. In to-day's *S.T.* he writes:

> When you diffidently suggest to one of the blind-spot Delians that
> one reason why Delius's operas, for instance, have not secured
> the place they deserve in the repertory may be that all his characters
> seem to speak much the same language, he will as likely as not,
> judging from my own experience, rejoin that the language is
> equally the same in all the Mozart or all the Wagner operas.

This is the flattest nonsense. I should never dream of saying this
about Wagner. Introduce five bars of the Prelude to *Lohengrin* into
the middle of the Prelude to *Tristan*, and I promise Ernest that I shall
twig it. Let King Mark break into the Steersman's song from *The
Flying Dutchman*, and even the Covent Garden audience would twig it.
But if I were to insert, say, fifty bars of "Song before Sunrise" into
"In a Summer Garden", I don't believe that one per cent. of the
Albert Hall audience would notice it. I don't believe Delius himself
would have noticed it. As a super-Delian put it at lunch to-day:
"Delius is all intoxication, but it's all the same intoxication. Wagner
has a hundred ways of making you tight." Of course Wagner has his
finger-prints, but he was also a mighty composer of tunes, whereas
Delius is all finger-prints and nothing you can hum. Musical thought?
But what musicologists like Ernest always fail to realise is that a
composer can cerebrate like six Senior Wranglers and argue like twelve
Immanuel Kants, but that it will avail him nothing if he can't think of a
tune; that what the ordinary music-lover is critical of is not pure reason
but pure sound. I had just written the last word when from the wireless
came the plaintive strains of "On Hearing the First Cuckoo in Spring".
Leo said, "This music moves me to tears, it's so *autumnal!*"

September 18 *Monday*

Looked again into Paul Wilstach's *Life of Richard Mansfield*, which
has a great deal about that actor's Richard III, including the Preface
to his version of that play. In this Mansfield puts the case not only
for Richard as a good-looking man—"The Countess of Desmond,
who danced with him at King Edward's Court, declared him 'the
handsomest man in the room, his brother, the King, excepted' "—but
as a non-criminal:

> The deformity of his mind, as drawn by Shakespeare, has to be
> adhered to, although history fails to corroborate it. Richard did
> not slay Edward, the son of Henry VI, he did not kill King Henry,
> he did not murder his Queen, the Lady Anne, and there are grave
> doubts as to his having been implicated in the deaths of Edward V

and his brother, absolutely no evidence existing that Henry VII did not find both Princes alive upon his succession.

This is indeed to make Richard the mildest-manner'd man that ever cut a throat. But I gather that Mansfield had the sense to act Shakespeare's man and not history's. When Mr G. produced *Macbeth* I remember discussing with him the length of time that is supposed to elapse between the murder of Duncan and the final catastrophe, in history a matter of some twenty years. His answer was the very good one that Shakespeare always wrote for swift performance, which corroborates *my* notion that in the play of *Macbeth* some two years elapse. Mansfield raises a similar point in connection with *Richard III*. The battle of Tewkesbury took place on May 4, 1471, and Henry's death, probably murder, some fortnight later. Mansfield points out that at this date Richard was only nineteen. Since the battle of Bosworth occurred on August 22, 1485, it follows that we must suppose fourteen years to elapse. I have never seen any Richard who conveyed this, and for the good reason that Shakespeare ignores the time-lag. I remember a production—I forget whose—in which Richmond dropped his sword and let the daggerless Richard claw the air and make in-effectual attempts to beat him down with his bare hands. I want something more. I want Richard to *hear* the words "The bloody dog is dead." I want to see him try to rise as Richmond puts his foot on him. I want to see in Richard's face the sense of defeat as well as the terror of dying.

September 19 *Tuesday*

From C. B. Cochran:

St James's Court
Buckingham Gate, S.W.
The Sunday of "King Richard III"

MY DEAR JAMES,

Since last Thursday afternoon, when I saw *Richard III*, I have been impatient for this morning. Your essay is masterly—I cannot imagine a more distinguished bit of criticism. It is so right and so very clear.

It is a superb achievement on the part of Olivier, but as I told Evelyn (she did not see the play with me), he plays it on the lines of Irving's Mephistopheles; and spoken as Larry speaks them, the lines lend themselves very well to this treatment. The funeral procession—Lady Anne scene—was in every particular strangely like my old governor's (Richard Mansfield's). I thought it very fine. R. M. always imagined that Kean played this scene on the same lines. Even the more anti-Mansfield critics admitted the beautiful quality of his voice, which, to his credit, he never over-played. I found the long afternoon at the New short and exhilarating. The whole Vic–Richardson–Olivier enterprise is tremendously interesting.

How right you are about the clothes! Everybody (except the Lord Mayor) had been to the same fashionable tailor, and they were all wearing their Sunday best for the first time. When Mansfield produced *Cyrano de Bergerac* I took over to him an exact reproduction of Coquelin's production—*i.e.*, the costumes. Five or six dress parades, with stage lighting, were held while Mansfield (a good painter) directed the breaking of them down until they lost all appearance of stage or fancy-dress costumes. The result was a series of real-life pictures of the period represented. I horrified Dulac when I did the same with his lovely costumes for the production I made at the Garrick with Bob Loraine. As one of the stage managers said: "In three hours the Governor's knocked three thousand quids' worth of costumes down to threepence!"

I have sold my last piano, my understudy pictures are on my walls, but I have the price of a lunch for you any day and place at your choice. A suggestion would give me great pleasure.

Yours as ever,
CHARLES B. COCHRAN

P.S. Shaw told me Barry Sullivan's *Richard III* was terrific. I think Wolfit's is grand, and I still think his *Lear* is the best Shakespearean performance I have seen in thirty years.

September 20 *Wednesday*

Ran into Malcolm Sargent at the Ivy. He said Delius had only one emotion—the expression of loveliness. "His music knows nothing about passion, hate, anger, jealousy, or the emotions of ordinary people; his concern is solely the expression of beauty. And I personally don't want it to be anything more." Somebody said, "But surely that limits the man as an artist?" SARGENT. "Why? I shouldn't regard a mystic who spent his life in an effort to achieve unity with the Deity as a limited being." J. A. "Perhaps not. But I should regard an evening spent watching a Buddhist contemplate his navel as a limited form of amusement. Ten minutes of it would be enough for me; and I have had my fill of Delius after ten minutes." Sargent went on to talk about modern idiom in music and the folly of believing that, because Man has invented the aeroplane, music should sound like a factory turning out Spitfires.

October 1 *Sunday*

To illustrate "that quality of elliptical association which so often, if not always, is so important a constituent in poetry which may legitimately be called 'pure' ", V. Sackville-West, in to-day's *Observer*, quotes the following from a volume of poems by Frederic Prokosch:

> When dusk caresses all our heads,
> When all the curtains touch the sill,
> When darkness cloaks the troubled beds
>   And torches dot the hill.
>
> When ships divide the intriguing night,
> When lust new agonies explores,
> When sailors watch the flickering light
>   Along their luckless shores.
>
> When all the impassioned lovers kiss,
> When madmen count the stars anew,
> When whales in their gigantic bliss
>   Lie trembling two by two. . . .

V. Sackville-West then asks:

> What are the whales doing here? They startle us by their sudden appearance after the homely observation of curtains touching the sill, yet any appreciative reader will instantly recognise that they are exactly right in the place where they occur.

But why whales? Why not any other mammal? I spent half an hour this morning composing three verses where the equally unexpected seems to me to be equally right:

> When gum-trees droop a sleepy head,
> When bridegrooms first in earnest woo,
> When kangaroos hop into bed,
>   Twining a tail or two.
>
> When school-marms still their charges' fears,
> When kings and queens enjoy a romp,
> When crocodiles forgo their tears,
>   Canoodling in the swamp.
>
> When stable-doors are locked at night,
> When lechers brace their muscles tense,
> When pigs with wings are steep in flight—
>   Then singing whales make sense.

Note the "elliptical association" in the fifth and seventh lines. This presumes that modern school-marms still retain the 'crocodile'.

October 18 *Wednesday*

Went to-night to Mr G.'s fourth and most moving *Hamlet*. Beautiful production by George Rylands. Leslie Banks very good as the King, and Miles Malleson a superb Polonius. Hamlet is not a young man's part. Who wants or expects a stripling to hold forth on the life after death, the propriety of suicide, the nature of man, the exuberance or restraint of matrons, the actor's art, the Creator's "large discourse"? Mr G. has now reached the right age; he is at the height of his powers; and the conjunction is marvellously happy. When, fourteen years ago at the Old Vic, the curtain went up on the new *Hamlet* there was perhaps not very much there except infinite grace. Four years later, after the production at the New Theatre, I find that I wrote: "The impression gathered is that of a Hamlet who can fly into the most shattering of pets." Five years later (Lyceum): "One's impression of this brilliant performance does not outlast the moment of its brilliance. It is cometary. That's Hamlet, that was! And the sky is empty again." I was delighted to find to-night that our First Player has, at last, stopped all the gaps. He is now unchallengeably this generation's rightful tenant of this "monstrous Gothic castle of a poem". He has acquired an almost Irvingesque quality of pathos, and, in the passages after the play scene, an incisiveness, a raillery, a mordancy worthy of the Old Man. To-night he imposed on me all this play's questing feverishness; the middle act gave me ninety minutes of high excitement and assured virtuosity; I don't remember that Forbes-Robertson was more bedazzling in the "O, what a rogue and peasant slave" soliloquy. Indeed, I think there is no doubt that this is, and is likely to remain, the best Hamlet of our time, and that is why I shall urge John to stick to the mantle of tragedy and leave lesser garments to others. For, like John Philip Kemble, he is not really a comedian. J. P. had the notion that by taking thought an actor can qualify himself for the lighter as for the more serious side of his art. This is rubbish. All the trying in the world would not have turned, say, Matthew Arnold into a dinner-table wit. It is the same with acting. Whenever I see John in a comic part I bethink me of Kemble, and Hazlitt's tale of his "unaccountable abstracted air, the contracted eyebrows, and suspended chin of a man about to sneeze". No, despite the Congrevian antics, I cannot see or hear the comedian in Mr G., who for comedy substitutes a wonderful line of something that is half superciliousness and half moral priggishness. He would be admirable as Sir Willoughby Patterne or Aubrey Tanqueray. If Dickens had cast his novels in the form of plays he would have made a magnificent Dombey, a superb Mr Littimer (always supposing he had not cast himself for Steerforth), and a devastatingly subtle Mr Mould. "How much consolation may I have diffused among my fellow-creatures by means of my four long-tailed prancers, never harnessed under ten pund ten!" As a comedian our First Player has no warmth, whereas as a tragedian he is all fire. He lives up to G. H. Lewes's dictum: the greatest artist is he who is greatest in the highest reaches of his art. And that is why I conjure him to stick to those rôles which entitle his critics to pronounce him a great actor. I shall make something of all this on Sunday.

October 21 *Saturday*

Went again last night to *Richard III*. Olivier has heightened and deepened and widened his performance out of recognition; it is now a masterpiece of *gouaillerie*, and the death scene is as tremendous as, judging from Hazlitt, I take Kean's to have been. Took Larry and Vivien Leigh to supper afterwards, when the Café Royal provided a banquet of roast partridges washed down with burgundy, which I can't drink, and champagne, which I find I still can. V. L. turns out to be as intelligent as she is pretty. Over and over again she said how much she preferred theatre to screen, and was backed up by Larry saying that film-acting is no job for an actor. He denied that Jock, who has arranged the text for the *Henry V* film, has painted the leaves of the trees yellow. "It's going to be a very green Agincourt."

November 14 *Tuesday*

> *D2 Albany*
> *Picadilly*
> *November* 13*th*, '44

MY DEAR JAMES,

If you can manage it, you will give me much pleasure by reporting for duty at La Corvette (Arlington Street, just behind the Ritz) at 7.15 on Friday, the 17th. I want you to be punctual because (*a*) restaurants now wait for no man, and (*b*) being kept waiting puts me into an unbuddhistic rage.

Now, Jimmie Agate, you critic of plays,
Here's a subject made to your hand.

A lady has offered to put up £10 000 after the war if I like to start a kind of Super-Stage-Society. What plays would you choose from those that we know about already? At present I have not got further than *Sakuntalā* (Binyon's version is said to be good), *Paolo and Francesca* (Phillips), *The House of Borgia* (Bax), *The Fair Maid of the West* (Heywood). I should exult in presenting *'Tis Pity*, but the praiseworthy Wolfit has done it recently enough. I should do my best, of course, to find distinguished contemporary foreign plays, but will Europe write such plays until another twenty years have gone? And by that time I shall be pleading with St Peter to allow you just occasionally to come up and see how the angels can interpret the Baxian masterpieces.

> Yours with friendship and admiration,
> C. B.

Queen Alexandra Mansions, W.C.2.
November 14th, 1944

My DEAR CLIFFORD,

I shall be there on Friday, and if not on the dot, then on a neighbouring one.

Yes, I think your Super-Stage-Society is a very good notion. Nobody can be induced to go to a plain cinema, whereas every one will flock to a Super-Cinema. But your present programme leaves me cold. I am horrified at the prospect of anything with a name like *Sakuntalā*, which smacks of India and anklets. To sit through *Paolo and Francesca* is like making a meal of pineapple cream. *The House of Borgia.* Non, mon vieux! The play of yours which ought to be revived is *Socrates*, but only if you can get Lewis Casson. Last, I don't care two hoots whether the Fair Maid came from the West, the East, the North, or the South. But then I know exactly what will happen to your Society. You will begin with a revival of *Twelfth Night*. You will follow this with the revival of some piece of Shavian talkativeness, and wind up with a reproduction of whatever masterpiece by Jack Priestley came off in the West End the week before.

But if you were serious! Of the great plays I have seen and should like to see again, here are one or two. Shakespeare's *Titus Andronicus*, which in the theatre I prefer to either *Cymbeline* or *Troilus and Cressida*. Beaumont and Fletcher's *The Maid's Tragedy*, with Sonia Dresdel as Evadne. Colman's *The Clandestine Marriage*. Do you remember Hazlitt? Ogleby, he says, "is as crazy a piece of elegance and refinement, even after he is wound up for the day, as can be well imagined; yet in the hands of a genuine actor his tottering step, his twitches of the gout, his unsuccessful attempts at youth and gaiety, take nothing from the nobleman. He has the *ideal* model in his mind, resents his deviations from it with proper horror, recovers himself from any ungraceful action as soon as possible; does all he can with his limited means, and fails in his just pretensions, not from inadvertence, but necessity." O. B. Clarence was superb in this part when I saw him sixteen years ago. He is, I am glad to say, alive and hearty, and could still play Ogleby. I am particularly fond of this play and this performance, and would think ten thousands pounds well spent on a venture which began and ended with this. And how about Drinkwater's *Robert E. Lee*, Richard Pryce's *Frolic Wind*, and Jean Cocteau's *Les Parents Terribles*?

Now a few plays I have never seen but want to. What about Olivier in Massinger's *A New Way to Pay Old Debts*? Judging from his Richard III, his Sir Giles Overreach should be very fine. Then why not Mr G. and Wolfit as Jaffier and Pierre in Otway's *Venice Preserved*? The main difficulty would be to get these two actors on to the same stage at the same time, John taking fright at Wolfit's over-plus of power, and Wolfit shying at John's elegances. "Two stars keep not their motion in one sphere."

And then Belvidera would be another difficulty. Byron was right
to describe her as a "maudlin bitch"; nevertheless the part takes
acting, and is beyond the reach of our modern ninnies about
four foot six inches high and weighing four stone three. Lastly I
want to see Ibsen's *Pillars of Society*. If you guarantee me the
above programme without any deletion you can put me down for
the sum of one guinea.

Ever your
James

P.S. A remark I overheard to-day may amuse you:
1ST YOUNG HIGHBROW. At least you must allow that Gielgud
is a good actor.
2ND YOUNG HIGHBROW. I just wouldn't know. I'm allergic to
Hamlet.

November 15 *Wednesday*

Went to see Hollywood's version of Van Druten's *Old Acquaintance*.
Shall burst into prose in the *S.T.* Something on these lines:
Consider great whales. Think of tumbling oceans. Of lazy, tropic
beaches and feathery trees. Of mountain-tops that freeze. Of earth-
quakes and cataclysms. Of all the things the film can do magnificently
and the theatre cannot look at. And then the time came when even the
film-makers got tired of looking at it, and decided there was more "to"
the pictures than the mere presentation of the outdoor and the outsize.
Hence those warning shadows, those garrets under Paris roofs, that
swirl of skirts above a dropped dance-programme, those enigmatic
sledges, those equivocal glooms. The decision once taken that the
pictures should cease being a paranoiac panorama and become
"cinema", the ensuing coquettings with famous novels were inevitable.
Would Mea Culpa look well in Lydia Bennet's sprigged muslin?
Would Thea Culpa find Dora Spenlow's bonnet sufficiently becoming?
Would Maxima Culpa shine at the Duchess of Richmond's ball? Of
course. Wherefore these things came to pass. I have never been able
to make out who's who in *Wuthering Heights*, but it didn't prevent
Olivier from being extremely effective in the snow and among gorse.
I was never able to get through *Gone with the Wind*, which didn't
prevent me from revelling in Vivien Leigh's presentation of some
swaying, tossing tulip.
Later the theatre was laid under contribution. And foolishly people
said, "How Shakespeare would have welcomed the films!" quoting in
support Chorus's

Think, when we talk of horses, that you see them
Printing their proud hoofs i' the receiving earth.

Either Shakespeare wrote this in a hurry or he just wasn't an intellectual. Anyhow, a moment's reflection would have convinced him that when you can see horses prancing and curveting there ceases to be any need to put that prancing and curveting into words. "You've had it." Neville Cardus once wrote of Woolley's off-drives that they were "like butter-flies going into the flame". But he was writing for a public which had not seen Woolley's innings. I had been with Cardus at Lord's that after-noon, and what he said was not "Look at that butterfly going into the flame!" but "Well played, sir!" Consider *Hamlet*, and what an appalling amount of extraneous stuff the film will have to show if it is going to be something more than a strict photograph of the acted play. We shall be shown the young Fortinbras sharking up his lawless resolutes; Claudius taking his rouse; the morn, in Technicolor clad, walking o'er the dew of yon high eastward hill, the glow-worm paling his uneffectual fire; the wind setting in the shoulder of Laertes' sail; what Danskers are in Paris; Hamlet's voyage to England, with his first and last essay in pocket-picking; Ophelia pull'd to muddy death; and flashbacks showing Hamlet *père* sleeping in his orchard, and Yorick bearing Hamlet *fils* on his back.

The itch to reproduce A in terms of B knows no cure. Witness the cinema organist in full blast at something composed for the violin, radio fiddlers scraping away at something written for the piano, and concert pianists hammering out pieces devised for full orchestra—for example, the Overture to *Tannhäuser*. It is partly this mania for transformation and partly the paucity of original ideas which has driven Hollywood into its versions of stage plays. Here it resembles the sailor who, in the lady's novel, steering for both Scylla and Charybdis, was in danger of missing both. The essence of the theatre is that everything is happening in a small, artificially lighted box: the essence of the cinema is that it has the whole daylight world to play about in. Scylla is the mere photographing of the play, in which case the cinema loses everything it stands for. Charybdis is going outside the play and showing you in action that which on the stage is merely related; this brings to nothing all the art and craft of play-making. In the theatre Van Druten's comedy was reasonably exciting because it fulfilled expectations aroused in a theatre, and because it was a comedy of good manners to which Edith Evans brought a whole armoury of wit and irony, while Marian Spencer, fortified by some preposterous hats, was the embodiment of delicious and fluffy riot. The film made the play seem dull because, while happening in a cinema, it turned its back on the cinema's peculiar qualities of change, variety, and excitement, and partly because the play had been turned into a comedy of bad manners. Bette Davis elected to make several appearances in pyjamas lacking the lower half, and indulged in the solecism: "Let you and I talk it over." (Shade of Millamant!) As for the goose-like little novelist, methought Miriam Hopkins's performance the last thing in tedium.

November 16 *Thursday*

Spent the day correcting the proofs of *Immoment Toys*. Particularly pleased with the suggestion, which I had forgotten, that Gracie Fields should play St Joan.

Violet Loraine told me at lunch that it was to her that Mrs Pat made that one of her sallies which I regard as the least expected and most glorious. It was at a soirée at Claridge's or somewhere, at which a famous coloratura singer was to perform. She came on. Mrs Pat, taking one look at the singer's enormous jowl, stopped chatting to the duchess on her other side and said to Vi, "My God! She looks like I do in a spoon!"

November 23 *Thursday*

Part of a letter from a lady:

Have been three times lately to see Mr Gielgud's *Hamlet*. And, each time, have been as rapt and enthralled as the rest of the audience—those lovely words—that lovely voice and diction— that princely bearing—noble conception! Came out, feeling as one imagines some musical enthusiast would do on hearing a Paderewski or Kreisler perform his favourite piece.—*Perfect* work—*perfect* interpretation—*perfect* instrument!—And then—as you yourself said of his previous presentation, "That's Gielgud— that was!" Was it Mr Gielgud's reputation, dazzling one, and causing one to concentrate on the actor's virtuosity, rather than the woes of Hamlet?—Twenty years ago I saw the same play at the same theatre. The star was John Barrymore, and I was twenty, and had only seen one Shakespearean play before. Surely, more of an occasion for confused and englamoured dazzlement and distraction—but I cried for Hamlet! Barrymore was smaller— hardly as princely in bearing, with a lighter voice. Nor had he the same way with poetry. He said: "Things rank and gross in nature possess it *mee-eerely!*"—and things like that, stressing unexpected words with great and inexplicable vehemence! And what a cold he had! His speeches were punctuated with the most resounding sniffs and snorts heard in any theatre since. His Hamlet was a *much* coarser fellow than Mr Gielgud's, too. But I only have to read my *Hamlet* now to hear and see him! Do you remember him in the closet scene? (Mr MacCarthy faulted it—said it was too intense, with Freudian implications, or something! Freudian fiddlesticks!) Do you remember how he launched himself, still kneeling, at Gertrude, as he besought her to lay not that flattering unction to her soul?—he *pommelled* the floor with his knees, a desperate, impotent little action, like a very small child whose emotions have gone past its powers of expression. A youthful action, most calculated to pull at the mother's heart.

November 30 *Thursday*

Here is the result of four days' agonising labour about the *Henry V* film. I would remark here that while there is an art of writing on a threepenny bit there is also an art of reading such writing.

FROM THE THEATRE ANGLE

He goes but to see a noise that he heard. . . .
A Midsummer Night's Dream

No, I do not believe that you can take a lot of Home Guards, dress them up in chain-mail knitted out of wool and sprayed with gold or aluminium paint (real armour would be no better), set them on a lot of horses, turn a handle, and blandly announce *Henry V.*

What is the object of a Shakespeare film? Is it to popularise Shakespeare? But with me he is already popular. Or to popularise our national poet with a public of which 95 per cent. has never seen a Shakespeare play, and 5 per cent. the inside of a theatre? First let us consider the matter of seating capacity. If every seat in every theatre in the United Kingdom were taken for every performance throughout the year the maximum number of playgoers that could be accommodated is under 100 millions. Yet according to the figures published in 1921 by the Parliamentary Commission on the Cinema, the number of persons who visited the films in the previous year was 1078 millions! (To-day increased, I suggest, to 3000 millions.) Seeing that all these non-playgoers have taken to the films like Donald Ducks to water, why not, runs the simple-seeming argument, use the films as a means of getting Shakespeare to the people? And I say: Not so fast. Are we sure that what is ultimately got over to the cinema audience will be Shakespeare? Or will it be something else? Chorus, you remember, says in this play:

> Still be kind,
> And eke out our performance with your mind.

But is the film public possessed of the kind of mind which is necessary to eke out a Shakespearean performance? "Sir," said Dr Johnson, "if you talk of *Cecilia* talk on." The reverse is, I fancy, the attitude of the filmgoer in the matter of *Henry V.* "Cut the cackle and come to the 'osses" is the unspoken demand here. In this connection the reader might like to be reminded of that dinner-party in which Saki's Stephen Thorle, recounting his slum experiences, said: "The gratitude of those poor creatures when I presented them with a set of table crockery apiece, the tears in their eyes and their voices when they thanked me, would be impossible to describe." And how Comus Bassington replied: "Thank you all the same for describing it." I do not think the filmgoer will thank Shakespeare for his descriptions of the joys of battle or the worries of kingship, unnecessary verbiage keeping him from the 'osses.

As a Shakespearean I care nothing for these battle-orgies. They are magnificent, and they are undoubtedly war. But they are not Shakespeare, who neither enacts the Battle of Agincourt nor describes it. He takes the playgoer straight from

> Now, soldiers, march away:
> And how thou pleasest, God, dispose the day!

to the Constable's "O diable" and Orleans's "O seigneur! le jour est perdu." Unless we count the comic episode with Pistol and his French prisoner there is nothing to show how the English came to win and the French to lose the day. As a Shakespearean I no more want interpolated cavalry charges in this great play that I want to see seascapes and naval fights in *Antony and Cleopatra*. Shakespeare put all of the Battle of Actium that matters dramatically into four an a half lines:

> She once being loof'd,
> The noble ruin of her magic, Antony,
> Claps on his sea-wing, and like a doting mallard,
> Leaving the fight in height, flies after her:
> I never saw an action of such shame.

I refuse to believe that model ships careering about in a tin bath, or even two actual-size, carefully reconstructed fleets manned by sailors bronzed by Blackpool's sun and wind, shaking out topgallants and swearing good, round Latin and Egyptian oaths, are going to add anything to those four and a half tragic lines. Or that Hamlet's "There are more things in heaven and earth, Horatio," would be enhanced by sequences depicting Halley's comet and San Francisco's earthquake. For me these actualities defeat their purpose. When Olivier stood up in his stirrups with sword upraised waiting to give the signal to the attent bowmen, I thought not of Shakespeare's Henry but of some modern conductor with baton poised ready to start the din in "Helden-leben". And fell into contemplation of an essay which should be called "Sir Thomas and the Aldershot Tattoo".

All the early part struck me as enchanting. But when the film flew, so to speak, out of window, Shakespeare, as far as I was concerned, walked out of door. The maker of any Shakespeare picture must, in my opinion, choose between photographing the acted play, as the first half of this film does, and taking the camera out of doors and shooting the *raw material* of the drama as the second half of this picture does. If the first choice is made then I see no harm in enlarging the scope of the film to include shots of the London of 1600 and the audience at the Globe Theatre. If the second choice be preferred then let us be allowed to *forget the playhouse altogether* and open with that "antechamber in the King's palace" furnished as it conjecturally was in 1415. And after that to France, at the risk of mistaking Agincourt for Sunningdale or St Andrews! "The centuries kiss and commingle". But I won't have them mingling; the result can only be a jumble of planes. Which is fatal. Only by strict choice and adherence, by

knowing its mind and sticking to it, can the screen hope to techni-
colour the lily and re-gild Shakespeare's gold.

The acting? As a critic of the theatre I must praise Olivier for a
superb performance throughout and in particular for that *geniality*
which makes "A little touch of Harry in the night" credible in
connection with Shakespeare's cold, calculating prig. (How many
filmgoers—or playgoers for that matter—ever give full value to the
infamous soliloquy in Henry IV, Part 1, about imitating the sun
hiding behind base contagious clouds? How W. S. came to write
this knavish, political stuff I don't know. A little touch of Francis
in the script?) As a dramatic critic who has strayed into the
cinema I must award the palm to that steed (White Surrey's
progenitor?) from whose back Henry orates. This animal has
perfectly realised that

> In films there's nothing so becomes a horse
> As modest stillness and humility.

For here Henry's mount kept very, very still, though it was lively
enough later on. Which means that I, even I, have cut Shakespeare's
cackle and come to the 'oss.

December 4 *Monday*

Queen Alexandra Mansions, W.C.2.
December 4th, 1944

DEAR JOCK,

Did you ever go with me to the Ring in Blackfriars? If so you
may remember the pub opposite. It had a snack-bar in which hung
a remarkable picture. This was an oil painting of a caged lion.
The landlord had removed the painted bars and substituted real
ones containing chicken-bones off which the lion was supposed
to have dined. Your film is exactly like that. Fashions in art may
and do change; one of them—surrealism—has come and is
already going. But fundamental principles are unchanging and
everlasting. The first of these is that a work of art must be consistent with itself, choose its plane, and stay there. Not principalities
nor powers, nor things present, nor things to come, nor height,
nor depth, nor any other creature shall gainsay this.

You cannot have Chorus first regretting that he cannot produce
"the very casques that did affright the air at Agincourt", and then
producing them. You cannot just add the thing described to the
description and enjoy the sum of both. Or would you have Othello
deliver his speech to the Senate followed by a sequence of all
those moving accidents by flood and field? Would you have Octavius
Caesar remind Antony that at Modena he drank the stale of
horses and then show him doing it? Or follow Enobarbus's barge
speech with an Alma-Tadema-ish view of the same? Or switch
from Friar Laurence to Mantua and show the Mantuans bringing
out their dead? Go to! A play's a play and a film's a film and
there's an end on't.

To fall into the Amanda Ros vein, I am surprised that you can think that the mighty cannon of my argument is puncturable by the puny grapeshot of contemporary film criticism. Do you quote *The Times* at me? Very well, I will quote *The Times* at you: "Miss Renee Ascherson, as Katharine, matches Mr Olivier's intelligence with a subdued coquettishness which makes the final scene perhaps the best of all." What would be thought of a *stage* production of *Henry V* in which the most effective thing was Henry and Katharine carrying on, as Edward would have said, like twitter-mice? No, Jock, I wired you after the performance that Olivier, or you, or somebody, had done an impermissible thing, and done it brilliantly. There is one line of argument open to you. This is the sociological line that it is better the mob should have bastard Shakespeare than none at all. But let us not confuse this with the suggestion that bastard Shakespeare is Shakespeare. A sofa is not a bed because you can sleep on it. A film is not Shakespeare because it entertains an audience.

Tell me, Jock, when the film was first mooted did you and Larry, realising that this was the first English filming of Shakespeare (not counting the Bergner), have a grand pow-wow on the subject of first principles? Or did you just dash into the thing with the notion that it would be "rather fun" to do half of it indoors and half in the open air? My guess—and I am writing like Brother Mycroft, except that he never guesses—is that first principles were never considered at all.

Here is the crux of the whole matter. Because film audiences know nothing about planes and wouldn't notice anything odd if you inserted half an hour of the Battle of Trafalgar into a film of a Jane Austen novel—presumably her naval officers fought somebody, somewhere, some time—am I to agree to your picture being made in the way it has been made rather than not at all? This raises the whole of Ivor Brown's "theatre and life" business. If it is better for the mass to have bastard Shakespeare than no Shakespeare, then I must hold that "I'm always chasing rain-bows", sung to the second subject of the Fantaisie Impromptu, is better than no Chopin. I don't say that Shakespeare's plays should not be screened, and I have pointed out two ways in which they can be screened. Having adopted one of these two legitimate ways, it then becomes lawful to lead the public to the Shakespearean well and see whether it will drink. But I insist that that well be Shakespeare's and nobody else's. I will have nothing to do with compromise. *Que je pactise? Jamais, Jamais*!

Ever your
JAMIE

December 21 Thursday

The question is not what we are to do with Germany after the war but with this country. My idea is to sentence the upper classes to the same fate as the lower—perpetual hard labour without imprisonment.

December 27 Wednesday

"The frog he would a-wooing go." But I doubt whether he courted his mistress as assiduously as I have courted fame, and now appear to have won it, or some measure of it, judging by the awards in this week's *Time and Tide* Literary Competition. The subject was a suggested Académie Anglaise of forty members, comparable to the Académie Française. G. M. Trevelyan heads the list with 80 votes— the English will always fall for a writer who is good in the sense that Mrs Baines's furniture was "good"—followed by Shaw with 60. H. G. Wells and E. M. Forster have 52 votes each, Masefield and Maugham 47 each. And so on and so on, with lots of Sitwells. I just scrape in with 18 votes, in company with H. E. Bates, Lord David Cecil, Noel Coward, C. S. Lewis, Desmond MacCarthy, and Harold Nicolson. I confess I am mightily gratified.

And think of the lovely people who are not in! G. W. Bishop, G. W. Stonier, and anybody who thinks the *Ego* books dull and repetitive. As Beetle said: "*Je vais gloater. Je vais gloater tout le* blessed afternoon. *Jamais j'ai gloaté comme je gloaterai aujourd'hui.*"

December 28 Thursday

Overheard in a bar:

AMERICAN SOLDIER: "You can't argue with me I'm ignorant!"

EGO 8

1945

January 8 *Monday*

Lunch with Hamish Hamilton at the Ivy, the other guests being Malcolm Sargent and Horace Horsnell. What was the best play written since the last war? The talk went something like this:

> SARGENT. *St Joan*, of course.
> J. A. There's no "of course" about it. We're trying to find the best *play*, and *St Joan* isn't a play, whatever else it may be.
> HAMILTON. Well, what do *you* say is the best play, James?
> J. A. *Juno and the Paycock*. Shaw's play second.
> HORSNELL (*sepulchrally*). Third.
> SARGENT. Why third?
> HORSNELL. Well, if you put *Juno* first you must put *The Plough and the Stars* second; you can't separate the two.
> J. A. I agree.
> HAMILTON. What do you say to that, Malcolm?
> J. A. (*before Malcolm can answer*). What is the most perfect opera you've ever heard?
> SARGENT. *Carmen*.
> HORSNELL, Attaboy!
> J. A. And the second?
> SARGENT. I suppose it would have to be *Meistersinger*. But there's always Mozart, you know!
> J. A. (*cold-shouldering Mozart*). Would you consider putting *Rosenkavalier* third?
> SARGENT (*humouring him*). I might consider it.
> J. A. Suppose that these are not operas but show-horses, and the class as it stands is headed by *Carmen, Meistersinger*, and *Rosenkavalier*. Now tell me. What do you do with that great, hulking forceful brute now coming into the ring—whose name, by the way, is *The Ring*?
> SARGENT. Well, I've no choice—I should have to put it either first or fourth. Or perhaps not even fourth. There's still Mozart.

209

J. A. Mozart be blowed!

HORSNELL. Anyhow, Malcolm, you've made James's point and mine. Shaw's play is either first or third, it can't be second.

SARGENT. What do you say, Hamish?

HAMILTON. I think we ought to leave it to the dramatic critics.

HORSNELL. It's up to you, James.

J. A. Well, if you want my serious opinion, I should put *Juno* first, *St Joan* second, and *The Plough and the Stars* third.

(*There is a general outcry at this, and a chorus of* "But you agreed . . .")

J. A. I know what I agreed. But I've told *St. Joan* to move down to third place, *and she won't budge*!

January 18 *Thursday*

The capture of Warsaw and the advance of the Russians have put me in mind of something which I am sending to the *S.T.* for its "Famous Retorts" series. This concerns one Népomucène Lemercier, the friend of Legouvé, the part-author of *Adrienne Lecouvreur*. According to Talleyrand, Lemercier was a brilliant chatterbox; when he was not chattering he exuded tragedies with names like *Agamemnon*. It was Lemercier who, at Malmaison, taught Napoleon the history of France. Later on the two quarrelled, and when Napoleon sent his old friend one of the first Crosses of the Legion of Honour it was returned. In revenge the Emperor forbade the performance of Lemercier's plays: Népomucène said nothing. Driven from his house, he took refuge in a garret and stopped both chattering and playwriting. And then one day, at the Tuileries, the Emperor perceived his old crony in a corner with other members of the Institute. Waving the crowd aside, Napoleon went up to him and said, "*Eh bien*, Lemercier, when are you going to write a new tragedy?" "*I am waiting, Sire!*" replied the poet. Surely a magnificent remark to make in 1812 on the eve of the Russian campaign!

February 27 *Tuesday*

Two ways of saying the same thing:

> I am dying, Egypt, dying; only
> I here importune death awhile, until
> Of many thousand kisses the poor last
> I lay upon thy lips.

> SHAKESPEARE, *Antony and Cleopatra*

Jean Gabin as the deserter in *Quai des Brumes* shot by bandits and saying to his sweetheart: "Embrasse-moi. Vite. On est pressé!"

March 7 Wednesday

Again two ways of saying the same thing:

> For myself I confess to have the smallest possible pleasure in a
> French actor when he is "profond et rêveur."
>   G. H. LEWIS, *On Actors and the Art of Acting*

> Furthermore, the guy seems to be improving right along, and
> gets so he can box fairly well and punch the bag, and all this and
> that, but he always has that far-away look in his eyes, and per-
> sonally I do not care for fighters with far-away looks.
>   DAMON RUNYON, *Bred for Battle*

April 27 Friday

The old heart-breaking subject has turned up again. A sergeant
in the Buffs submits a poem, "not with a request for advice on publication, nor for suggestions of how to break into the big money, but merely
for an opinion so as to confirm my worst fears, *i.e.*, that I am just
wasting my time, or to uphold what my friends tell me, that there is
merit in the effort." The letter has this postscript: "I may add, as a
point of interest, that I wrote the poem whilst engaged in tank fighting
in Normandy. We were standing by to go in, and it passed an hour
away." The poem is valueless. I have sent the following reply:

> *Queen Alexandra Mansions, W.C.2*
> *April 27th, 1945*

DEAR SERGEANT,

It seems to me—and I have thought about it a good deal—
that any work of art must have two functions. If you write a book
the first function is to get something off your chest; the second
is to give pleasure to the reader. The same thing applies to a
painting, a bust, or a piece of music, and equally to acting, singing,
playing a musical instrument, dancing.

Your poem is valueless as regards its secondary function,
which does not mean that it is valueless in its first function. I
doubt if you could have been better employed during that hour
before going into action. Look at it this way. Take the following
lines:

> Matthew is in his grave, yet now
> Methinks, I see him stand,
> As at that moment, with a bough
> Of wilding in his hand.

And now the following:

> He trudged along through copse and brake,
> He trudged along o'er hill and dale
> Nor for the moon cared he a tittle,
> And for the stars he cared as little,
> And for the murmuring river Swale.

Magic is in the first but not in the second. Yet it is quite possible that Wordsworth, getting the second off his chest, felt as much relief as he did with the first. You wanted to write those lines before that battle, and you wrote them. Yot got them off your chest, and you felt the better for it. That means that your poem fulfilled its first function. But it is not poetry. Are you going to ask me to define poetry? My dear Sergeant, better men than I have spent a lifetime over this and failed. Asked for a definition, that great minor poet A. E. Housman replied that he could no more define poetry than a terrier could define a rat, but that he thought both he and the terrier recognised the object by the symptoms which it provoked in them. These symptoms differ with the individual. The great critic Montague said that the sight or sound of a beautiful thing gave him gooseflesh. The form this emotion takes with me is a shiver at the base of the spine. I have no other criterion. Here are one or two specimens, and they all have to do with arms. First I choose Herbert Asquith's poem which begins:

> Here lies a clerk who half his life had spent
> Toiling at ledgers in a city grey,
> Thinking that so his days would drift away
> With no lance broken in life's tournament:

and ends:

> And falling thus he wants no recompense,
> Who found his battle in the last resort;
> Nor needs he any hearse to bear him hence,
> Who goes to join the men of Agincourt.

Next a poem by Patrick Shaw-Stewart, beginning:

> I saw a man this morning
>   Who did not wish to die;
> I ask and cannot answer
>   If otherwise wish I.

and ending:

> I will go back this morning
>   From Imbros over the sea;
> Stand in the trench, Achilles,
>   Flame-capped, and shout for me.

Third and last you might like to know John Pudney's *For Johnny*, of which most effective use is made in the film *The Way to the Stars*. Here it is:

> Do not despair
> For Johnny-Head-in-Air
> He sleeps as sound
> As Johnny underground.
>
> Fetch out no shroud
> For Johnny-Head-in-Cloud,
> And keep your tears
> For him in after years.
>
> Better by far
> For Johnny-the-Bright-Star,
> To keep your head
> And see his children fed.

I cannot tell you, nor can anyone tell you, why these things are poetry, and why

> Can this be then the purpose of it all,
> That woman shall go through the jaws of Hell
> To give another victim to the call,
> Of Naziism and the Fascist cult as well?

is not. But let me stress this equally—no man should tell you, and you must not allow any man to tell you, that the effort of writing your lines wasn't worth while. There are some things of which the act of doing is the real reward.

Yours sincerely,
JAMES AGATE

I have decided, whether it is cynical or not, to have some five hundred copies of this printed for dispatch to all those soldier, sailor, Air Force, and civilian scribblers who pester me.

June 9 Saturday

A letter:

Officers' Mess
North-West Army Signals
Rawalpindi
India Command
29th May 45

DEAR MR AGATE

You do not know me, nor have we ever met. I have been trying to write to you ever since I landed in this extraordinary country several weeks ago—but what with the heat and Beverley Nichols, it has been impossible to concentrate on matters that did not daily surround me. However, I am now on leave, 7000 feet above sea-level, in the blessed cool of a hill station.

I had the fortune to leave England on the same ship as Donald Wolfit and his company on their way to the Middle East. Being a struggling pre-war (and, God willing, post-war) actor, I found myself with the job of Ship's Entertainment Officer. While I was in the throes of trying to organise the very assorted talent on board, Wolfit asked, almost shyly, if he and his company could be of any assistance! Naturally, I was greatly impressed by this very generous offer. With some hectic weeks at the Winter Garden behind them, and a Middle East tour before them, Wolfit and his team had obviously been looking forward to the complete rest which is normally offered by a sea-voyage. But, confronted by a ship full of troops on their way to India, and with the knowledge that there was no theatre on board, and that all costumes and "props" were locked and sealed in the hold, there was only one thought in the great actor's mind—to do as much as possible for the troops in the time allotted.

Within what seemed a matter of hours, the ship's dining-room was packed (and I mean packed) with troops. There was a small space at one end of the room on which we had managed to focus some of the existing lights. By this time the ship had started to roll very badly; I was excited and, at the same time, puzzled—how on earth (or at sea) could a full performance of *Much Ado about Nothing* be given in this minute space, *sans* costumes, *sans* props, *sans* scenery—in fact, *sans* everything but actors in E.N.S.A. uniform? The answer was easy—to Wolfit. He made a brief speech to the effect that *Much Ado* would be played exactly as it had been played at the Winter Garden, and that all costumes, props, etc., would be imagined to be complete—also, that he believed that this was the first time since the seventeenth century that a full Shakespearean play had been given at sea. Within two minutes of the start of the play the mass-illusion was complete, the audience were held in pin-drop silence, the absence of props, etc., was not noticed or mentioned again—even old Neptune realised the importance of the occasion, and stopped rolling the ship. At the finish Wolfit and his company received an ovation such as only a mass of really grateful British Tommies can give.

Much Ado was done several times so that the whole ship could see it. This was followed by several performances of *The Merchant of Venice*—a memorable one being given on deck in the middle of the Mediterranean to a really vast audience, who were perched on every conceivable part of the ship—and for two and a half hours the only sound that could be heard (apart from the magnificently audible performers) was the slight throb of the engines, and the gentle swish of that amazingly blue sea as we sped through it. This courageous and unselfish hard work was completed by a grand performance of *Hamlet*. The success of the whole effort can be judged by the send-off that was given to this valiant company at their post of disembarkation. The ship had a distinct list to starboard as every soldier on board cheered and sang them down the gangway.

With best wishes,
Yours sincerely,
DAVID DODIMEAD (Major)

P.S. You may be interested to know that I have just purchased *Immoment Toys* and *Ego 6* from the oddest little bookshop in the oddest Indian bazaar.

June 15 *Friday*

Cedric Hardwicke accused me to-night of hypocrisy. Why did I blame him for making pictures while I myself was wallowing in them? I said, "Boy, you've got me wrong. I don't in the least mind your making pictures. I think you make them very well. What I object to is your coming over here and reviving old successes when you ought to be creating new ones." He said, "Let's get everything clear. First, I am not one of those intellectuals who, when war was declared, ran away to America. I was in America two years before the outbreak of war, and you will remember that we met in New York in the summer of 1937. I was officially asked to stay on in Hollywood, and I stayed. They have given me a year's leave of absence, and that is why I am in England. At the end of the time I shall go back to Hollywood, because I am one of those odd blokes who think a contract should be adhered to. When I return to England for good I shall try to do the kind of plays you want. But it will have to be with my own money. When you're tied to a management you commercialise yourself and can't help it (I am transcribing roughly) because you are in a way responsible to them for their money. This means that you have to put up with some silly ass of a producer or play with some wildly unsuitable actress because she's box-office." This conversation took place on the way to Cedric's sumptuous flat in South Street. On arrival, found Lady H. awaiting us with wonderful cocktails and a really remarkable supper. Cedric was in immense form and full of stories. How a famous Hollywood star, who poses as a great art connoisseur, bought a vastly expensive fake Manet or Renoir—C. couldn't remember which. Only to find, when he got home, the original hanging on his walls! Apropos of a former English actor, now a Hollywood star, C. remarked, 'God made him a good actor; he has turned himself into a bad one." He was full of theories about himself. "I can't act. I have never acted. And I shall never act. What I can do is to suspend my audience's power of judgment till I've finished. There are good actors and there are great actors. The great actor takes care that the audience shall have eyes and ears for no one else." I was delighted to find that he has exactly my views about producers—"They just get in the way"—

and even more pleased when he confessed that from the first night to the last of the New York production of Paul Vincent Carroll's *Shadow and Substance* in which he was such a success as Canon Skerritt, he hadn't the vaguest notion what his part was all about. We discussed my ideal cast for *Hamlet*, and C. agreed, with one exception. He said he thought the best King there had ever been was Oscar Asche. "When he looked at Gertrude the corners of his lower lip hung down like mutton chops." He said that never before or since had the atmosphere of the court of Denmark been properly conveyed. "It should be gross and licentious. Nowadays the place is so prim and Claudius so proper that you wonder what the fuss is all about." The talk then switched on to broadcasting, and both C. and Lady H. animadverted against English snobbery in the matter of sponsored programmes. They assured me I couldn't imagine the magnificence and variety of American wireless; live performances by best orchestras, with plenty of Toscanini. "After all," said C., "what does it matter if between the movements of a Beethoven symphony you are recommended to take somebody's cure for acidity? You get used to it, and after a time pay no more attention to advertisements you hear over the air than you do to those you see in the English *Times*. What do you care if a well-written notice of last night's play is flanked by a puff of Sal Hepatica?" We talked till the small hours, then these nice people sent me back in a car. Snuggled in the corner of the back seat was a bottle of whiskey.

July 10 *Tuesday*

Enjoyed last evening more than any other since the war. Occasion: a reception given by the French Ambassador and Madame Réné Massigli to the actors of the Comédie Française—I owe my invitation to the fact that my French goes a little beyond that of the young gentleman with the lumpy forehead at Mr Podsnap's party who said "*Esker*" and then stopped. I sat in a corner for two hours with Jean Yonnel and Pierre de Rigoult. Yonnel, off the stage, looks every inch an actor; you couldn't possibly mistake him for anything else. Wit and the grand manner, to which must be added his superb voice. Said that to put paint on one's face, learn another man's words, simulate another man's passions and go on the stage to court the applause of an ignorant rabble must always be a despicable business unless the actor knows and holds himself to be in touch with beauty. Said his first appearance had been as Hippolyte to Sarah's Phèdre. "I have played Hippolyte to many Phèdres, and with all the others I felt that when the Queen had declared her passion there was no reason why I should stay to hear the rest of the speech except that I was paid to do so. With Sarah it was different. She hypnotised me—I couldn't move. It was only when she took her eyes off me that I recovered the use of my limbs." Said later that when he was finished as an actor he had one ambition—to be a concierge. "In that profession there is no housing problem." Presently Pierre Dux joined us and asked whether I knew any witty English comedy which would translate. Tentatively I suggested *The Importance of Being Earnest*, of which he had never heard. Delightful evening, the champagne taking second place to the elegance of the setting and the fascination of hearing great artists discuss themselves and their art. "X is exactly right as Hippolyte; his voice is not dark enough for Ruy Blas." "Y has the voice for R. B. but not the shoulders." And so on.

July 11 Wednesday

The Eskerites were in great force at the British Council's treat last night. Again a notable absence of critics. Perhaps they are saving themselves for Lord Bessborough's party on Saturday? Got jammed in a corner with the charming but voluble gentleman who runs the principal theatre in Cairo, in which I had to simulate interest.

July 12 Thursday

The only way with miracles is to make them happen. When I first conceived the idea of luring Tartuffe and Hippolyte to Angus McBean's studio I renounced the idea as altogether too ambitious. To ask of overworked actors that they should transport themselves and their props, make up and pose for the benefit of *Ego*, seemed to me to ask too much. And then I took my courage in both hands and went all out for it. I addressed a supplication to the Contrôleur-Général, in which I suggested that since the *Ego* books go all over the world, my account of the visit of the Comédie, embellished by such photographs as McBean proposed to take, would help to spread knowledge of civilisation's most precious possession—French culture. As a letter of this sort must be elegant, and as my written, as well as my spoken, French leaves something to be desired, I sent the letter to a translation bureau and received in return a screed which the French Académie could not have bettered, and far more ornate than my draft. Gaily I signed this, and sent my houseboy with it to the theatre. It was only when the messenger was beyond recall that I remembered that the envelope bore the stamp: "Berlitz School of Languages"! On my arrival at the French Embassy that evening Yonnel came up to me and said, "J'ai grand plaisir à rencontrer l'auteur d'une prose si majestueusement belle!" The séance at Angus's took place this morning, and succeeded beyond expectation. After which we adjourned to the Ivy, where we were joined by Pierre de Rigoult, the Contrôleur-Général. Luncheon was a trifle hurried—they were due at a matinée—but *very* gay, though I am not quite sure that I liked Angus saying, "I understand Mr Agate's French, but not anybody else's." If there is such a thing as a terrestrial paradise then I inhabited one to-day. There had been a moment in the studio when I raised Hippolyte's arm an inch. Dacqmine said, "You find it better like that?" I said, "No, young man, worse!" "Then why?" "So that I can write in my diary: 'To-day, July 12, 1945, I directed the Comédie Française!' "

July 13 Friday

To-day has been hell. I told Angus McBean that I should call last night some time after eleven to see the negatives of the French players. I called, and at my first knock all the lights in the place were turned out. I knocked half a dozen times, but nobody answered. This morning I began getting into touch soon after nine o'clock. Hopeless. I tried the 'phone; no reply, though I could hear the ticking of the clock on the wall, which meant that somebody had taken the receiver off. I sent messengers. No admission. Finally, I sent Leo over. Not at home. All day we got the most conflicting reports. Angus was sick. He was lunching with a duchess. He had gone to photograph a herd of Hereford cattle. I was in despair until, very late at night, he turned up at Alexandra Mansions to explain the whole thing. It seems that, twelve out of twenty exposures being ruined owing to a faulty box of plates, he hadn't dared to meet me until he had developed the remainder. He then produced eight superb heads—seven of Dacqmine and only one of Yonnel. But what a one it is!

July 14 Saturday

Excellent supper at the Savoy, given by the Franco-British Society to the French players. We ate *Les Quenelles de Saumon Nantua* (only mine was lobster), *La Volaille en Cocotte Grand'mère*, and *Le Mont Blanc aux Fruits Frais*. Asking whether I would take *vin rouge*, the waiter whispered, "It's the same thing as *red wine*, sir." I demanded whiskey and soda. The seating arrangements were, in my view, entirely right and proper. Lord Bessborough had on his right the wife of the French Ambassador, and on his left Phèdre, and then me. Phèdre, who was dressed entirely in black, turned out to be of the Hamlet's Aunt persuasion, and I got through by enlarging upon the one line in which she had been better than Sarah—the one favourable point in to-morrow's notice. She inclined her head and said, "Votre Lady Macbeth n'est pas un rôle difficile." To which I replied that some of our English actresses found it difficult enough.

No sign of the critics, who, throughout the entire stay, have put up an extraordinarily poor show, the Critics' Circle, from which I resigned some time ago, doing nothing whatever about our visitors, and most of the popular papers ignoring them. Knowing that they were feeling strongly about this, I intimated that I should like to say a few words. What I proposed to do was to remind our French guests of, and acquaint our English hosts with, the story of John Philip Kemble's visit to Paris in 1800, and the dinner given to him by the Théâtre Français. The conversation turned upon the respective merits of English and French drama. The French actors being for Corneille, Kemble naturally countered with Shakespeare. Whereupon one Michot said, "Molière, sir—whom have you to show against Molière?" "Oh," said Kemble, "but Molière is not a Frenchman." "What" said the actor. "He is an Englishman, perhaps?" And Kemble replied, "No, sir, he is not English." And then, according to Auger, Kemble went on, "Les petites divisions de royaumes et de siècles s'effacent devant Molière. Tel ou tel pays, telle ou telle époque, n'ont pas le droit de se l'approprier. Il appartient à l'univers; il appartient à l'éternité." Yes, I had it all nicely memorised. It would seem, however, that what I call the Agate-As-Public-Speaker Resistance Movement is making progress. Anyhow, I wasn't called upon; and perhaps the evening was running late. Recovered my equanimity on emerging from the Savoy into the biggest thunderstorm for years. Even I don't pretend to compete with the elements!

July 15 *Sunday*

Clifford Bax, unburdening his heart about the critics, recently wrote:

The fact is, though nobody has perceived it, that a professional play-critic is a monstrosity—a sow with five legs or a man with four thumbs. Nature did not intend him, and that is why we have to conceal our repulsion when he confronts us. A keen playgoer may see, perhaps, ten, fifteen, or even twenty plays a year, and it is for him that dramatists write and that managers dangle their bait. Your newspaper-critic may see a hundred productions in a year. The result is—let me put it with unmistakable simplicity— that he does not see any play as a normal citizen would see it. He is therefore as fantastic a freak as the Yorkshireman who ate half a dozen ordinary breakfasts. However, I must give you an example of my contention. Some years ago I glanced at a play-notice by X.Y.Z., whose conceit would be pathetic if it were tolerable, and in his notice he wrote, 'Then the usual quartet of lawn-tennis players came on, with the usual racquets', and, we deduce, immediately bored X.Y.Z. Not until I had read these words did I realise, being only an average playgoer, that several playwrights must have recently used the convenient device of a tennis-party for getting their characters on and off the stage. Does not this example demonstrate in a twinkling that X.Y.Z. may black-mark a play for some effect which will seem to me and you unobjectionable and even adroit? He sees too many plays, eats too many breakfasts, is a monster.

For "play-critic" read "film-critic," and I imagine that C. B.'s complaint still holds. Far be from me to admit that my old friend, throughout a long and distinguished career, has ever been right except about three things—the compelling fascination of Henry VIII, the wit of Nell Gwyn, and his own passion for clumping indifferent bowling out of the ground for six.

July 19 Thursday

Opened the second Sixth Form Conference of the Schools of King Edward's Foundation at the ghastly hour of ten-something. Audience of about three hundred. Spoke for sixty minutes, after which they— both the boys and the girls—heckled me for ninety more. Some fifty questions, of which here are the first three.

1. *Q. What is a good play?*
   A. A play which doesn't make you yawn or fidget is a good play relative to you. A play at which only a numskull would yawn or fidget is a good play absolutely.
2. *Q. Must a good play have a moral?*
   A. No. *Twelfth Night* has no moral. But no play can be *great* unless it sends you out of the theatre feeling you have undergone a spiritual experience.
3. *Q. What are the rules of dramatic criticism?*
   A. Only two that matter. One. Decide what the playwright was trying to do, and pronounce how well or ill he has done it. Two. Determine whether the well-done thing was worth doing at all.

The conference may or may not turn out to be a feast of reason; at lunch the only flow was soul! This annoyed me so much that when K. P. Tynan, my boy-chairman, told me that the programme included a concert, a cricket match, and a performance of *Hamlet* with himself in the title-rôle, I said, "And how, pray, will visitors know which entertainment is which?"

July 20 Friday

Letter to Hamlet (*see above*), who had asked my opinion of a prose poem on the subject of "L'Art pour L'Art".

> *Queen Alexandra Mansions, W.C.2*
> *July 20th, 1945*

MY DEAR HAMLET,

Of course you can write. You write damned well. You write better than I have ever attempted to write. The mistake you make is the old one of trying to do too much. Why sow with the whole sack? Why say: "The *avant-garde* harks grimly back to the *splendours and miseries* of de Sade"? Must you drag in Balzac? Why, when you are in full spate of discussion about Huysmans, lug in Voltaire? Why tell us that Mallarmé "was passing proud and rode in sorrow through Persepolis"? I see no connection between the French poet and the Elizabethan one.

I don't believe George Moore ever thought of Rimbaud as "a consumptive youth weaving garlands of sad flowers with pale, weak hands". Rimbaud described himself at that period as "surly of aspect, ungainly of figure, with huge red hands like a washer-woman." And I conjure you, now and for ever, to put a stop to your punning. Say, if you must, of Guillaume Apollinaire that "devout and donnish, here was Phoebus Apollinaire turned fasting friar". But to say that "Verlaine was always chasing Rimbauds" is just *common*. Like cheap scent.

My dear boy, in a prose poem of less than a newspaper column's length you undertake to tell us about Gautier, Montesquieu, Heredia (without the accents, please), de Sade, Huysmans, Moore, Verlaine, Rimbaud, Proust, Apollinaire, Mallarmé, and Flaubert. Don't you think that these are enough without dragging in Balzac, Voltaire, Meredith, and Marlowe? If it helped I should be the last person to object. But it hinders. Read what Montague in *A Writer's Notes on his Trade* has to say about quotation, and be guided by him. It is only old cripples like me who have to use the crutches of another man's wit to get along from paragraph to paragraph. You don't need this.

One more small thing. Remember "Saki": "Stephen Thorle said, 'The gratitude of these poor creatures, when I presented them with a set of table crockery apiece, the tears in their eyes and in their voices when they thanked me, would be impossible to describe.' 'Thank you all the same for describing it.' said Comus". Why talk of Proust as "indescribably leisured" and then go on to describe that leisure? "The jaws of his memory were ponderous indeed and marble." Even so, what possible connection is there between Proust's memory and the tomb of Hamlet *père*? This is just plain showing-off. Take my advice. Absent thee from quotation (four syllables, please) a while.

Yours sincerely,

JAMES AGATE

Black Thursday

My first reaction to the Election result was to make the following entry in my Diary:

Death robbed Roosevelt of his triumph, and now the mob has stolen Churchill's glory and trampled it underfoot. "The decision of the British public has been recorded in the votes counted to-day. I have therefore laid down the charge which was placed upon me in darker times." Words which should make Englishmen blush for a thousand years.

My next reaction was to 'phone Edgar Lustgarten and tell him that I was applying for naturalisation as a Patagonian. He said, "I shouldn't if I were you—they might make you President!" And then I pulled myself together. There is no question of scurviness towards the greatest Englishman since Queen Elizabeth. The seed of to-day's affair was contained in something Lady Oxford said at lunch at Gwen Chenhalls's a few days after Churchill became Prime Minister: "Winston is the one man who can lead this country to victory. When he has got it he will cry like a baby. He is a fighter who loves fighting; nothing else really interests him, though he may pretend it does. He is the last man to handle the reins of peace." Many electors must have asked themselves this question: Am I to vote for Winston and abandon my principles, or should I stick to my principles at the risk of seeming ungrateful? For once in a way Churchill seems to have lacked a sense of the stage. His proposal, turned down by the Socialists at the Blackpool Conference, that the Coalition should continue until the end of the war with Japan, when there should be an election, was a mistake. What he should have said was: "Leave me in power till we've finished off the Japs, when I will retire and not embarrass the country with any nonsense about gratitude." He should not have risked defeat. Incidentally, it is no use the Tories thinking they are going to get back in six months' time because the Socialists are going to make a mess of things. The new Government won't make a mess of things, and there is enough way on the ship to keep it going for a year or two whoever is in control on the bridge.

I rang up the head waiter at one of my favourite restaurants and said, "Listen to me carefully, Paul. I am quite willing that in future you address me as 'comrade' or 'fellow-worker', and chuck the food at me in the manner of Socialists to their kind. But that doesn't start until to-morrow morning. To-night I am bringing two friends with the intention that we may together eat our last meal as gentlemen. There will be a magnum of champagne and the best food your restaurant can provide. You, Paul, will behave with your wonted obsequiousness. The *sommelier*, the table waiter, and the *commis* waiter will smirk and cringe in the usual way. From to-morrow you will get no more tips. To-night you will all be tipped royally." The head waiter said, "Bien, m'sieu." That was at a quarter-past six. At a quarter-past nine I arrived and was escorted by bowing menials to my table, where I found the magnum standing in its bucket, and three plates each containing two small slices of spam! Who would have thought a head waiter to have so much wit in him?

August 1 *Wednesday*

Every lifetime has its peak days, and yesterday was one of mine. At 2 A.M.—I was working at *Ego*—the telephone rang. It was Pierre de

Rigoult, Contrôleur-Général of the Comédie Française, saying he was just back from Scotland, and that he and Pierre Dux, the Administrateur-Général, wanted me to dine with them that night as they had something to give me. The dinner took place at the Ambassadors, and I was presented with a scroll signed by all the members of the visiting company of the Comédie in order of seniority.

The conversation over dinner—the food was exquisite—was very animated, if sometimes a little difficult. My hosts plied me with embarrassing questions. "Is Gielgud a great actor?" (They had seen him the night before in *The Circle.*) I got out of this by saying that the piece is not one by which they should judge Mr G., who is not a comedian. De Rigoult said, "You can't see his eyes." Next question: "Has he the scaffolding for a great actor?" I told them that Mr G. has more poetry than any other actor of our day. "Have you any great actresses in the sense that Clairon, Rachel, and Bernhardt were great?" I wriggled out of this by asking whether there are any of that kind in France to-day. "Who is your worst good actor?" Ten names trembled on my lips, and I suppressed them all. (De Rigoult gave a lightning and instantly recognisable imitation of the worst of modern good French actors.) "What, M. Agate, has been your greatest moment in the theatre?" I said, "Bernhardt as Pelléas rushing on and saying in reply to Mélisande's 'Qui est là?' in a voice halfway between famished tigress and strangled dove, 'Moi, moi, et moi!' " "And your next greatest?" I replied, "Any moment in all the hours I spent watching Henry Irving." De Rigoult said, "You meant that Irving's worst was better than anybody else's best?" I said, "Je vous le jure!" They made the point that to them our English actors have no "jeu". That they do nothing with their lines *qua* actor, and are content to speak them as the author wrote them. I agree, with the exception of Seymour Hicks. Not one English playgoer in a hundred will understand what is meant here. In boxing a blow starts at the back of the heel, travels along the entire torso, and culminates at the point of contact. A French actor delivers each and every line with his whole body, from his toes to his eyebrows. Our theatre is manned by signposts; theirs has the animation of a puppet show. On the political side I gathered that while there is a 1000 to 1 chance that Laval was aiming at circumventing the Hun by *roublardise* (I don't think they believed this), Pétain is the resolute, unforgivable traitor. As for de Gaulle, he is a *maître-gaffeur*, whose career is over.

Having arranged for a car, I enticed my hosts to the Maison McBean, where the Presentation of the Scroll was photographed. Then bundled them with Angus to Grape Street, where we toasted each other's countries in my last bottle of champagne, brought over from France by "Curly", who had charged me to drink it only on a noble occasion. And then I showed them round the Musée Sarah. Dux had not seen S. until the year after her operation, when, in Racine's *Athalie*, she was brought on in a palanquin. (He surprised me by saying that the drama of Corneille is more alive than that of Racine. About the latter: "C'est la tragédie de salon." I told him Edmund Gosse's remark about Racine's verse: "Poetry in silver chains.") De Rigoult didn't see S. until just before her death, and both were very anxious to hear my record of her in Phèdre, saying that, so far as they knew, nobody in France, and certainly not the Comédie, possessed it. Now I have two records of this: one very old and worn, the other, hardly used, given me by Ivor Novello. It was, of course, the latter that I presented to Dux, who formally accepted it on behalf of the Comédie. Further libations being indicated, my last bottle of whiskey but one was now requisitioned. Here I had the happy idea of ringing up Jock, telling him to jump out of bed, huddle into some clothes, and run "like the swift hare" to Grape Street. This he did, saying, on his somewhat breathless arrival, "If it's to meet anybody less than George Nathan or Pare Lorentz I'll be gey fashed wi' ye." He was, of course, enchanted, and talked to my visitors in excellent French, with not a little of his native brilliance. The party broke up about 1 A.M., Dux and de Rigoult having to be at Croydon Aerodrome at seven o'clock this morning. By the way, they took with them a certificate from me assuring the Censor that Racine never wrote anything subversive or in any way connected with current affairs! Dux has enormous charm—but it is almost as though there were no face of Dux but merely a rallying-ground for all the scamps in Molière. De Rigoult speaks little, but to the point.

The others having departed, and the last bottle of my whiskey now handsomely in action, Jock says, "Jamie, you've ten minutes in which to write down the names of the hundred best players, male and female, of all nationalities since Roscius. And I'll do the same." We finish on time, and comparison shows eighty names common to both lists. There are gaps, of course—I forgot Stanislavsky, Joanny, Mrs Oldfield, Sada Yacco, and Adrienne Lecouvreur. Jock's omissions include Macklin, "Little" Robson, De Max, Kitty Clive, Mrs Jordan, Jeanne Granier, and Duse (!!). The concernancy? An idea Jock is going to put up to the Imperial Tobacco Company against the time when they resume their cigarette-cards. To bed about 4 A.M., entirely sober, which I attribute to the greater intoxication keeping the champagne and whiskey within bounds.

August 8 *Wednesday*

Letter from George Lyttleton:

> Let me end with a bit of treasure trove which at any rate I know you will like if you have never seen it. Some one told it to the late John Bailey as the sort of specimen of Swinburne's humour which Gosse ought to have put in his Life and didn't— an invention of Swinburne's of Queen Victoria's confession to

the Duchess of Kent of her one lapse from virtue, put for some Swinburnian reason into French: "Ce n'était pas un prince; ce n'était pas un milord, ni même Sir R. Peel. C'était un misérable du peuple, un nommé Wordsworth, qui m'a récité des vers de son *Excursion* d'une sensualité si chaleureuse qu'ils m'ont ébranlée— et je suis tombée". Perhaps it was a good thing he was not made Poet Laureate.

Yours ever,
GEORGE LYTTELTON

PEACE

VJ Day

It is twenty minutes past eleven in the morning of the Greatest Day in History. H.M. the King has driven in procession to Westminster to open Parliament, and on the air nothing but antiquated musical comedies with the alternative of "X and his Apache Band" in "Fête Tzigane". Wonderful! Amazing! *Gigantesque*! Where, in God's name, are the L.P.O., the L.S.O., the Hallé Orchestra, the B.B.C. Orchestra? What has become of Beecham, Cameron, Barbirolli, Boult? Why weren't orchestras and conductors standing by? *Everybody, even Cabinet Ministers, knew it was about to happen.* Here, I suggest, is a programme the German wireless might have sent out if Germany had won:

DEUTSCHLAND ÜBER ALLES
DIE WACHT AM RHEIN
HITLERMARSCH
SIEGFRIED'S FUNERAL MARCH
(*In Memory of the Fallen*)
RIENZI: OVERTURE
EROICA SYMPHONY
EIN HELDENLEBEN
EIN FESTE BURG IST UNSER GOTT

The programme to begin at seven A.M. and continue till midnight, with relays of live orchestras and conductors and no nonsense about recording. People tell me the English win wars because they like musical comedy, and the Germans lose wars because they like music. I don't believe it. In the meantime my staff has the day off. I hate crowds, the Café is inaccessible, and it is raining. Nothing remains except to munch some stale bread and staler cheese, break my rule about the day-time non-consumption of alcohol, *and work*!

225

August 21 *Tuesday*

At the revival to-night of *Lady Windermere's Fan* I asked Lady
Alexander, exquisite as ever and looking like the lids of Juno's eyes,
whether in the 'nineties peeresses at private dances wore tiaras. She
said, "They wore them at the tea-table!"

August 22 *Wednesday*

Lunch with Bertie van Thal at the Savoy, where a really extraordinary
coincidence happens. (First let me say that Bertie's life at the Food
Office is one unbroken sea of milk troubles. Either London is drowning
in milk and there are no bottles to put it in, or there is an avalanche of
bottles and no milk.) Now for the coincidence. At the next table is
Kay Hammond with her little boy. Gathering that he is fond of cricket,
I beckon him over and tell him how I once bowled out W. G. Grace.
Whereupon John Clements leans across and says, "This is unbelievable.
In the lounge before lunch I was telling John how at a public dinner
my father heard W. G. say that on the sands at Blackpool he had been
bowled first ball by a little boy of seven whose name he never knew!"

September 2 *Sunday*

Letter to Jock:

*Queen Alexandra Mansions, W.C.*2
September 2nd, 1945

DEAR JOCK,

If I had not passed a self-denying ordinance in the matter of work
I should now be setting about a formal essay entitled "A Gossip
on a Novel of Charles Dickens". However, I compromise with a
letter. And naturally a letter to you, who awakened my too-long-
dormant interest in *Dombey and Son*. I have read this in bed every
night since your letter to me in the earlier part of this summer.
What a masterpiece! Twenty times have I had to put it down
through sheer excess of admiration.

Were you at any time struck by the resemblance of Edith Granger
to Hedda Gabler? This first occurred to me when Cleopatra says,
"The sword wears out the what's-its-name." And Edith says
coldly, "The scabbard, perhaps". On the next page is Cleopatra's
superb remark about Henry VIII: "Such a picture, too, he makes,
with his dear little peepy eyes and his benevolent chin!" You
remember that Chesterton singles this out? It is, I think, the best
thing in the book, with the possible exception of Cousin Feenix's
remark on the occasion of his call to apologise to Dombey for
his "lovely and accomplished relative's" behaviour: "I have been
in a devilish state of depression ever since; and said indeed to

Long Saxby last night—man of six foot ten, with whom my friend
Dombey is probably acquainted—that it had upset me in a
confounded way, and made me bilious". Do you remember
G. K. C. on Cousin Feenix?—"As consistent and as homogeneous
as wood; he is as invincible as the ancestral darkness". But I won't
quarrel if you prefer the reply of Mr Toots on being told by Susan
Nipper that Florence will never love him: "Thank'ee! It's of no
consequence. Good night. It's of no consequence, thank'ee!"
One of the most moving things to me in the book is the fact that
Dickens does not forget the dog, Diogenes. "Autumn days are
shining, and on the sea-beach there are often a young lady and a
white-haired gentleman. With them, or near them, are two
children—boy and girl. And an old dog is generally in their
company".

The last page suggests something which will infuriate you—
that there are too many pages. Arthur Bates, who looks after me,
said the other evening on seeing me immersed in *D and S*, "Should
I like that book?" I at once asked him what kind of books he
liked. He said any kind. Could he tell me the names of some of their
authors? After thinking for a few minutes he said—and I give
you my word I'm not inventing or improving—"Shakespeare,
Byron, Keats, Tennyson, Damon Runyon, Sherlock Holmes,
Alan Dent". When I had recovered I read a page of *D and S* at
my topmost reviewing speed and found it took me two minutes.
(Nobody can beat me at reading quickly when I want to.) Allowing
Arthur three minutes—it would be nearer four—the result must
be thirty-four solid hours of reading. As I don't suppose he gets
more than half an hour to read each day, which includes newspapers, it follows that it would take him between three and four
months to get through *D and S*. And that is too long. Do you
realise that in thirty-four hours he could read a dozen crime
stories?

The point is how to get young people to read Dickens, and I
suggest by cutting him. The characters I should leave out of any
shorter *Dombey* would be Sol Gills, Capt. Cuttle (who is desperately unfunny), good Mrs Brown, Alice Marwood, the Toodle
family (in part), John and Harriet Carker. I should reduce Walter
Gay to a minimum, and cut at least half of Florence, whose value
largely disappears with the death of Paul. I feel too that those
interminable colloquies when Dombey, Edith, and Carker go into
conference might be shortened.

Look again at chapter XX—"Mr Dombey goes upon a
Journey"—and tell me whether it should not end at "He had seen
upon the man's rough cap a piece of new crape, and he had assured
himself, from his manner and his answers, that he wore it for his
son". This is superb, worthy of Balzac at his most transcendent.
Why go on? Isn't it better to shorten masterpieces—written in
an age when there was more time on hand—with a view to getting
the present age to read them, than to leave them in their integrity
and the certainty that they will not be read? (There is always the
full text for whoever wants it.) I know all about Tennyson and
his "I wish there were a great novel in hundreds of volumes that I

might go on and on". Our young bank-clerks are not Tennysons. Why, out of a too-nice regard for punctillio, should the next generation—or this—be deprived of all knowledge of Miss Tox, Mr Toots, Cleopatra, and Joey B.?

Of course, shortening needs to be done not only with care but with a touch of genius. There would be no re-writing, and the plot would be kept together by italicised résumés. Why don't *you* do it? You could do all the novels in something under three years. Please don't send me a MacStingerish reply. They've already cut Shakespeare's *Hamlet*, Boswell's *Johnson*, and Handel's *Messiah*. And I've just cut Agate's *Ego*!

Ever,

JAMIE

September 9 Sunday

From Jock:

Spooncreel
Maybole
Ayrshire
September 7th, 1945

DEAR JAMIE,

A Very Happy Birthday!

And now about this not-easily-defensible notion of your abridging Dickens—or my abridging Dickens—or anybody's abridging Dickens. It *could* be done—I might even permit myself to go so far even as to say it *should* be done—for schoolchildren between twelve and sixteen (who read drastically abridged Swift and Defoe anyhow). Even there I would insist on its being done (if it must be done), not by any one person, but by a committee of six highly sensible Dickensians. For a random suggestion:

(1) J. B. Priestley
(2) W. H. Salmon (editor of the *Times* weekly, with whom I had a wondrous Dickens pow-wow at the Press Club the other night)
(3) Robert Lynd
(4) Rebecca West
(5) James Bone, and
(6) either You or Me.

For adults I would not give the scheme any sanction. Any adult worth a hoot tries Dickens once and, if he finds him palatable at all, re-reads his own favourite sections *à son gré*. Here are we, Jamie, you and I, two adults; both presumably worth several hoots in some respects, and we don't begin to agree in detail about a novel which finds us both madly enthusiastic—*Dombey and Son*.

You want to cut Captain Cuttle (who is "desperately unfunny" to you and G. K. Chesterton, but delightful in all he says and does to the rest of the world); the Toodle family in part (and I wholly adore it); half of Florence (who is to me the most tolerable and touching of all of Dickens's maidens); and (more understandably) good Mrs Brown and one or two minor characters.

But, look you! some of your likes are my aversions. What do
you, or we, or our committee, do about that? I have always
found Joey Bagstock exceedingly tiresome, and I skip (when I
re-read) the innumerable descriptions of his incipient apoplexy—
just as most people probably skip the nauseating references to
James Carker's teeth. *No, no, no!* And no again—the more I
think of it! He would be a very brave man who should abridge
a Dickens novel for adult readers. You try it, if you dare. It would
be like trying to kidnap Master Alexander MacStinger! (And
did you observe, by the way, how Mrs MacS. quietened that
masterful mite during her wedding to Captain Bunsby?)

> Ever thy
>
> JOCK

P.S. Boswell's *Johnson*, Handel's *Messiah*, and *Ego* are beside
the point. They are not fiction. Or are they?

> *Queen Alexandra Mansions, W.C.2.*
> *September 10th, 1945*

DEAR JOCK,

Ye'll dae a fine letter, and Rubicon will be proud of his Gemel.
Erudite allusion for the use of German editors later on.

Yes and no about your Dickens suggestions. I would trust
Rebecca West with an abridgment of Shakespeare but not Dickens.
No woman has ever laughed at C.D., and the sex is not going to
start now. On the whole I think I am against a committee. My plan
would be one novel, one abridger. As follows:

Pickwick	J. A.?
David Copperfield	J. B. Priestley
Bleak House	Bernard Darwin
Great Expectations	Neville Cardus
Dombey and Son	Alan Dent
Martin Chuzzlewit	George Lyttelton
Nicholas Nickleby	Robert Lynd
Little Dorrit	Hugh Kingsmill
Our Mutual Friend	D. B. Wyndham Lewis

November 29 Thursday

In a letter from a lady:

> I saw Henry Irving twice only. The first time was in *The Bells*
> at Swansea. The only picture remaining in my memory of that
> performance is that of Irving taking off his gaiters. Before the
> play began, the crowd of people in the gallery, mostly young
> Welsh men, whiled away the waiting time by singing. Irving sent
> out a message from his dressing-room to say that he was sorry
> he could not hear well enough from that distance to appreciate
> the music fully, but he would be honoured if the audience in the

gallery would remain after the performance and sing again for him. They did. Irving came before the curtain and listened for twenty minutes to the harmonies of *Aberystwyth*, *Cwm Rhondda*, and *Dafydd y gareg wen*. You know them. Irving then spoke his thanks and said that the evening would always live in the store-house of his memory. "I wish you all a very good night". That was Irving, the man. The second time I saw him was not long before his death. I was walking along the seafront at Minehead, when I became conscious that the people ahead were parting to stand at the sides of the pavement. Strolling along between them, bowing slightly to right and left, came Irving. It was a royal procession of one. That was Irving, the actor.

December 11 *Tuesday*

Took Jock to the Press view of *Caesar and Cleopatra*. So bored that I didn't know where to look! Caesar like an elderly Peter Pan, and Cleopatra just out of Roedean. Apollodorus the apple of every shopgirl's eye, and so on. Poor use of the camera which prompted Jock to whisper, "This is the first time I've thought of Alexandria as a rose-red city half as old as Denham."

EGO 9

January 1946–June 1947

January 13 *Sunday*

Peter Brook, the stage director, has an interesting letter in to-day's
S.T. about his recent production of *King John* at the Birmingham
Repertory Theatre:

> It was obvious from the first that the audience would miss the
> meaning, and thus the force, of the whole of the great soliloquy
> about "Commodity" because of the complete change of sense that
> this word has undergone. Yet, to substitute another word through-
> out would have been unpardonably irritating to those who knew
> the speech. Consequently we introduced an extra phrase on the
> first appearance of the word to "plant" its meaning:

> That smooth-fac'd gentleman, *Expediency*,
> *Or, as they say*, tickling Commodity,
> Commodity, the bias of the world. . . .

P. B. seems to be worried about the legitimacy of this. On the whole
I am for rather than against, *when strictly necessary*. In the Bastard's
speech there is no great poetry to be interfered with, and no familiar
passage, But are we to have the emendation

> Thus conscience—*meaning thereby consciousness*,
> *Awareness*—does make cowards of us all?

or

> Season your admiration—*since you start*,
> *And all your visage cries astonishment*—
> With an attent ear, etc., etc.

I strongly suspect that when Lady Macbeth told her husband he
had "broke the good meeting With most admired disorder" she was

not using "admired" in the modern sense. But I should boggle at some such elucidatory rewriting as:

> LADY M. You have displaced the mirth,
>   broke the good meeting,
> With most admired disorder—*going off*
> *The deep end at a silly, peevish ghost*
> *Strongly suggests that Scotland's majesty*
> *Should get a hold on's self.*

And I should certainly not allow any Macbeth I directed to enlarge thus-wise:

> Thou hast no speculation—*naught to do*
> *With throwing sprat to catch your mackerel,*
> *Nor yet debating if to be or not,*
> *Nor e'en that perlustration Walkley loved,*
> *But used in purest sense of optic power,*
> *The opposite of nictitation,*
> *Ablepsy, amaurosis, and the like—*
> *Let me repeat: horrible shadow, know*
> Thou hast no speculation in those eyes
> Which thou dost glare with.

But enough of babble, as Gilbert's Lady Jane remarked.

April 13 *Saturday*

The theatre managers are at it again, and once more there is talk of barring me from first-nights. In a way I sympathise. Many of them have not been taught to see beyond the box-office. They fuss because I have no patience with rubbish. When you tell them that just as there are swing and jive concerts at which nobody would expect Newman to look in, and trashy novels that nobody would expect Desmond to look at, so there are theatrical entertainments that I just can't sit through—when you tell them this they goggle. They have spent weeks, months, in dressing, lighting, and providing a setting for something they don't recognise as inanity. Why should they? To this type of mind nothing on which money has been expended is inane. Anyhow, the storm is on; I may weather it, or I may not. The *Observer* once patted me on the back for having "with the minuteness of a Himalayan surveying-party charted the highlands of Ibsen." Wonderful if I am hurled to destruction because I couldn't sit through *Song of Norway*!

May 13 *Monday*

Spent last Saturday morning diarising and answering letters. No,

I will not go down to Bristol and lecture for a fee of three guineas plus expenses. No, I will not talk to East Anglians for no fee and no expenses. No, I do not know why brass bands are always out of tune. No, I cannot tell a young man how to become a "litiry" critic. Yes, I will write an advertisement for a commercial firm, and supply a photograph, if (*a*) the stuff they are selling is something I can reasonably be connected with, and (*b*) they give me £100 free of tax. No, I do not know the value of a complete set of the Waverley Novels, edition unknown. Yes, I will lunch with the representatives of the French film industry and talk for as long as they like in return for a glass of cognac. No, I am not on the staff of *Punch*, and what makes the blasted idiot think I am? Yes, I am prepared to say which are the best twelve books in the English language, and do so. Tell a literary society in Cheshire that the best way to find out why Ibsen was a great dramatist is to read his plays. Yes, I will write 1200 words at one-quarter my usual rates for a paper published in Moscow to help its readers to some knowledge of the English theatre. Yes, I will talk free of charge to some East End boys and girls. Thirty-one letters, plus two manuscripts returned, also a book on Beddoes lent me by a Bloomsbury intellectual and which unaccountably turns out to be the property of a public library in the Midlands. Item, a signed photograph to please a Miss Boakes who cannot endure life in the Mendips unless she has my picture to look at.

And then an extraordinary thing happened. Some time before the War Clement Scott's daughter gave me her father's newspaper-cutting book containing several thousand dramatic criticisms covering the period 1811–33. I turned this into a little book called *These Were Actors*. Then, during my stay at Oxford in 1940, an anonymous donor presented me with four small volumes of theatrical press-cuttings for the years 1885–93. Bound in shiny black stuff and falling to pieces. To me enormously interesting, but not enough for a volume. On Saturday morning I received an enormous parcel, which turned out to contain one hundred and twenty large envelopes, each holding ten and sometimes twenty cuttings about some play or production. Period 1897–1906. In less than ten minutes I had decided to make another little book out of these and the black books. Unfortunately the original collector—a covering letter explained that they had been bequeathed to the sender, who had chosen me as an alternative to the salvage dump—had in nearly all cases cut off the name of the paper and the date. This obviously called for a lot of niggling work, and I had given Booth-Palmer the week-end off. And then the doorbell rang, and a young man carrying a lot of *Egos* presented himself. Would I sign them, please? Now I have a shark's eye for anybody to get me out of a jam. "Come in. Who and what are you?" "John Compton. Air Force". "Hobbies?" "James Agate and cricket. I'm pretty good at the first and not bad at the second." "How bad at the second?" "Before the War I won one of Jack Hobbs's bats. Took 8 wickets for 4 runs. Was given a trial at the nets at Canterbury. Last week I did the hat-trick

with the first three balls of the season. Also made top score." "Going in
for cricket when you get demobbed?" "No. Not good enough. I was
better at sixteen. What I'm looking for is something connected with
the theatre." "Where are you stationed?" "St. Athans. On leave till
Monday night." "My secretary's on leave. Care to do a locum? Three
guineas plus hotel bill." "My hotel's fixed up and I don't want money."
"Well, what do you want?" "To be in *Ego*."

And so the bargain was struck. We worked for the rest of Saturday,
all Sunday, and all to-day till the boy had to leave. By that time all the
1500 cuttings had been dated and arranged in their proper order.

May 14 *Tuesday*

Last night after the young man had gone I sat on working. At 4 A.M.
the book was finished. Sixty thousand words plus forty illustrations,
some from my private collection and some as the result of rummaging
in the shops on my way back from lunch yesterday and to-day. There's
always time to do a thing if you want to do it hard enough.

May 23 *Thursday*

I once knew a murderer. He was a charming young man, of a gay
and debonair manner, and a free and open-handed disposition. Excellent
company. Alas! that when funds ran short he conceived and executed
the notion of insuring and setting fire to his mother. Had I been briefed
for the defence I should have argued that Sidney Harry Fox was a
Dickensian who had been led away by Sam Weller's, "Wery sorry to
'casion any personal inconwenience, ma'am, as the housebreaker said
to the old lady when he put her on the fire." He certainly did not belong
to the more revolting type of murderer, the poisoner. The point to
make about these gentry—not, of course, the kind which poisons for
money—is the exquisite depravity of their satisfactions. Neill Cream
liked to talk about women, music, money, and poisons. Teignmouth
Shore ends his account in the "Notable British Trials":

> His actions were probably governed by a mixture of sexual
> mania and sadism. He may have had a half-crazy delight in feeling
> that the lives of the wretched women whom he slew lay in his power,
> that he was the arbiter of their fates. Sensuality, cruelty, and lust
> of power urged him on. We may picture him walking at night
> the dreary mean streets and byways of Lambeth, seeking for his
> prey, on some of whom to satisfy his lust, on others to exercise
> his passion for cruelty; his drug-sodden, remorseless mind exalted
> in a frenzy of horrible joy. Whatever exactly he was, the halter
> was his just reward.

This Famous Trial used to be my favourite bed-book; there was a time when I knew the names of all his victims in chronological order—Ellen Donworth, Matilda Clover, and so on. The point about this morning's film at the Gaumont is the sexual gratification accorded to any strangler by the act of strangling. Which means that anybody who attempts to make a film on this subject is at once up against the film censor. The strangler's motive being strictly unavowable, some other must obviously be found. What about making him the son of a public hangman, whose fingers owe their peculiar habits to heredity? That this is all my eye and the late respected Mr Billington won't trouble the one-and-nine-pennies. What might a little incommode them is that the widow of the common hangman should be living in one of Belgravia's costlier mansions. Wherefore it becomes necessary to make the strangler the grandson of a hangman, with a father (deceased) who also showed signs of "strangler's twitch" fortunately kept in control. In other words there is no harm in a film about sexual mania so long as the maniac's motive is not sex. Eric Portman very good.

May 26 Sunday

Decided to put my "Shorter Dickens" problem to George Lyttelton, promising myself to abide by his decision. Here it is:

> *Finndale House*
> *Grundisburgh*
> *Suffolk*
> *May 24, 1946*

MY DEAR JAMES AGATE,

This is very difficult!—because, *me judice*, you are absolutely right, and so is Alan Dent (thus proving that John Morley was right when he spoke of "the plain maxim that it is possible for the same thing to be and not to be").

You say that half a loaf, etc. *He* says, "No, because it is currant bread, and, however you divide it, many epicures will say that the half you have thrown away contains the tastiest currants". A mean metaphor. Let us rise higher and say, Doesn't it all come to this: Are the Dickens novels to be regarded as Holy Writ, which is the argument against abridging the Bible?—though how we should be spiritually poorer by not knowing that Huz was the brother of Buz I don't know. If you had a committee of Dickensians sitting on each novel the result would be that when they had finished (*a*) they would not be on speaking terms, and (*b*) they would have eliminated about 750 words. I agree with you too about R. West. Dickens is not for very clever women any more than Boswell is. Did, *e.g.*, Virginia Woolf ever mention either, though she had plenty to say about Defoe and Swift and Donne and Hardy?

It is mainly the length (and the sentiment) which puts off the modern reader. Those who also say that his characters are not true to life and that his humour is long-winded wouldn't read him whether abridged or not, and in Browning's words may be "left in God's contempt apart".

So on the whole I am definitely with you in your arguments. And I should very much like to do one, *Martin Chuzzlewit* for choice if you have not earmarked him. How potent is environment! Three miles away FitzGerald spent much time cutting down for his own amusement all the masterpieces of English poetry and prose—except Browning, whom he would not read at all.

I hope that my postcard did not make you very cross, and that you will not blast me, as you did that poor man from Berkhamsted, with some withering words about sheer (or pure) pedantry. And you will be quite right.

Yours ever,

GEORGE LYTTELTON

May 28 Tuesday

To-day has been what I call a full day. Up before nine and wrote 1200 words, being the script for a wireless debate sometime in June on "What is the Value of Dramatic Criticism?" Lunch with Bertie van Thal and a Big Noise in the book-distributing trade, to whom we put up the "Shorter Dickens" proposition. He said that the moment we started on it some big publisher would rush out a complete reissue of the full text and swamp us. Or else some common little fellow would undersell us with a still shorter version, cut by some hack, vilely illustrated, and flaunting a hideous cover. Which means that in current slang 'we've had it'. All I can do now is to break the news of our disappointment to Lyttelton. Back to flat and do so. Rewrite the stuff about Dramatic Criticism. Rush down to Broadcasting House to record my share in to-morrow's "How not to make a Historical Film." (Nothing like a switch of subject to keep the mind active.) Back to flat and have a last look at proofs of *Ego* 8, which Frank Dunn has returned with hundreds of 'marks'! Then to the Unity Theatre to see revivals of the films *The Battleship "Potemkin"* and *Kameradschaft*. Slight giddiness, but pull myself together with a watercress sandwich! Take Gwen Chenhalls to supper and on to a party at Harry Kendall's, where I meet Franklin Dyall and we talk about Irving and what to-day's young playgoers would think if they saw the dying Louis XI come crumbling through the curtains in sky-blue silk.

Whit Monday

A letter from a W.R.N.S. officer:

With reference to *Ego* 7, Page 302 (this is the Naval formula for every sort of letter), you, for once, are wrong and Dean Inge is right. The bad man never does reach satiety: instead of sating his desire he destroys it. It's all in *Macbeth*, from the murder of Banquo onwards. I know one ought not to think of Iago outside the framework of the play, but suppose he had got away with it and tried again: he would have been caught by the law of Diminishing Returns and found that he got less and less excitement out of it all each time.

". . . The Metaphysicals, and Milton beyond them, went even beyond Shakespeare, for they imagined hell, and whatever may be thought of the doctrine of hell theologically and morally, it is a very great poetic idea. Shakespeare's people were able—they were compelled—altogether to die. Lear, outraging nature, was outraged by nature, but he died. Macbeth, self-robbed of sleep, found a living somnambulism, but he died. They glanced at that other vision in moments—'Hell is murky'. But it is Satan whose everlasting and hopeless desire restored the full vision to English verse, the 'perishing everlastingly' of that great ode the Athanasian Creed.

> I would be at the worst: worst is my port,
> My harbour, and my ultimate repose,

and he cannot be."

(New Book of English Verse, Introduction)*

See an imbecile film called *Bedelia*, in which a husband will not believe that his wife, who has already disposed of three husbands for their insurance money, is proposing to murder him, until he sees the cat, which has eaten of the fish intended for supper, turn on its back and die under his nose. Spend half the evening wondering by what economic or ethical or aesthetic law I should be compelled to waste my time. And then something clicks in my brain, I take down Wilde's *Intentions*, and I read:

> Criticism is no more to be judged by any low standard of imitation or resemblance than is the work of poet or sculptor. The critic occupies the same relation to the work of art that he criticises as the artist does to the visible world of form and colour, or the unseen world of passion and of thought. He does not even require for the perfection of his art the finest materials. Anything will suit his purpose. And just as out of the sordid and sentimental amours of the silly wife of a small country doctor in the squalid village of Yonville-l'Abbaye, near Rouen, Gustave Flaubert was able to create a classic, and make a masterpiece of style, so, from subjects of little or no importance, such as the pictures in this year's Royal Academy, or in any year's Royal Academy for that matter, Mr Lewis Morris's poems, M. Ohnet's novels, or the plays of Mr Henry Arthur Jones, the true critic can, if it be his pleasure so to direct or waste his faculty of contemplation, produce work that will be flawless in beauty and instinct with intellectual

subtlety. Why not? To an artist so creative as the critic, what does subject-matter signify?

Had Wilde been living to-day he would doubtless have added films to the base metal which a creative critic can turn into gold.

June 19 Wednesday

Here is a bit of my broadcast debate on the Value of Dramatic Criticism.

A YOUNG MAN. It would be very interesting, Mr Agate, if you would tell us your opinion of the value of dramatic criticism.

AGATE. Young man, are you sure that you're not confusing 'value' with 'function'? For half a crown I can buy a pair of braces. I suggest that braces, considered functionally, are worth more than half a crown. Do you mind if we talk about the function of criticism? It might make what we're discussing clearer.

Y.M. All right. Let's put it that way. What is your view of the function of dramatic criticism?

AGATE. Dramatic criticism has three functions. The first is to let the world know what the previous night's play has been about. There's no reason why a report of this kind should not be written by the same man who describes how in the afternoon he saw a man knocked down in Oxford Street trying to stop a runaway horse. The second function is to tell the public whether the new play is good, bad, or indifferent. This means that the critic must know his job. That is if you hold with my dictionary, which defines criticism as "the art of judging with knowledge and propriety of the beauties and faults of a work of art".

Y.M. But just how do critics know a good play from a bad?

AGATE. A play is good when the playgoer wants to know what some character—let us call him A—is going to do next, what B will say to C, and what is C's come-back.

Y.M. But, surely, even a cheap melodrama can have this effect on a popular audience?

AGATE. Then the cheap melodrama is a good play for that audience.

Y.M. This brings me to my next point. How would you tell a good play from a great play?

AGATE. That fine critic William Archer settled this years ago. In the case of a good play the spectator leaves the theatre in very much the state of mind in which he entered it. In the case of a great play he goes home feeling that he has undergone an experience. That he has been spiritually enriched by, say, a performance of *Everyman*, emotionally enriched by *King Lear*, intellectually enriched by *St Joan*.

Y.M. Yes, I follow that, but what is your third function of criticism?

AGATE. Reporting the theatre in terms of the art of writing. It is one hundred and fifteen years since Mrs Siddons died, and it still gives me exquisite pleasure to read that great passage in Hazlitt which runs: "She was Tragedy personified. She was the stateliest ornament of the public mind. She was not only the idol of the people, she not only hushed the tumultuous shouts of the pit in breathless expectation, and quenched the blaze of surrounding beauty in silent tears, but to the retired and lonely student, through long years of solitude, her face has shone as if an eye had appeared from heaven; her name has been as if a voice had opened the chambers of the human heart, or as if a trumpet had awakened the sleeping and the dead".

It is fifty years almost to the day since I read Shaw on Mary Anderson, an extremely beautiful woman who wasn't a very good actress. Shaw wrote: "The position our Mary wanted to begin with, in her teens, was that of Mrs Siddons. It is useless to gasp at such presumption; for she got what she demanded. She knew that it was childish to cry for the moon; so she simply said with quiet dignity, 'Be good enough to take that moon down from its nail and hand it to me.' Which was accordingly done. The world which once sent Mrs Siddons back to the provinces as a failure prostrated itself like a doormat to kiss the feet of Mary Anderson".

It is forty years since Walkley wrote about *The Doctor's Dilemma*: "A thoroughly 'Shavian' play, this, stimulating and diverting, occasionally distressing, now and then bewildering. O philosopher! O humorist! you say with gratitude. And then you whisper, with a half-sigh, O Pierrot! O Faun!"

It is thirty-five years since I read C. E. Montague's estimate of Bernard Shaw: "Mr Shaw is one of the cyclonic kind of talents that charge through their time as an express train tears through country stations, and if your mind be only a piece of straw or an empty paper bag, or is not pulled in any special direction by something else, it leaves all and follows the express until the express drops it a little farther on".

Y.M. Reading dramatic criticisms, I am sometimes inclined to think a great deal of it is destructive. Oughtn't criticism to be constructive?

AGATE. Will you tell me how to write constructive criticism about a building after it has been erected?

Y.M. Not of the finished play, perhaps. But shouldn't criticism of the production and the acting be constructive?

AGATE. Neither producers nor actors take the slightest notice of critics. There is a famous scene in Ibsen's *A Doll's House*. The persons on the stage are Torvald Helmer, his wife Nora, and Dr Rank, their old friend, a dying man. Rank asks Torvald for a cigar, and Ibsen's stage direction is: "Nora hands match. Rank lights his cigar at it." Rank then makes his exit on the words "Thanks for the light" uttered to Nora, and obviously a reference to the solace and comfort which her friendship has brought him over the years. At a West End production some time ago it was the husband who gave the cigar and struck the light. And Rank taking no notice of the wife, went out saying to the husband, "Thanks for the light," jauntily, as we should say to-day, "Ta, old man". I pointed out in my paper that this was all wrong. Was any notice taken? No. A fortnight later I saw the performance again. No change had been made.

Y.M. But surely actors would benefit by constructive criticism?

AGATE. Once a mumbler always a mumbler. That's all there is to be said about actors.

Y.M. Well, is criticism any use from the box-office point of view?

AGATE. You mean: Does criticism help to drag the public in? I could tell you an old story of how many years ago, the then dramatic critic of the B.B.C. so taunted and goaded the public by telling them that to give it Sherriff's *Journey's End* was like casting pearls before swine—so enraged the public that, to prove the critic wrong, on the day the booking opened Maurice Browne had enough applications for seats to fill the theatre for three weeks.

Y.M. Ah, but that's a long time ago.

AGATE. Well, then, I'll tell you a story of to-day. The takings for *No Room at the Inn*, produced at the Winter Garden Theatre some six weeks ago, were £35 on the Monday night and £105 on the Saturday night. Then Alan Dent got busy and wrote a magnificent eulogy of the play in his paper. On the Sunday I did my little bit. On the following Monday the takings were £104 as against £35, and on the Saturday £350 as against £105. I have a letter from the management saying the result of those two articles was to treble the play's takings.

Y.M. Do you think a young man can be a good dramatic critic?

AGATE. There may be the makings of a good critic in a young man. But you would not say that a beginner who had ascended only Snowdon was as good a judge of a mountain as a more experienced climber who had tackled the Matterhorn and Mount Everest.

Y.M. Would it be wrong to say that one man's opinion is as good as another's?

AGATE. Let's talk sense. Suppose you found a bit of shiny stuff in the gutter and wanted to know whether it was diamond or glass. Would you take it to Hatton Garden or Covent Garden?

Y.M. Is there anything else that you can say to young playgoers?

AGATE. Yes, a great deal. But nothing that can *usefully* be said. In my day young people knew they didn't know; now they are certain they know. I was turned thirty before I wrote my first dramatic criticism, having spent twenty years getting to know about plays and acting. The modern young man has no notion of educating himself for his job, or that he needs educating. He leaves Oxford by the morning train, and goes straight from Paddington to get himself appointed dramatic critic to some highbrow weekly. And on the following Saturday he has a column telling me Irving was ham. Good night!

July 2 Tuesday

The Secretary of the Hallé Concerts Society having asked me for an article for their new magazine, I have sent them the following:

ALBUM LEAF

The Pleasures of Listening. Yes, but why seek the opinion of a dramatic critic almost entirely preoccupied with the Pains of Looking, a book critic stifled with the Plagues of Skipping, a film critic asphyxiated with the Penalties of Technigazing?

Presumably because I am an old Hallé fan. I shudder at the last
word, and could almost break off to write an essay on the Decline
of Taste.

The joy of great music? Too big a subject for an essay let. Let
me take refuge in reminiscence. I attended my first Hallé concert
at the age of seven. Yes, the year was 1884. I was taken by my
nurse to the Reform Club in King Street, and deposited in the
hall to wait until my father had finished his dinner. Then in a yellow
four-wheeled cab with red plush seats to the Free Trade Hall
and a seat in the gallery with a view of Hallé's left profile and,
when he was playing the piano, a full view of his back, the idea
being that I, as a commencing student of that instrument, might
observe the fingering. I thought Hallé a nice old gentleman, but a
tame player, with less than half my mother's fire. It is only fair
to say that she had studied under Madame Heinefetter, a pupil of
Chopin.

Later on came the Christmas performance of Handel's *Messiah*.
Edward Lloyd looked to me as though he wore a *toupet*—but
nobody else has ever sung "Comfort Ye" so well. Santley's voice
was gone even then (I don't believe there was ever a time when it
wasn't gone!) He sounded like a lion in *delìrium tremens*, and in
"Why do the nations" his head and hands shook with something
which was half daemonism and half palsy. Albani was always
tremendous in ruby velvet, which made me feel sorry for Ada
Crossley, who, as became her inferior station as a contralto,
generally moped in black. I adored Norman-Neruda long before
she became Lady Hallé. I thought her ugly but supremely elegant,
and still can see that thin gold bangle slide up and down her
bowing arm.

Enfin Richter vint. And I remember how, at the first performance
in Manchester of Tschaikowsky's Pathetic Symphony, Richter
laid down his bâton in the second movement and let the orchestra
conduct itself. Carreño in the Tschaikowsky Piano Concerto in
B flat minor. There, if you like, was fire and force and a walloping
pair of arms, and the proper atmosphere of a blacksmith's shop.
Lots and lots of great pianists—Busoni, d'Albert, Rosenthal,
Backhaus, Petri, Pachmann, whom I thought a charlatan, and
one or two Englishmen I didn't think much of because (*a*) they
were English and (*b*) I didn't think they could really play. Piano
quartets, yes; but the Concerto in the grand style, no. I remember
crying when on one occasion the pianist turned out to be Leonard
Borwick.

The meandering Delius. Was ever anything less like a fair?
Or less like Paris? And I remember my Daudet:

> Maison Bénie! Que de fois
> je suis venu là, me reprendre
> à la Nature, me guérir
> de Paris et de ses fièvres.

Did Daudet in very sooth desire to be cured of Paris and its fevers?
Did Delius ever have fevers of which to be cured? My first

Symphonic Poem, Strauss's *Don Juan*. My first Elgar. And, of
course, lots of Wagner, conducted in the heavy, beer-and-tobacco
stained, German and proper manner.

But those were the days of *tune*, when, as likely as not, the
season would open with the *Euryanthe* Overture of Weber, always
provided it was not Cherubini's *Anacreon* or Nicolai's *Merry
Wives*. And once at least during the season we should be given the
Oberon and *Freischütz* Overtures, and some stout lady in yellow
satin would sing "Ocean, thou mighty monster," and look as
though she was prepared to swallow as well as aspostrophise it.
Or shriek a greeting to some Hall of Song, and later, after clapping
on more tulle, send out an SOS in the shape of Senta's Ballad.
But all this was the age before Bartók.

In those days the leader of the orchestra was Willy Hess. At the
same desk sat Siegfried Jacoby, who taught the violin to two of
my brothers and was a great consumer of tea and buttered toast,
and a mordant wit. I remember being called in to play the piano
part in a *concertante* by somebody, and being in a state of terror
the entire time and hardly reassured by his "Vell, ve finished
together, und dat is something." Yes, mine is a musical family.
It is not given to every young man to have got lost on Snowdon
in company with the grandson of the great Manuel Garcia. Or to
have met Carl Fuchs, the 'cellist, on the top of Helvellyn. Or even
to have played the piano to Henry Wood two years before his
first promenade concert.

But I must be getting back to Manchester and the Free Trade
Hall. Of what did I think as my legs dangled and my cream socks
fell over my black shoes, which fastened with a button and strap?
Well, I used to weave romances about the people in the gallery
opposite. And I conceived a violent hatred of the man on my
other side, who never spoke to me throughout eight years and sat
stiff as a poker, rather like a male Betsey Trotwood.

With my dislike of him I connect certain distastes which have
remained with me all my life. Nearly all slow movements, *because
they go on too long*. Beethoven, in my early view, was a great
offender, particularly in the Seventh Symphony, where I still
think he should have wound up the Allegretto three minutes
earlier. Anything called a recitative, nearly all Bach, vast quantities
of that dry pedant Brahms. All the piano pieces of Schumann,
and most of all that loathsome thing called "Grillen". As against
this I had my special favourites. There was Adolph Brodsky,
who didn't seem to me to be very good as soloist, leader, or
conductor, but whom I liked for his genial expression and tummy.
Singers, too. Marie Brema; a lady who was always known as
Miss Fillunger; that great bass singer George Henschel, whose
"Spring" is one of the most beautiful songs ever written; a colossal
Swede of the name of Lundquist.

With these goes the memory of the best musical criticism this
country has ever seen:

"Mozart has done more to debauch the critical sense of musicians
than any composer who ever lived; practically no one ever mentions his name except in words of absolutely undiscriminating

eulogy. . . . But those who do not lose their heads over Mozart are constrained to point out that no organism can have such qualities as his without having the correlative defects. If the stream of speech runs so easily and so unceasingly, it is bound at times to run a little thin; and it is this thinness that wearies some people after a day or two spent in going not merely through the half-dozen masterpieces of Mozart but through a large quantity of his work of all kinds. One rather tires of seeing what is almost nothing at all said with such perfect grace and such formal impeccability. . . . The Mozart fanatic rhapsodises about Mozart, but does not think enough about him".

That was written by the musical critic of the *Manchester Guardian* on the hundred and fiftieth anniversary of the birth of Mozart. It comes in my first newspaper-cutting book, and the date is January 27, 1906. Is anybody writing stuff as good as this to-day in London, Sydney, Kamchatka, Colwyn Bay? No. The *Manchester Guardian* and the Hallé Concerts are the last remaining glories of a city which, when I last visited it, seemed entirely given over to motor salesmen.

And here I must stop. All that I have been writing about happened many years ago. And I am still listening to music. As the great poet so nearly wrote:

> The Child is Father of the Man;
> And I could wish my days to be
> Bound cach to each by natural melody.

And no Bartókery, if you please!

July 4 *Thursday*

Ivor Brown laid it down recently that a critic who finds himself allergic to any department of entertainment "ought to stay away from these, to him, foolish things". I agree, with the reservation that if he is allergic to too many things he should chuck his job and go in for something else. Fortunately I am not allergic to much. Modern British music, modern poetic drama, Shaw's plays, ballet, mime, musical comedy, Fred Astaire, skating films, and British film acting—this is very nearly the lot. Remains only Walt Disney. There is nothing on land or sea, nothing in the air or in the bowels of the earth, that bores me so abysmally as the later pictures of Walt Disney. Which goes for Donald Duck too. I would rather sit at the bottom of a coal-mine, in the dark, alone, and think of nothing, than go to see any of the successors to *Fantasia*. 1 would rather listen to Bloch's String Quartet played in a goods-yard, with shunting operations in full swing and all the Jews trying to get into or out of Palestine (I never remember which) wailing up against the walls—there is no noise known to me, including the road drill and the later compositions of Béla Bartók, that I execrate so deeply as the squawking of that abominable fowl. Wherefore I have told the *Tatler* that I will not go near *Make Mine Music*.

July 11 *Thursday*

Vignette. Hermione Gingold at the Ivy wearing a hat like a Martello tower with cascades of veiling, putting a bunch of carnations in her mouth à la Carmen, and saying with an atrocious leer, "Any gentleman like to strip to the waist?"

July 19 *Friday*

Supper to-night to Lillian Gish, looking lovely in a cowl and opals. I had asked Jock, Wilfred Rouse, and Bertie van Thal, and we were like fervents at the shrine of a young and witty saint. An enchanting evening, in the course of which she gave me her handkerchief, now being put under glass, and I told her that fame rested not upon her art, but upon the lovely, *baby* contour of her forehead.

August 9 *Friday*

Bored G.I. at repertory performance of *The Cherry Orchard*: "Cripes, if I'd known there was going to be all this fuss about a bloody orchard I'd have bought it myself in the first act."

August 13 *Tuesday*

One evening last week a personable and strangely clean young man came up to me in the Café Royal and said, "Where is Wiltshire?" I said, "Next county to Hampshire. Why?" He said, "That's odd; I thought it was somewhere in the Fen District. The reason I ask is because I've just been posted to the Wiltshire Regiment. (Grunts from J. A.) My name is Peter Forster, Second Lieutenant. It seems that the cradle of civilisation—Egypt, you know—is rocking, and they want me to steady it."

J. A. Who's 'they'?
Y. M. The War Office.
J. A. (*waking up*) What the devil has all this to do with me?
Y. M. Only that I'm going to succeed you on the *Sunday Times*.
J. A. The hell you are! What are your qualifications?
Y. M. That I'm a first-class dramatic critic.

    J. A. How old are you?
    Y. M. Twenty.
    J. A. Then what you mean is, you are a potentially first-class
critic.
    Y. M. I'm a jolly good writer.
    J. A. When do you start for the Middle East?
    Y. M. Wednesday morning next.
    J. A. Lunch with me here Tuesday next, and bring with you 3000
words establishing that you are not just a conceited young fool.

Devas Jones arriving at this point, I said "Let me introduce a young
man I don't know to my Commanding Officer in the First World
War." Forster said, "I hope I am on speaking terms with my C.O. in
thirty years' time. It's more than I am now!" To-day he turned up on
time with an essay of exactly 3000 words entitled *A Very Short View
of the English Stage.* I cull:

> I have never seen a great actor. Of course I have never seen a great
> actor. Nobody has since 14th October 1905. But then in these
> days we set genius at a discount and concentrate on the Lowest
> Common Denominator. O you reformers! Is it not enough that a
> communal hand should rock the child in a communal crèche;
> that individual lives should become no more than Vital Statistics?
> Would you also take away my gilt and plush? Would you abolish
> boxes? Would you have me sit in some civic shed and listen to
> solemn tracts about the economic problems of ploughmen in the
> Caucasus? And must I consider this good drama because you
> consider it good politics? O City Corporation Censor! Dost thou
> think because thou art communist there shall be no more Somerset
> Maughams? . . .
>   Ralph Richardson's portrait of the scruffy, frowzy stage of
> early middle age, the age when for the first time a man doesn't
> bother to put on a clean collar: that was wonderful acting. And
> the final realisation that "Vouloir ce que Dieu veut, est la seule
> science qui nous met en repos", as Vanya and Sonia began work
> again, was most moving. His Falstaff I thought a wonderful piece
> of bluff, all brilliant overtones, with every resort of comic tech-
> nique; a spoiled-baby Falstaff, bigger, brighter, funnier than
> ever before. He is the least extraordinary of actors in the front
> rank to-day. His performances are on view, with all credentials in
> order; and all of the highest integrity; "no offence i' the world,"
> he seems to say; hard-working self-effacing interpreter of difficult
> rôles; his face the face of Everyman—meeting him casually on
> a bus the last thing you would take him for would be a distinguished
> actor. . . .
>   By his Hamlet Gielgud will be best remembered. He played
> him not like Wolfit, as a private detective watching over the
> Danish Royal Family; nor in the Clunes manner, like Young
> Woodley on the eve of expulsion; nor yet in the style of Maurice
> Evans's new version, broadened and abridged for soldiers, as a
> Yankee at the Court of King Claudius. With Gielgud it was the

ruin of a noble nature. Exquisite in delivery, in action liquid grace, he sustained the excitement and tension right up to the sad heroics of the sword play, until finally the rest was silence, save for the heavy breathing of the dead.

Good enough for twenty years of age. We shook hands on the understanding that he is to save £150 before he comes out of the Army next spring. This will give him £3 a week to starve on for a year, during which time I undertake to find him a job as a fledging critic.

August 19 *Monday*

Have been reading John Dover Wilson's new edition of *King Henry IV, Parts 1 and 11*, and find him a little less than sound on a point that is, to me, of intense interest—the real character of Prince Hal:

> If Hal be the cad and hypocrite that many modern readers imagine, or even if he seem merely "dimly wrought" by the side of his gross friend, then the whole grand scheme of the Lancastrian cycle miscarries, since it is the person and reign of King Henry V which gives the bright centre to that dark picture, a brightness that by contrast makes the chaos that follows all the more ghastly.

"Tellest thou me of 'ifs'?" In all English literature I do not know a more revolting passage than that in Part 1, Act 1, Scene 2, beginning: "Yet herein will I imitate the sun." The gorge of Pecksniff himself must have risen at the hypocrisy of:

> And like bright metal on a sullen ground,
> My reformation, glittering o'er my fault,
> Shall show more goodly and attract more eyes
> Than that which hath no foil to set it off.
> I'll so offend, to make offence a skill;
> Redeeming time when men think least I will.

Quiller-Couch said that this speech, if we accept it, poisons all of Henry that follows:

> Most of us can forgive youth, hot blood, riot: but a prig of a rake, rioting on a calculated scale, confessing that he does it coldly, intellectually, and that he proposes to desert his comrades at the right moment to better his own repute—*that* kind of rake surely all honest men abhor.

("Q", whom this greatly bothered, tried to throw the responsibility upon Burbage, who, he half-heartedly suggested, came to the poet and said at a later date: "Look here, the audience aren't going to stand for a rapscallion turned Sunday-school teacher. You've got to get them right about him in the beginning!" Whereupon Shakespeare went back and obediently inserted the miserable stuff.) The Professor says: "The anointed King who emerges from the Abbey is a different *man* from the Prince who entered." Who, then, is right? "Q" who condemned the anointed Henry as a cad, or J. D. W., who talks of spiritual change?

When literary critics differ, who shall decide? Obviously, a dramatic critic. In his earlier book *The Fortunes of Falstaff* J. D. W. put forward the thoery that Shakespeare intended Falstaff to appear in *Henry V*, thus fulfilling the promise in the Epilogue to *Henry IV*. That Shakespeare made this promise in the belief that Kempe would be there to play Falstaff, and that, Kempe having left the company and no other Falstaff forthcoming, Shakespeare had to kill off the big fellow. I'm sorry, but I don't believe a word of it. I prefer "Q" 's manly, direct:

> Shakespeare could not bring Falstaff upon the stage in *King Henry V*, because he dared not. . . . Henry must not be allowed to meet Falstaff. For Falstaff can kill him with a look. . . . It was Henry who wronged Falstaff and killed his heart; Falstaff had never a thought of hurting Henry: and therefore, or ever you can present Henry of Agincourt as your *beau idéal* of a warrior king you must kill Falstaff somehow and get his poor old body behind the arras: for, as Hazlitt said, he is the better man of the two.

Let me put it that J. D. W. is right in the study, and "Q" a hundred times right on the stage.

August 29 Thursday

KAFKA. Am thinking of starting a movement to be called "Kafka Is Balls," with a club of which I propose to make myself Perpetual President. Not on the strength of having read Kafka—indeed, I have never opened him—but because of what the high-brow magazines tell me about him. Am considering a button with the letters P.P.K.I.B.C. Perpetual President Kafka Is Balls Club.

CANNES FILM FESTIVAL

September 19 Thursday

Osbert Sitwell would have been the best writer to describe our experience of this afternoon—visit to the Villa Sardou, in the Boulevard Carnot at Le Cannet, where Rachel died. The house is strictly closed to the public, and we were only allowed to inspect it on the representations of the Mayor that I have written a book about Rachel. For years I have dreamed of such a visit. The place was untouched. Here was the marble bed with its antique sculptures at the head and the figure of Tragedy at the foot. Here was the *salle-à-manger*, with the decanters and glasses Rachel used. The salon is a very dark, long narrow room with a ceiling representing the firmament. Exquisite stained-glass windows everywhere. Rachel's piano. The fireplace, in the shape of the trunk of a marble tree whose branches enclose the whole room, still black with smoke. Ceremonial chairs. Statues in every corner. Hearing of our visit, the owner of the house next door which was formerly part of the Villa, showed us round an extraordinary affair of terraces, balconies, stairs, and towers, from which a hundred years ago there was an uninterrupted view of the sea. A miniature and baroque version of Tower Bridge with a faint suggestion of Mr Wemmick's Castle. It was all extraordinarily impressive, like a last act of Victor Hugo. We were shown round by a remarkable old lady of great age, who said, with finality, "Voici le lit de mort de Rachel. N'y touchez pas!" No plaque. Nothing to tell the passer-by that here, jealously guarded, are the last links with the world's greatest actress.

September 20 *Friday*

This morning there arrives for me at the hotel a photograph of Rachel's balcony, kindly sent by M. Marcel Lenormand, the owner of the other half of the villa. I wonder whether the dying Rachel ever climbed this and said sepulchrally:

Soleil, je te viens voir pour la dernière fois!

Later. The Festival is in a complete state of disorganisation. *There are no tickets.* Willie [Wilfred Rouse] has this afternoon received a letter addressed to "Madame le Recteur Roussy", at the wrong hotel, containing invitations for last night's reception and an aviation meeting to be held after we have left. Six attempts to attend to-day's showing of *Caesar and Cleopatra* have failed, and *The Times* is sitting in the corner with its head buried in its hands. In the meantime the aircraft carrier *Colossus* has arrived, and a plague of ants has broken out in my bedroom.

Still later. Attended a cocktail party given by the film producers in spite of not having received an invitation. Met the delicious Public Relations Officer, who, like Mrs Erlynne in Wilde's play, explained everything. And we agree that no woman can be expected to cope single-handed with twenty-four different Government Departments.

September 21 *Saturday*

Yesterday's opening day at the Film Festival was a fiasco. In the morning *Caesar and Cleopatra* bored everybody stiff and sent British stock down to zero. The evening's principal film was the Mexican *Les Trois Mousquetaires*, a travesty of Dumas's story in the Bob Hope manner. In Spanish, without sub-titles, and, as far as we could gather, totally unfunny. After two hours of this, in sweltering heat, the audience began to pour out in hundreds, preferring to stroll about in the open air till it was over. Willie and I went across to La Jetée, a charming café where, under the lime-trees, we drank some cool beer and listened to an orchestra of eight deal with Liszt's *Les Préludes* and selections from Grieg, Wagner, and Sibelius. We returned an hour later to find the wretched film still going on to an almost empty hall! Some time after midnight they put on the new Hitchcock film, *Notorious*. At a quarter to one this was discontinued and re-started, as they had got the reels in the wrong order. Too much for us, and we left in search of supper, or anyhow a drink. We found this at the Zanzi-Bar, where a furious *bagarre* suddenly started, somebody saying that any Frenchman who allowed himself to submit to Buchenwald was *un lâche*. This was violently resented by two ex-Buchenwalders. Things were beginning to look ugly, when the barman rapped on the counter and said, "M'dames et M'sieurs, j'ai une triste nouvelle à vous annoncer, Raimu est mort ce soir." And at once the quarrel was submerged in the general grief.

This morning I attended a *conférence*, the idea being to set up an International Critics' Circle. On the adoption of the motion that delegates should not give their own personal views of films, but act as mouthpieces for the majority view, I left. Eric Dunstan motored us to lunch at his charming little estate, called Le Moulin de la Mourrachoux, about ten miles from Cannes. I cannot imagine a more lovely little house, situated on the banks of a stream and waterfall. "My nearest neighbour lives a mile and a half away," said Eric. "I have no idea who she is." Here we met Commander Tommy Thompson, personal atten-dant to Winston Churchill throughout the War, and Tommy Partington, whom somebody described as looking like a tame eagle accustomed to playing poker in church. What we ate and drank I don't remember, but it was exquisite. Everybody in very good form, the best remark being Eric's "I remember Sarah Bernhardt's funeral perfectly. I have never had so long to wait to cross the street." Still no letters and no English papers. But the French sheets are a joy. One of them, after noting the presence of Margaret Lockwood, Schiaparelli, and Duff Cooper, gets out of last night's fiasco with the headlines: "Bing Crosby, Fred Astaire, et Erroll Flynn brillent par leur absence."

ENGLAND

October 14 *Monday*

DEAR GEORGE LYTTELTON,

I have decided that *Ego* 9 shall be the last. My Publishers say that if I deliver now what stuff I have got ready and the balance at the end of the year there's a chance that they may be able to publish on my seventieth birthday. E. V. Lucas said that one of the marks of a gentleman is never to show that he is tired. That's as may be. I am sure that one of the marks of an artist is not to let his work show signs of fatigue. I am very weary. Yesterday afternoon Gwen Chenhalls took me to Harold Holt's box at the Albert Hall. We arrived in time for my favourite piano concerto, Beethoven's C minor. This begins, as you know, with a long exposition by the orchestra. Half-way through this I fell asleep to wake only with the applause at the end, and not having heard a note of Pouishnoff. And this after a lunch of monastic simplicity—meaning two double whiskies and an omelette. Now here's the point. In this state of tiredness some of my work must necessarily suffer. I am determined that it shan't be *Ego*, and by any code of fairness it mustn't be my papers. I am not overlooking the possibility of a postscript, to be published if and when my literary executors—horrid phrase—think fit. I might even call it *Postscript to Ego*, or *Letters from Grundisburgh*.

November 13 *Wednesday*

"The measure of choosing well", wrote Sir William Temple, "is whether a man likes what he has chosen." This applies particularly to one's friends. It is twenty years since I chose George Mathew, and I have been amply repaid. At least four nights a week, and often five and six, he looks in for an hour's chat on his way to Regent's Park. In that hour we discuss practically everything, though the subject which most crops up is the exact meaning and use of words. Fowler is our Bible here, though a Bible of which one can be critical. Said George to-night, "Why doesn't he come down heavily on those people who say 'infer' when they mean 'imply'?" I said, "What about Shakespeare, who uses the two indifferently?" "Oh, Shakespeare," said George, "He was an ignorant b——, anyway!"

November 28 *Thursday*

Letter from Roger Machell:

> 90 *Great Russell St.*
> *London, W.C.*1.
> *Nov.* 27, '46

DEAR MR AGATE,

Discussing your broadcast about the Hays Office and film censorship, a Hollywood magnate who is now in London told me, quite casually, that the use of the word behind, whether as a noun or a preposition, is banned in American films. As a preposition, the phrase 'in back of' is substituted. He instanced "the garden is in back of the house." When I asked whether in its next Biblical epic Hollywood would make our Lord remark, "Get thee in back of me, Satan," he nodded gravely and said he thought so.

Yours ever,
ROGER MACHELL

Boxing Day

In my mail this morning:

Date..................

1. I *have/have not
   received your last three letters
2. I have not replied owing to my
   *Absence from home ⎫
   Change of address ⎪
   Indifference ⎪
   Forgetfulness ⎪
   Laziness ⎬
   Rudeness ⎪
   Illness ⎪
   Imprisonment ⎪
   Insanity ⎪
   Death ⎭

3. I *Apologise for ⎫
   Commiserate with you over ⎪
   Laugh at ⎪
   Gloat over ⎬
   Regard with indifference ⎪
   Intend to continue ⎪
   Intend to discontinue ⎭

the inconvenience caused to
you by para. 2 above

Signed........................

* Strike out words not required.

The sender is a Naval captain who has never allowed charm to undermine authority.

December 28 Saturday

In *The Times*:

Queen Alexandra Mansions
Grape Street, W.C.2
December 27, 1946

To the Editor of "The Times":
SIR,
Your obituarist says of W. C. Fields that he was "an almost ideal Mr Micawber in the film of *David Copperfield*". Sir, you will

permit me to say that he was not, and demonstrably not, and could not be. Consider Micawber's first appearance in the novel. " 'This,' said the stranger, with a certain condescending roll in his voice, and a certain indescribable air of doing something genteel which impressed me very much, 'is Master Copperfield. I hope I see you well, Sir?' " There was nothing remotely genteel about Fields's Micawber, who in the film made his first appearance by a highly ungenteel fall through the roof of his own house.

Consider again. " 'Under the impression that your peregrinations in this metropolis have not as yet been extensive, and that you might have some difficulty in penetrating the arcana of the Modern Babylon in the direction of the City Road—in short, that you might lose yourself—I shall be happy to call this evening, and install you in the knowledge of the nearest way.' " Fields's Micawber would not have used the word "peregrination" or known the meaning of "arcana".

Mr Micawber's manners which "peculiarly qualify him for the Banking business"? Not even Mrs Micawber at her most doting could have said this of Fields. Micawber is a gentleman who keeps his fallen day about him, and if he is not played like this is not played at all. Fields was a glorious buffoon. But being possessed of no more gentility than a pork pie he could do no other with Micawber than turn him into an obese Ally Sloper, with very much the same nose and hat. And that, I submit, is not Dickens's character.

> I am, Sir,
> Your obedient servant,
> JAMES AGATE

December 30 *Monday*

An anonymous letter:

W. C. FIELDS AS MICAWBER

> De Mortuis nil nisi bonum
> You
> Self-advertising
> Flamboyant
> Swollen-headed
> &
> Utterly bloody
> Bastard.
> God wither your right hand!

> To James Agate,
> Queen Alexandra Mansions,
> Sour Grape Street,
> W.C.2.

December 31 *Tuesday*

My Year's work:

Sunday Times	.	.	57 000 words
Daily Express	.	.	42 000 ,,
Tatler	.	. .	55 000 ,,
Ego 8	.	. .	100 000 ,,
Odd articles	.	.	10 000 ,,
			264 000 ,,

Now let me repeat a little sum which fascinates me. Turning up *Ego* 4 (page 152) I find that between September 1921 and December 1939 I had written a total of 5 000 000 words. Again I do the little sum:

December 1939	.	.	5 000 000 words
,, 1940	.	.	350 000 ,,
,, 1941	.	.	250 000 ,,
,, 1942	.	.	265 000 ,,
,, 1943	.	.	300 000 ,,
,, 1944	.	.	316 000 ,,
,, 1945	.	.	311 000 ,,
,, 1946	.	.	264 000 ,,
			7 056 000 ,,

Whaur's your Balzac and your Bennett noo? In the scales of quantity, not quality, idiot!

1947

January 7 *Tuesday*

Spent the day jotting down notes for article on *The Master Builder*.

January 8 *Wednesday*

Tore up yesterday's notes. Too much like 'prentice work—allusions to Shaw, Arnold, Montague. Wrote a new article and delivered it at *S.T.* offices.

January 9 *Thursday*

Retrieved article and destroyed it. Wrote another and, I hope, final one.

January 10 *Friday*

It wasn't final.

May 31 *Saturday*

Letter to Brother Mycroft.

One thing, my dear Whiskers, that irks me is the extraordinary combination of fatigue and insomnia. Owing to the pain all my body cries out for sleep, and I just can't catch it—probably something to do with the asthma. Fortunately, however, my flat faces two ways, so that I put an extremely comfortable, high-backed, well-pillowed chair in the windows of two rooms with different aspects. Both windows have ledges which will take a cushion. I go to what I call bed at eleven o'clock, sit in the dark, and get amusement out of Holborn's cats and other late *noceurs*. Quite frequently, round about four, I put my head on the cushion and drop off for a couple of hours, after which there is the delight of seeing Holborn wake up. To get the best of this entertainment I go into the room which has a view of a lot of little shops, including a tyre-dealer's and it is fun to watch dust-carts jostling Rolls-Royces for priority. And when the doctor comes in the morning and asks what sort of night I have had, I say, "Splendid!"

I can't read new books because of the fatigue, but I can still quote Micawber in chunks. I don't play the gramophone much, as I find the noise hurts, but I can sit and nurse the records and play them in my head. When friends come round I like them to be more or less silent, while I recall the witty things they have said in the past. I have an immense amount to be thankful for, and never cease marvelling that a contentious and truculent fellow like me can have acquired, without angling for it, so much that gives old age its value. To-day I have had telephone messages from Lilian Braithwaite and Helen Haye; Abel of the Ivy sent me a dozen peaches; Gwen Chenhalls's kindness is not to be believed; my room is almost as full of flowers as Sarah Bernhardt's *loge* on a first night. I could have cars here every hour of the day, but the doctors say I am not strong enough to go for drives. So I sit and muse and am thankful that, so far as I can perceive, my intellectual vigour has not abated. It shows itself best in this, I think—the realisation that it is not within the power of present pain to lay a finger on past ecstasy. I thank God that He has made this world more perdurable than any but a poet's view of it—that a thousand poets could fall off a mountain without doing anything except add to its grandeur. What does it matter if my spirits droop a little now and then so long as the butcher-boy can whistle, or how many aches and pains I groan under so long as the cherry blossoms in the Park?

So don't worry about me. I have had enough happiness and

excitement and joy of work to fill ten lifetimes. Don't come up to London to see me; so long as you stay put I shall feel that "There's sap in't yet".

My best love to yourself, Lizzie, and Mary.

Ever,

JIMMIE

June 1 Sunday

There was a time when I planned to end this Diary on my seventieth birthday—a project no longer feasible. I think I should have finished with something like this:

> I thank Thee, God, for all the things life has meant to me. For the seaside and cricket on the sands which made up my childhood. For the golf-courses and show-yards of my youth and middle age. For the books, acting, and music, recollection of which makes my old age rich and enviable. For the stone walls of Derbyshire, the dales of Yorkshire, Welsh mountains, and English lakes. For fun, good talk, and enjoyment of the minds of others. For Brother Edward's wit and courage. For Brother Harry, who has taught me what unselfishness may be. For Leo Pavia. For those great spirits—Montague, Monkhouse, Mair. For the loyalty and devotion of my friends everywhere. For the humble friends and helpers who have made my work possible. For any talent I may have possessed, and the gift of energy to prosecute it. For never having utterly lost the sense of the glory and the freshness of a dream. For never having for one instant believed that there hath pass'd away a glory from the earth. For the power of being two persons.

> I loved the garish day, and, spite of fears,
> Pride ruled my will: remember not past years.

June 2 Monday

On the first page of *Ego* there is a cutting from an evening paper which, first with the news, was overjoyed to tell its readers how James Agate, "described as a dramatic critic", at some police-court in Essex had been committed to prison for a debt of twenty pounds. Well, history repeats itself; or at least mine does. Received this morning a court communication from the Revenue saying that unless I find £940 within a week everything in my flat except the bed I lie on will be taken away. The fact that since the War, despite reduced income and increased tax, I have paid off some £6000 of arrears appears not to weigh with these gentry, who do not rise above a twopenny bus-ride view of existence. Any why should they? It takes one Balzac to write, and another to comprehend, "La dette est une oeuvre d'imagination que les créanciers ne comprennent jamais." It would be absurd to expect tax-collectors to think on these levels. Or on any level. One of these paper-cuffed, inky-fingered gentry said to me the other day. "Mr Agate, with all the money you have made you ought to leave nine rows of houses." I said, "Mr Inspector, with all the money I have spent I am going to leave nine volumes of *Ego*." But it was lost on him, just as the Revenue threat is lost on me. I am not unduly perturbed because in three months' time they are going to demand another £940, plus £300 for Amusement Tax or something. I am just not worrying. Something has always turned up, and something will turn up now. I have lived for so long on the edge of so many precipices that for me *terra firma* has become *terra incognita*. In the meantime I cannot think of a better note on which to end my Diary. "The deadest deaths are the best," said old Montaigne, and I hold the same about quick endings. So, with a friendly nod to the readers who have kept me company during the last fifteen years, I set about my final sentences. As I pen them I see Brother Edward rubbing his long nose as though wondering how a man who has written so much can have said so little. While over my shoulder comes the voice of Leo, saying, "Tell me, James; will your *Ego* 9 be Choral?"

FOOTNOTE TO "EGO 9"

by
Alan Dent

James had definitely and finally decided to make this volume the last of the *Ego* series. We therefore have here the strange and, I should think, unprecedented spectacle of a man coming to the virtual conclusion of his autobiographical diary at the moment when Death's hand—without his knowing it—was upon him. He terminated his autobiography even as his life was ending.

The end came suddenly, just before eleven o'clock on the evening of Friday, June the 6th. He had a heart-attack, collapsed, and died beside his bed. I last set eyes on him on the previous Monday evening, when I called to see him and found him sitting up in his study, in some pain and discomfort, yet zealously correcting the early galley proofs of this same volume. He was by no means pessimistic, and did not mention death.

Exactly a fortnight earlier there had been a very remarkable incident in the lives of both of us. Newspapers have to be unsentimental, and to envisage possibilities of the dissolution of any and every celebrity. One of my editors had asked me to prepare an obituary notice of James. In spite of his being so obviously ill, it had never occurred to me he was going to die in my own lifetime, and I was therefore a shade alarmed at the request. I telephoned him to ask how he was, and he insisted on my breaking a previous appointment and lunching with him. "The Ivy at one, and not a minute later. I have to see a film at two," he said. I was in his favourite restaurant at onc o'clock sharp, and sitting at the corner table on the right as one enters. No James! So there and then, alone at the table, and with most of the theatrical celebrities that matter in full view, I took out my tablets, and then and there, and full of the subject, wrote my obituary of James—straight on to the page, as is my wont, modelling each sentence in my mind before committing it to writing.

This article appeared, eventually, in *The Manchester Guardian* on the Monday after James's death. I was setting down the last words of its last sentence—this is plain and simple truth—when he looked round the door and, grey of face but smiling, said, with a flash of his uncanny percipiency, "Fifty minutes late, I know, but it takes me a time to dress. What are you writing there, Jock—*my obituary, I suppose?*" I did not deny the fact, but put my papers away. We ordered food and drink, and when I was beginning my soup he startled my by saying, "Come, boy—as one journalist to another—let me read what your really think of me!" I think anyone in my shoes must have found this an agitating experience—indeed, a distressing one. With his great horror of death he might there and then have had his fatal heart-seizure. He might, at the least, have taken violent exception. I therefore hesitated—

but he firmly insisted. I thereupon gave him the article to read and continued to eat my soup, though with a trembling hand.

Never have I felt so foolishly like James Boswell, and never in his life did James so resemble Dr Johnson. He read the piece through with a kind of beaming solemnity, paused only when he came to the list of his enthusiasms to entreat me—yes, entreat me—to make mention of "golf", and then handed me back my manuscript with a single observation: "I'm proud, Jock, to have that written about me, and you've written it well!" Thereupon he changed the subject, and never again throughout the hurried luncheon—or in the remaining three weeks—made any mention of the following obituary, which I wrote in those circumstances, which he read in those circumstances, and which duly appeared in that great newspaper to which, to our pride, we have both belonged:

"Death hath this also, that it openeth the gate to good fame and extinguisheth envy. *Extinctus amabitur idem.*" (How James would have chuckled over an appreciation that begins with a quotation involving both Bacon and Horace!)

Now that he is dead, few will deny that he was the leading dramatic critic of our time. He was the chief of our craft, and a warrior chief, and a working chief right up to the end. As a critic he was cogent, never smooth, often belligerent, often capricious too, but always forthright, and sound and consistent in his standards; angrily impatient of the slipshod, the gimcrack, the pretentious, full of words and notions and allusions and audacities, full of sound and fury too, but always signifying something. And he used everything he had to write about or around—even the most trivial and unpromising play, book, film, or essay-topic—as as occasion for spilling the words and ideas with which his large mind so generously overflowed.

For fifteen years, which seemed like five, I served my apprenticeship with him in the craft of criticism, and never once in that time did I see him, when well and working, 'dry up' for lack of anything to say. He was extravagant in all ways, and did not pretend to be anything else. He had a large amount of that self-knowledge which the Greeks called ultimate wisdom. He loved praise even more than most of us do, and would let you call him all the things he was—witty, immensely readable, discriminating, irresistible provocative, Pepysian, Johnsonian, Hazlittean, and even Shavian—till the sun went down (or rose) and the wine-bottle was empty. But if any commentator, or any mere flatterer, praised his writing style the critic in him invariably ousted the inordinate vanity. His prose was lively and prickly, but not that of a great stylist. He knew this and admitted it honestly. He slaved all his life to express himself in a style comparable to that of his lofty models and ideals—Hazlitt, C. E. Montague, and the critic Shaw. He was genuinely satisfied with his writing only when it seemed to him a passable approximation to any one of these.

In his later life he turned to diary-making—writing, naturally, far more loosely than in his criticism—and produced nine big volumes of the celebrated autobiography *Ego*—a kind of huge vat to catch all that overflow of the verbal energy that was in him or which he occasioned in his followers, friends, and enemies. Like Falstaff in more ways than one, he was not only witty in himself, but the direct occasion of wit in his inferiors.

In his person as in his work he could be over-bearing, brow-beating, blunt, and then "incalculably he could do the nicest things", as some one once phrased it to me in a letter. In my secretarial time I have called him many things to his face—a monster, a ton of saturated self, a "bletherin' blusterin' blellum" (just to tease and just to be Scots), but he easily forgave and was easy to forgive. He had, beside true and unexpected kindness, a formidable amount of charm (a valuable gift even when one trades on it), was full of delightful surprises, and was never a bore (except about personal health, a subject on which Dr Johnson himself was probably a bore).

In fine, we are mourning a great character, undeniably a great dramatic critic, and possibly a great diarist. Only time can determine his status in the last faculty. How he would have beamed at my triple and considered application of the word 'great'—a word he wisely taught me to use with the most critical discretion!

He was at his consummate best—either writing or talking—on the subject of great acting, and was almost unique in his profession in having seen some! The ruling passions of his life were for the stage, for informed and witty conversation, for the language and literature of France, for golf and Hackney ponies, and for all that goes with urbane living. He loved life dearly, and "the vasty hall of death" can seldom have had a more unwilling visitant.

CONCISE BIOGRAPHIES

Brown, Ivor (1891–1974). Author and critic. Dramatic critic of the *Manchester Guardian,* also *The Observer* 1928–54 during part of which time he was also editor.

Chenhalls, Gwen, née Teagle. Widow of Alfred Chenhalls, one of J.A.'s financial advisers who was killed in the same aeroplane crash as Leslie Howard. One of J.A.'s few women friends and a violinist of ability.

Dent, Alan "Jock" (*b.* 1905). Author, critic and journalist, J.A.'s secretary 1926–41. London dramatic critic of the *Manchester Guardian* 1935–43. *News Chronicle* 1945–60.

Lyttelton, George (1883–1962). Younger son of Lord Cobham and Assistant Master at Eton.

Mathew, George (*b.* 1897). Journalist, on *Country Life* when J.A. started writing for that magazine. Friend and literary executor of James Agate.

Montague, C. E. (1867–1928). Journalist and author; dramatic critic of the *Manchester Guardian* 1890–1925.

Morgan, Charles (1894–1958). In addition to being a novelist, playwright and essayist, Morgan was dramatic critic of *The Times* 1926–39.

Pavia, Leo (1875–1945). Infant prodigy pianist, unsuccessful composer, music teacher. Translated Wilde's plays into German 1906–9. J.A.'s secretary 1941–5. "A Jewish Dr Johnson."

Rubinstein, Stanley (1890–1975). Author and solicitor. Friend and literary executor of J.A.

Shearman, Montague (1886–1940). Barrister and Progressive Member of the LCC for Bermondsey before the First World War. Foreign Office thereafter. Collector of modern paintings and Hon. Secretary of the Contemporary Arts Society.

Walkley, A. B. (1855–1926). Dramatic critic of *The Times* 1900–26.

INDEX

261

INDEX

INDEX

INDEX

265

INDEX

266

INDEX